WORD STEMS

WORD STEMS

A Dictionary

JOHN KENNEDY

The first edition of this work was published by the American
Book Company, New York, in 1890.

Published by
Soho Press Inc.
853 Broadway
New York, NY 10003

Library of Congress Cataloging-in-Publication Data

Kennedy, John, fl. 1870–1914
Word stems : a dictionary / John Kennedy.
    p.   cm.
Rev. ed. of: A stem dictionary of the English language. 1971.
ISBN 1–56947–051–0 (alk. paper)
1. English language—Etymology—Dictionaries. 2. English
language—Word formation. I. Kennedy, John, fl. 1870–
1914. Stem dictionary of the English language. II. Title.
PE1580.K43   1996
422'.03—dc20   96-9783
                                                       CIP

Manufactured in the United States

WORD STEMS

EXPLANATIONS

In the word list the stem is indicated by dark italic type. Where the stem has been corrupted or has undergone any change, the regular stem form is given in a parenthesis beside the word. The immediate purpose is to render the central meaning. A full analysis may be obtained by reference to the lists of prefixes, stems, and suffixes for the modifying elements in a word.

ABBREVIATIONS

Arab.	Arabic	Icel.	Icelandic
A.S.	Anglo-Saxon	It.	Italian
Bret.	Breton	L.	Latin
Dan.	Danish	Low. L.	Low Latin
Du.	Dutch	M.E.	Middle English
F.	French	O.F.	Old French
G.	Greek	Pers.	Persian
Ger.	German	Port.	Portuguese
Goth.	Gothic	Skt.	Sanskrit
Hind.	Hindoostanee	Sp.	Spanish

Low Ger.	Low German
O.H. Ger.	Old High German
M.H. Ger.	Middle High German

DEVELOPMENT

The English language in familiar speech consists mainly of words of Anglo-Saxon origin. But of the words constituting the English language, fully three fifths are of Latin origin. The Latin element was first introduced into England by the armies of Julius Cæsar and his successors. The conquests of Cæsar resulted in displacing entirely the Celtic language in Southwestern Europe from the Rhine to the Strait of Gibraltar, and establishing in its place the Latin language. This was due to no deliberate attempt, but to the operation of natural laws. The superior civilization overcame the speech of the inferior. The conquest of England by the Romans, however, was only nominal, never amounting to more than an armed occupation, and therefore affected the speech of the country but slightly. The Latin language was again introduced, and with more effect, in the fifth and sixth centuries, by Christian missionaries from the South of Europe, who re-established Christianity on the island. The literature of the period was exclusively Latin, and all instruction came from a Latin source. But the great inundation of Latin words came with the Norman Conquest; for the Norman French was but modified Latin. The eleventh century after Christ completed the conquest undertaken in the first century before Christ. But it failed to overthrow entirely the speech of the land, and resulted only in a language compromise.

The presence of words of Greek origin in the English language is due to several interesting causes. In the first place, the Greeks made early progress in the arts and sciences. Being originators in both fields, they were enabled to designate important distinctions by the words of their own language, as in the case of geometry, discovered and developed by Euclid, of logic and rhetoric, developed by Aristotle, and of astronomy, founded by Hipparchus and Ptolemy. As these and other sciences passed to foreign lands, they retained the Greek terminology fixed with such exactness. The Romans were instructed by the Greeks; and in appropriating Greek thought they likewise appropriated a large range of Greek terms. It was a Greek-laden Latin which the conquerors of the world spread over the Roman Empire. The Latin speech took complete possession of Gaul (now *France*). French is but Latin more or less corrupted and modified by the vicissitudes of two thousand years; and as such it has its Greek element. When, therefore, French became incorporated into English, the inseparable Greek element likewise came in.

But many words have come into English directly from the Greek tongue, owing to the revival of letters and the close study of the noble literature of Greece. Moreover, modern scientists have found it expedient to express new sciences in terms of Greek origin for the following reasons: 1st. It is natural to adhere to a settled system of nomenclature (Greek terms first had the field). 2d. A uniform terminology is necessary, that students of different nations may follow each other's discoveries without confusion; and to no other language would they all be so ready to defer as to the transcendent Greek. 3d. Great exactness is necessary in the expressing of scientific distinctions, and no other language has so fully met this requirement as the language of the highly cultivated and consequently subtle and acutely discerning Greeks. 4th. Scientific terminology must have a fixed value, the shifting uses of words in popular use would introduce confusion into science,—the scientific term must be as unchangeable as the imbedded fossil; the Greek, being a dead language, has this fixity of form.

The Low Latin is the Latin of the later times, after it had received large admixtures from the Teutonic languages of the north of Europe. It assimilated its Teutonic elements more or less and subjected them to Latin inflections. It was succeeded by the Romance languages of modern times.

The French language that came to England with the Normans in A.D. 1066 was not the French of today. The latter embodies the vast development and the modifications of eight hundred years. It is, therefore, mainly with an *Old French* that our English language connects.

Iceland as a region contributed nothing to the formation of the English language. Scandinavia, from whence the Icelanders came, did, however, contribute largely by the inroads, conquests, and settlements of the Danes or Northmen, and also to a slight extent through the Normans, who were of Scandinavian origin. The migration of the Icelanders to such a distant region cut them off from the language development of the mother country, and their speech, therefore, remained almost stationary. As this migration occurred soon after the Danish conquests, we are enabled to cite Icelandic words as the antecedents of the Scandinavian elements in English. A similar arrest of language development occurred in the case of the French settlements in Canada. The French settlements, however, were not so completely isolated as were the Icelanders, nor did they occur at so early a period. Otherwise we should have today almost a living example of the French of the Norman Conquest period.

As the several invading and conquering races left their impress on the language of England, so likewise the Arabian or Moorish conquest of Spain left a broad impress on the geography and language of that country. The Moslems were taught to extend their religion by the power of the sword. In accordance with this mandate, they exterminated Christianity and every other belief at issue with Islam in southwestern Asia and northern Africa. In due time they invaded Europe, first appearing in Spain, and effectually conquering the peninsula. They entered from Africa, from the region of Morocco, and were hence called Moors. They crossed the narrow Strait of Gibraltar, and signaled their entrance into Europe by immediately re-christening its geographical features. The great rock (the Pillar of Hercules), which had borne for centuries the name of the renowned mythical hero, was destined to bear thereafter the name of the conquering Moorish chief, Tarick (Gibraltar—Geber-al-Tarick, the rock of Tarick).

The wave of invasion crossed the Pyrenees, but its onward progress in that direction was arrested forever by the decisive victory of the French on the plain of Tours. Confined to Spain, the Moors or Arabs immortalized their occupation of the region by the diligent cultivation of the arts and sciences and the number of Arabic terms prominent in scientific nomenclature.

ALPHABETICAL WORD LIST

abate
abbot
abbreviate
abdicate
abdomen
abduct
aberration
abeyance
abhor
abject
abjure
ablative
ablution
abnegation
abnormal
abominate
abolish
aboriginal
aborigines
abound (und)
abrade
abrasion
abridge (brev)
abrogate
abrupt
abscind
abscond
absent

absolute
absolve
absorb
absorption
abstain (ten)
abstemious
abstract
abstruse
absurd
abundant
abuse
abyss
acalephoid
acanthaceous
acanthus
acaulous
accelerate
accent (cant)
accept (capt)
access
accident (cad)
accipitres
acclaim (clam)
acclivity
accommodate
accomplice
accord
accost

accoutrement
accretion
accrue (cresc)
accumulate
accurate
accuse (caus)
accerval
acephalous
acerbity
acetic
aehene
achieve (chief/
    chef)
achromatic
acinaciform
acicular
acid
aciform
acme
acoustic
    (a cow'stik)
acoustics
acquaint
    (cognit)
acquiesce
acquire (quer)
acquit (quiet)
acrid

*acri*mony
*acri*tude
*acro*bat
*acro*gen
*acro*polis
*acro*stic
*acule*ate
*acu*men
*acu*te
ad*age*
ad*amant*
ad*apt*
ad*dict*ed
ad*dress*
ad*duce*
*aden*ose
adept
ad*equ*ate
ad*here*
ad*hes*ion
ad*hes*ive
adieu
*adip*ose
ad*jac*ent
ad*ject*ive
ad*journ* (*diurn*)
ad*judic*ate
ad*junct*
ad*jure*
ad*just*
*adjut*ant
ad*minister*
ad*mire*
ad*miss*ion
ad*mit*

ad*mon*ish
ad*monit*ion
ad*olesc*ent
ad*opt*
ad*ore*
ad*orn*
ad*roit* (*direct*)
*adul*ation
adult
*adulter*ate
ad*umbr*ation
ad*vance*
   (*avanc*)
ad*vant*age
   (*avant*)
ad*vent*
ad*vent*ure
ad*verse*
ad*vert*
ad*vert*ise
*advis*e
ad*voc*ate
a*dyt*um
*aer*ate
*aer*ial
*aer*iform
*aer*olite
*aer*onaut
*æsth*etic
af*fa*ble
af*fair* (*fac*)
af*fect* (*fact*)
af*fi*ance (*fid*)
af*fid*avit
af*fili*ate

*affin*ity
af*firm*
af*fix*
af*flat*us
af*flict*
af*flu*ent
af*front*
*ag*ent
ag*glomer*ate
ag*glutin*ate
ag*grand*ize
ag*grav*ate
ag*greg*ate
ag*gress*
ag*grieve* (*grav*)
*ag*ile
*ag*itate
*ag*nate
*ag*nomen
*ag*ony
*ag*rarian
*ag*ree (*grat*)
*ag*riculture
*aisl*e (*al*)
*alacr*ity
alb
*alb*ino
*alb*um
*alb*umen
*alb*urnum
al*che*my
*alder*man
al*ert*
*ali*as
*ali*bi

alien	**ambl**e (*ambul*)	ana**lyz**e
aliment	**ambros**ia	ana**pest**
alimony	**ambro**type	an**archy**
ali**quot**	(*ambrot*)	ana**the**ma
all**ege**	**ambul**ance	ana**tomy**
all**eg**ory	a**melior**ate	an**ces**tor
all**ev**iate	a**men**able	an**chor**ite
all**e**y	a**mend**	**ancien**t
all**eg**ation	a**men**ity	anec**dote**
all**iter**ation	a**merce**	**anem**one
allo**path**y	**ami**able (*amic*)	an**er**oid
all**oy** (*leg*)	**amic**able	an**eur**ism
all**ude**	**ami**ty (*amic*)	**angel**
all**us**ion	am**munit**ion	**ang**ina
all**u**vial	a**mne**sty	**angio**sperm
ally	a**mor**ous	**ang**uish
almoner	a**morph**ous	an**hel**ation
a**loft**	amphi**bi**ous	an**hydr**ous
alphabet	amphi**brach**	animad**vert**
altar	amphi**the**ater	**anim**al
alter	am**phor**a	**animal**cule
altercation	**ampl**e	**anim**ate
alternate	**ampl**ify	**anim**osity
altitude	**ampl**itude	**anim**us
alveolate	am**put**ate	**ann**als
a**man**uensis	**amygdal**oid	ann**ex**
amateur	**amyl**aceous	an**nihil**ate
amative	ana**chron**ism	**anni**versary
amatory	an**æm**ia (*haim*)	an**nounce**
ambassador	an**æsth**etic	(*nunci*)
ambi**dexter**	ana**gram**	**ann**ual
ambi**dextr**ous	ana**lemm**a	**ann**ul
ambi**ent**	ana**log**y	**ann**ular
ambi**g**uous (*ag*)	ana**lys**is	an**nunci**ation
ambi**t**ion	ana**lyt**ic	ano**dyn**e

anoint (*unct*)
anomaly
anonymous
anserine
antagonist
antecedent
antediluvian
antemeridian
antennæ
antepenult
anterior
anthology
anthracite
anthropogra-
 phy
anthropology
anthropophagi
anticipate (*cap*)
antidote
antipathy
antiphon
antipode
antipodes
antiquary
antique
antiquity
antiseptic
antithesis
antitype
anxious (*ang*)
aorta
apathy
aperient
aperture
apex

aphæresis
 (*hair*)
aphelion
aphorism
aphthong
apiary
Apocalypse
Apocrypha
apogee
apology
apoplexy
apostate
apostle (*stol*)
apostrophe
apothecary
apothegm
apotheosis
appall
appanage
apparatus
apparent
apparition
appeal (*pell*)
appear (*appar*)
appease (*pac*)
appellation
append
appetite
applaud
apply
apposite
appraise
 (*preci*)
appreciate
apprehend

apprentice
 (*prehend*)
apprize
approbation
appropriate
approve
approximate
appurtenance
apse
apsides
apterous
aptitude
aquafortis
aquarium
aquatic
aqueduct
aqueous
aquiline
arable
arbiter
arborator
arboreous
arborescence
arboret
arboretum
arboriculture
arc
arcade
arcanum
arch
archæology
 (*archai*)
archaic
archaism
archer

archetype
architect
architrave
archives
arctic
ardent
ardor
arduous
area
arefaction
arena
arenaceous
argent
argillaceous
argue
arid
aristocracy
arithmetic
armada
armadillo
armament
armipotent
armistice
aroma
arrest
arrive
arrogant
arrogate
arson
article
artifice
artillery
Aryan
asbestos
ascend

ascetic
ascetitious
ascribe
asinine
aspect
asperity
asperse
asphyxia
　(sphuz)
aspire
aspirate
assail (sal)
assault (salt)
assemble
assent
assert
assess
assets (satis)
asseverate
assiduous
assimilate
assist
assize (sess)
associate
assuage (suav)
assume
assumption
assure
aster
asterisk
asteroid
asthenic
asthma
astral
astriction

astringent
astrology
astronomy
astute
asylum
ataxic
atheist
athlete
atmosphere
atom
atrocious
atrocity
atrophy
attach
attack (tach)
attain (ten)
attempt
attend
attention
attenuate
attest
attire
attitude (apt)
attorney
　(atorn)
attract
attribute
attrition
auburn (alb)
auction
audacious
audible
audience
audit
augment

*aug*ust
*aur*eola
*aur*ic
*aur*icle
*aur*icular
*aur*iculate
*aur*if*er*ous
*aur*iform
*aur*ist
*auscult*ation
au*spic*e (*spec*)
au*spic*ious
(*spec*)
*auster*e
*authen*tic
*auth*or (*auct*)
auto*cracy*
auto*graph*
auto*matic*
auto*maton*
auto*nomy*
auto*ps*y
*aut*umn (*auct*)
*auxili*ary
a*vail* (*val*)
*aval*anche
*avar*ice
*aven*aceous
a*veng*e
a*ven*ue
a*ver*
*aver*age
a*vers*e
a*vert*
*avi*ary

*avid*ity
a*voc*ation
a*void*
*axi*al
*axill*ary
*axio*m
*axi*s
a*zo*ic
a*zo*te

*bacc*ivorous
*badin*age (azh)
bail
*bail*iff
*bail*iwick
ba*lance* (*bi*)
*ball*ad
ball*ast*
*ball*et
*ball*oon
*ball*ot
*band*it
bank*rupt*
*bany*an
*bapt*ize
barb
*barbar*ous
*barb*er
*bar*o*meter*
*barric*ade
bary*tone*
*basil*ica
*basil*isk
bass
bass-relief

(bä-relief)
*bast*ile
*bastin*ado
(*baston*)
*bast*ion
*bath*os
*bathy*metrical
baton
*batrach*ian
*batt*alion
*batt*er
*batt*ery
*batt*le
*batt*lement
*beat*itude
beau (*bo*)
*beau*ty
*bel*dam
be*leaguer*
*belemn*ite
bella*donna*
*bell*e
*bell*icose
*bell*igerent
Benedict
*benedict*ion
bene*fact*ion
bene*fact*or
bene*fic*e (*fac*)
bene*fic*ent (*fac*)
bene*fit* (*fact*)
bene*vol*ent
benign
benison
(*benediction*)

bestial
beverage
bias
bib
bibaceous
bibber
bibliography
bibliology
bibliomania
bibliopole
bibulous
bi**cephal**ous
bi**corn**ous
bi**dent**al
bi**enn**ial
bi**foli**ate
bi**furc**ated
bi**gam**y
bi**later**al
bile
bi**lingu**al
bill
billet
billiards
bi**man**ous
binary
bi**nocul**ar
bi**nom**ial
biography
biology
bi**part**ite
bi**ped**
bi**penn**ate
bis**cuit** (*coct*)
bi**sect**

bishop (*scop*)
bis**sext**ile
bi**valv**e
blanch
blanc-mange
bland
blank (*blanc*)
blanket (*blanc*)
blas**phe**me
blazon (*blazon*)
board (*bord*)
bombard
bombast
bona fide
bonbon
bonny
bonus
border
borough
botany
bounty (*bon*)
bovine
brace
bracelet
brachial
brachiate
brachycephalic
brachy**graph**y
brackish
branchial
brasier
breve
brevet
breviary
brevier

brevity
brief (*brev*)
brigade
brigand
brigantine
brilliant
brochure
   (broshoor')
bronchial
bronchitis
brumal
brute
buccal
bucolic
buffalo
bugle
bulrush
bulwark
burlesque
bursar
butter
butyraceous
byssoid

cable (*cap*)
cachinnation
cadaverous
cadence
cæsura
calamiferous
calamity
calamus
calcareous
calcimine
calcine

calcium
calculate
calculous
calculus
calculi
caldron
calefy
calendar
calender
calends
calisthenics
calligraphy
callous
calm
calomel
caloric
calorific
calumny
calx
calyx
camelopard
camera
camerated
camp
campaign
campanula
campestral
cancriform
candelabrum
candid
candidate
candle
candor
cane
canister

cannon
cañon
canon
cant
cantata
canticle
capable
capacious
caparison
cape
caper
capillary
capital
capitation
capitular
capitulate
capnomancy
caprice
capricorn
caprid
capsule
captain (*capit*)
captious
captivate
captive
captor
capture
caracole
carbon
carbunche
cardiac
cardinal
careen (*carin*)
caress
caricature

carinated
carnage
carnal
carnation
carnelian
carnival
carnivorous
carotid
carpenter
carpet
carpology
carrion (*carn*)
cartel
cartilage
cartography
cartoon
cartouch
cartridge
cascade
caseine
caseous
cashier
caste
castellated
castigate
castle (*castell*)
casual
cataclysm
catacomb
  (*cymb*)
catalepsy
catalogue
cataplasm
cataract
catarrh

catastrophe
catechise
category
catenate
caterpillar
cathartic
cathedral
catholic
catholicon
catoptrics
caudal
cauliflower
cause
causeway (*calx*)
caustic
cauterize
caution
cavalcade
(*cavall*)
cavalier
(*cavall*)
cavalry (*cavall*)
cave
cavern
cavil
cavity
cede
ceiling (*cel*)
celebrate
celerity
celestial
celibacy
cemetery
cenobite
(*coino*)

cenotaph
(*ceno*)
censer
censor
censure
cent
centenary
centenarian
centennial
centesimal
centigrade
centipede
centrifugal
centripetal
centuple
centurion
century
cephalic
ceraceous
ceramic
cerate
cere
cereal
cerebral
cerebrum
cerement
ceremonial
ceriferous
certain
certify
certitude
cerulean
ceruse
cervical
cervine

cessation
cession
cetaceous
chafe (*chauf*)
chagrin
challenge
chameleon
chamomile
champagne
(*sham*)
chandelier
(*candel*)
chandler
(*candel*)
chant (*cant*)
chaos
character
charlatan (sh)
charm (*carm*)
charnel (*carn*)
chart
charter
chasm
chaste (*cast*)
chasten (*cast*)
chastise (*cast*)
chemistry
cherish
chevalier (sh)
chief
chieftain
chicanery (sh)
chiliometer
chime (*cymb*)
chimera

(*chimair*)
chimney
(*camin*)
chiro**graphy**
chirology
chiromancy
chiropodist
chisel (*cæs*)
chivalry
(*cheval*)
chloral
chlorine
chloro**form**
chloro**phyl**
choir (*chor*)
choler
cholera
chondrology
choral
chord
chrism
Christ
chromatic
chrome
chromium
chromo
chronic
chronicle
chronology
chronometer
chrysalis
chrysanthe-
mum
chryselephan-
tine

chrysoprase
chyle
chyme
cicatrice
cicatrix
ciliary
cincture
cinerary
cineritious
cinquefoil
circum**ambu-**
late
circum**ference**
circum**flex**
circum**flu**ence
circum**fuse**
circum**jace**nt
circum**locut**ion
circum**scrib**e
circum**spect**
circum**stance**
circum**vall**ation
circum**vent**
circum**volve**
circus
cirriferous
cirrigerous
cirrous
cistern
citadel
cite
civil
claim (*clam*)
clamny
clamor

clandestine
claret
clarify
clarion
class
classic
clause
claviary
clavichord
clavicle
clavier
clef (*clav*)
clematis
clement
clerk
clergy
client
climate
climax
clinic
clinical
cloister
clypeate
clyster
co**adjut**or
co**agul**ate
coagulum
co**alesce**
co**alit**ion
coast (*cost*)
cocciferous
coccyx
code
codicil
co**erce**

cogent
cogitate
cognate
cognition
cognizance
   (*cognosc*)
cognomen
cohabit
cohere
coherent
cohesion
coign (*cune*)
coin (*cune*)
coincide
coleopteral
colewort (*caul*)
collapse
collar
collate
collateral
colleague (*leg*)
collect
college
collet
collide
collision
collodion
colloid
colloquial
colloquy
collude
collusion
colonel
   (kurnel)
colony

colporteur
   (*coll*)
columbary
columbine
column
coma
comatose
combat
combatant
combine
combustion
comedy
comet
comfit (*fact*)
comfort
comic
comity
comma
command
commemorate
commence
   (*initi*)
commend
   (*mand*)
commensurate
comment
commerce
commination
comminute
commiserate
commissary
commit
commodicus
commodity
common (*mun*)

commune
community
commute
compact
company
comparable
compare
compass
compassion
compatible
compeer (*par*)
compel
compend
compendium
compendious
compensate
compete
competent
competition
compile
complacent
complain
complaisant
complement
complete
complex
complicate
complicity
compliment
   (*ple*)
comply
   (*compli*)
component
comport
compose

composite
compost (*posit*)
compound
  (*pond*)
comprehend
comprehensive
comprise
compromise
compulsion
compunction
compute
comrade
  (*camer*)
concatenation
concave
conceal (*cel*)
concede
conceit (*capt*)
conceive (*cap*)
conception
  (*capt*)
concern
concert (*sert*)
concession
conchology
conciliate
concise (*cæs*)
conclave
conclude
conclusion
concoct
concomitant
concord
concourse
  (*curs*)

concrete
concur
concussion
  (*quass*)
condemn
condense
condescend
condign
condition (*dat*)
condole
condone
conduce
conduct
conduit (*duct*)
cone
confabulation
confect (*fact*)
confection
  (*fact*)
confederate
confer
confess
confide
confine
confirm
confiscate
conflagration
conflict
confluence
conflux
confound
  (*fund*)
confraternity
confront
confuse

confute
congeal (*gel*)
congenial
congenital
congeries
congestion
conglomerate
conglutinate
congratulate
congregate
congress
congruous
conirostral
conjecture
conjugal
conjugate
conjunction
conjuncture
conjure
connate
connect
connive
connote
connubial
conquer
conquest
consanguinity
conscience
conscious
conscript
consecrate
  (*sacr*)
consecutive
consent
consequent

conserve
consider
consign
consist
console
consolidate
consonant
consort
conspicuous
    (spec)
conspire
constant
constellation
consternation
constipate
constitute
constrain
    (string)
constrict
construct
construe
consult
consume
consummate
consumption
contact
contagion
    (tang)
contain (ten)
contaminate
contemn
contemplate
contemporane-
    ous
contemporary

contempt
contend
content
conterminous
contest
context
contiguous
    (tang)
continent (ten)
contingent
    (tang)
continue (ten)
contort
contortion
contour (tourn)
contraband
contract
contradict
contralto
contrary
contrast
contravene
contribute
contrition
contrive (trov)
controversy
controvert
contumacy
contumely
contusion
convalesce
convection
convene
convent
convention

converge
conversant
converse
convert
convex
convey (vi)
convict
convince
convivial
convolute
convolve
convolvulus
convoy (vi)
convulse
cooperate
coordinate
copious
copula
copy (copi)
corbeil
corbel
cordate
cordial
corduroy
coriaceous
corium
cornea
corneous
cornel
corner
cornet
cornice (coron)
cornicle
corniform
cornucopia

cornuted
corolla (*coron*)
corollary
   (*coron*)
corona
coronal
coronation
coroner
coronet
coroniform
coronule
corporal
corporate
corporation
corporeal
corps (*kor*)
corpse
corpulent
corpuscle
correct
corridor
corrigible
corroborate
corrode
corrosion
corrugate
corrupt
corsair
corse
corselet
corset
cortical
cortege
   (kor'tazh)
coruscate

corvette (*corb*)
corvine
cosmetic
cosmic
cosmical
cosmogony
cosmography
cosmopolitan
cosmorama
costal
costate
cotemporane-
   ous
cotemporary
cotyledon
cotyloid
count (*comit*)
countenance
counterfeit
   (*fact*)
country (*contr*)
couple (*copul*)
couplet (*copul*)
courage (*cor*)
courier (*curr*)
course (*curs*)
covenant
cranium
cranny
crasis
crassitude
crate
crater
crayon (*crai*)
create

creature
credence
credentials
credible
credit
credulous
creed
cremation
crenate
crenelate
creosote
crepitation
crescent
cretaceous
crevasse
crevice
criminal
criminate
crinite
crinoline
crisp
criterion
critic
crucial
crucify
crucifixion
crude
cruise (*cruc*)
crural
crusade (*cruc*)
crustacea
crypt
cryptogam
crystal
cubation

cube
cubit
cucullate
cuirass (*cori*)
culm
culminate
culpable
culprit
cultivate
culture
culvert (*col*)
cumulate
cuneal
cuneate
cuneiform
cupidity
cupola
cupreous
cupriferous
curate
curator
cure
curious
current
curriculum
cursory
curt
curtail
curvirostral
cuspidate
custody
cutaneous
cuticle
cutlet (*cost*)
cycle

cyclone
cyclopedia
cyclopædia
cyclops
cymbal
cymbiform
cynic
cynosure
cyst

dactyl
dame
damn
damsel
data
date
dative
datum
daunt (*domit*)
deal
debate
debenture
debilitate
debility
debit
debouch
    (daboosh')
debris (da bre)
decade
decadence
decahedron
decalogue
decamp
decant
decanter

decapitate
decapod
decastich
decastyle
decay (*cad*)
decease (*cess*)
deceit (*capt*)
deceive (*cap*)
decemvir
decennial (*ann*)
decent
deception
    (*capt*)
decide (*cæd*)
deciduous (*cad*)
decimal
decimate
decision (*cæs*)
decisive (*cæs*)
declaim (*clam*)
declare
declension
decline
declivity
decoct
decollate
decorate
decorous
decorum
decrease
    (*cresc*)
decrepit
decrescent
decretal
decumbent

decussate	**dei**st	**dendr**ometer
de**dicate**	**dei**ty	**dendr**ology
de**duce**	de**ject**ed	de**nomin**ate
de**duct**	**del**eble	de**note**
de**face**	de**lect**able	de**nounc**e
de**falc**ate	de**leg**ate	(*nunci*)
de**fam**e	de**lete**	**dens**e
de**fault**	de**leter**ious	**dent**al
de**feat** (*fact*)	de**lib**erate	**dent**icle
de**fec**ate	de**lic**ate	**dent**iform
de**fect** (*fact*)	de**lici**ous	**dent**ifrice
de**fend**	de**light** (*delect*)	**dent**ist
de**fens**e	de**line**ate	**dent**ition
de**fer**	de**linqu**ent	de**nude**
de**fer**ence	de**lir**ious	de**ny** (*neg*)
de**fic**ient (*fac*)	de**liver** (*liber*)	de**part**
de**fic**it (*fac*)	de**lude**	de**part**ment
de**file**	de**luge** (*diluvi*)	de**part**ure
de**fin**e	de**lus**ion	de**pend**
de**fin**ite	**dem**agogue	de**pict**
de**flag**ration	de**mand**	de**pil**ate
de**flect**	de**marc**ation	de**plete**
de**flex**ion	de**mean**	de**plore**
de**flor**ate	de**mean**or	de**ploy** (*pli*)
de**flux**ion	de**ment**ed	de**pon**ent
de**foli**ation	de**ment**ia	de**popul**ate
de**form**	de**mis**e	de**port**
de**funct**	demo**cracy**	de**pose**
de**gener**ate	de**mol**ish	de**posit**
de**glut**ition	de**monet**ize	de**prav**e
de**grade**	de**monstr**ate	de**precate**
de**his**cent	**dem**otic	de**preci**ate
deify	de**mur**	(*preti*)
deign (*dign*)	de**mur**e (*mor*)	de**pred**ate
deism	**dendr**iform	(*præd*)

depress
deprive
depute
derelict
deride
derision
derive
dermal
dermatology
dermoid
derogate
derogatory
descant
descend
  (scand)
describe
description
descry (scrib)
desecrate (sacr)
desert
deshabille
  (desabil)
desiccate
desiderate
desideratum
design
designate
desire (desider)
desist
desolate
despatch
  (pesch)
desperate
despicable
  (spec)

despise
  (spic, spec)
despoil (spoli)
despond
despot
dessert
destine
destitute
destroy (stru)
destruction
desuetude
desultory (salt)
detach
detail
detect
detention
deter (terr)
detergent
deteriorate
determine
detersion
detest
detonate
detour (tourn)
detract
detriment (trit)
detritus
detrition
detrude
detruncate
deuterogamy
Deuteronomy
devastate
develop (volup)
deviate

device (divis)
devious
devise (divis)
devoid
devolve
devote
devour (vor)
devout (vot)
dexter
dexterity
dextral
dextrorsal
diabolic
diabolical
diabolism
diacritical
diadem
diæresis (hair)
diagnosis
diagonal
diagram
dial
dialect
dialogue
diameter
diapason
diaphanous
diaphragm
diarrhea
diary
diatonic
diatribe
dicephalous
dictate
diction

dictionary
dictum
didactic
  (*didasc*)
dif**fer**
dif**fic**ulty (*fac*)
dif**fid**ent
dif**fus**e
di**gest**
digit
di**glyph**
dignify
dignitary
dignity
di**graph**
di**gress**
di**lacer**ate
di**lapid**ate
di**lat**e
di**lat**ory
di**lemm**a
di**lig**ent (*leg*)
di**lu**ent
di**lut**e
diluvial
dime (*decim*)
di**mens**ion
di**meter**
di**min**ish
di**minut**ion
di**miss**ory
di**mit**y
di**morph**ism
diocese
dioptrics

dio**ra**ma
diphtheria
di**phthong**
di**plo**ma
di**pter**al
dire
di**rect**
dis**aster**
dis**burs**e
disc
dis**cern**
disciple
dis**comfit**
  (*confit*)
dis**commod**e
dis**concert**
dis**cord**
dis**course**
  (*curs*)
dis**creet** (*cret*)
dis**crep**ant
dis**cret**ion
discriminate
dis**curs**ive
dis**cuss** (*quass*)
dis**dain** (*dign*)
dis**gorge**
dis**grace** (*grati*)
dis**gust**
dis**hevel**
  (*chevel*)
dis**integr**ate
dis**junct**ive
dis**loc**ate
dismal (*decim*)

dis**miss**
dis**par**age
dis**par**ity
dis**patch** (see
  des**patch**)
dis**pel**
dis**pens**ary
dis**pens**e
dis**pers**e (*spars*)
dis**play** (*pli*)
dis**port**
dis**pos**e
dis**posit**ion
dis**put**e
dis**quisit**ion
dis**reput**able
dis**rupt**
dis**sect**
dis**sembl**e
dis**semin**ate
dis**sensi**on
dis**sent**
dis**sert**ation
dis**sid**ent (*sed*)
dis**simul**ation
dis**sip**ate (*sup*)
dis**solut**e
dis**solut**ion
dis**solv**e
dis**son**ant
dis**suad**e
dis**suas**ion
dis**tain** (*ting*)
dis**tant**
dis**temper**

distend
distension
distich
distil (*still*)
distinct
distinguish
distort
distrain
   (*string*)
distress
distribute
district
disturb
ditto (*dict*)
ditty (*dict*)
diurnal
divaricate
diverge
divers
diverse
diversion
divert
divest
divide
dividend
divine
divisible
division
divisor
divorce (*vers*)
divulge
docile
doctor
doctrine
document

dodecagon
dedecahedron
dogma
dogmatic
dogmatical
dogmatize
dolorous
domain
   (*domin*)
dome
domestic
domicile
dominant
dominate
domineer
dominical
dominion
donate
donor
dormant
dormer
dormitory
dorsal
dose
doubt (*dubit*)
doxology
drama
drape
draper
drapery
drastic
dress
dromedary
drupe
dryad (*dru*)

dual
dubious
duct
ductile
duel
duet
duke (*duc*)
dulcet
dulcimer
duodecimal
duodecimo
duodenum
duplicate
duplicity
durable
duramen
durance
duration
duress
dynamic
dynamics
dynamite
dynasty
dysentery
dyspepsia
   (*pepi*)

ebriety
ebullient
ebullition
eccentric
ecclesiastic
echo
eclectic
eclipse (*leip*)

eclogue (*leg*)
economy
ecstasy
ecumenic
ecumenical
edacious
edible
edict
edifice
edify
edile
edit (*dat*)
edition (*dat*)
educate
educe
eduction
efface
effect (*fact*)
effeminate
effervesce
effete
efficacious (*fac*)
efficient (*fac*)
effigy
efflorescence
effluence
effluvium
efflux
effort
effrontery
effulgent
effuse
effusion
effusive
egoism

egoist
egotist
egregious
egress
ejaculate
eject
elaborate
elapse
elastic
elate
elect
electricity
eleemosynary
elegant
elegy
element
elevate
elicit (*lac*)
elide
elision
eligible (*leg*)
eliminate
elision (*læs*)
elixir (*iksir*)
ellipse (*leip*)
elocution
elope
eloquent
elucidate
elude
elusive
elusory
emaciate
emancipate
emasculata

embellish
emblem (*ball*)
embrace
embrasure
embrocation
embryo
emend
emerge
emetic
emigrate
eminent
emissary
emission
emit
emolliate
emollient
emolument
emotion
empale
emperor
   (*imperat*)
emphasis
empire
   (*imperi*)
empiric (*peir*)
employ (*pli*)
emporium
empyreal
empyrean
emulate (*æmul*)
emulsion
enamor
encaustic (*cai*)
encephalic
enchant

enchase (*chass*)
enclitic (*clin*)
encomium
encounter
   (*contra*)
encroach
   (*croc*)
encyclical
encyclopædia
endemic
endogen
endow (*dou*)
endue (*endo*)
endure
enemy (*inimic*)
energy
enervate
enfilade
enfranchise
engage
engender
   (*gener*)
engine (*ingeni*)
engross
enhance (*ante*)
enigma
enormous
ensconce
   (*schantz*)
ensiform
ensign
ensue
entablature
entail (*taill*)
enteric

enterprise
entertain (*ten*)
enthusiasm
   (*theos*)
entity
entomoid
entomology
entrails
entreat (*trait*)
enumerate
enunciate
envelop (*volup*)
envelope
   (*volup*)
environ
envoy (*vi*)
epact
epaulet
ephemeral
epic
epicarp
epicycle
epidemic
epidermis
epigastric
epiglottis
epigram
   (*gramm*)
epilepsy
epilogue
epiphany
episcopal
episode (*eisod*)
episperm
epistle (*stell*)

epitaph
epithet
epitome (*temn*)
epizootic
epoch
epode
equable (*æqu*)
equal
equanimity
equation
equator
equestrian
equilateral
equilibrium
equine
equinoctial
equinox
equipoise
equipollent
equiponderant
equity
equivalent
equivocal
eradicate
erase
erect
erode
erosion
erotic
err
errant
erubescent
eructate
erudite
eruption

erysipelas (*pell*)
escalade
e**scort**
e**sc**ulent
eso**phag**us
esoteric
e**speci**al
espionage
es**plan**ade
e**spous**e
e**ss**ence
e**stabl**ish
e**stat**e
e**sth**etic
e**stim**able
estival
estuary
e**tern**al
ethic
ethical
ethics
ethnic
ethnography
ethnology
etymology
etymon
eu**charis**t
(*chariz*)
eu**logy**
eu**phem**ism
eu**phony**
eureka
e**vacu**ate
e**vad**e
e**vanesc**ent

e**vangel**ist
e**vas**ive
e**vent**
e**vict**
e**vid**ent
e**vince**
e**viscer**ate
e**voke** (*voc*)
e**volut**ion
e**volve**
ex**acerb**ate
ex**act**
ex**agger**ate
ex**alt**
ex**amin**e
ex**ampl**e
(*exempl*)
ex**asper**ate
ex**cav**ate
ex**ceed** (*ced*)
ex**cel** (*excell*)
ex**cels**ior
ex**cept** (*capt*)
ex**cerpt** (*carpt*)
ex**cess**
ex**cis**ion (*cæs*)
ex**cit**e
ex**claim** (*clam*)
ex**clud**e
ex**clus**ive
ex**commun**icate
ex**cori**ate
ex**cre**ment
(*cret*)
ex**cresc**ence

ex**cret**e
ex**cruc**iate
ex**culp**ate
ex**curs**ion
ex**cus**e (*caus*)
ex**ecr**ate (*sacr*)
ex**ecut**e (*secut*)
ex**eges**is (*egeis*)
ex**empl**ar
ex**empl**ary
ex**empl**ify
ex**empt**
ex**equ**ies (*sequ*)
ex**erc**ise (*arc*)
ex**ert** (*sert*)
ex**hal**e
ex**haust**
ex**hibit**
ex**hilar**ate
ex**hort**
ex**hum**e
ex**ig**ent (*ag*)
exile
ex**ist**
ex**it**
ex**od**us
ex**ogen**
ex**oner**ate
ex**orbit**ant
ex**orc**ise (*orciz*)
ex**ordi**um
exoteric
exotic
ex**pand**
ex**pans**e

expatiate
  (*spati*)
expatriate
ex*pect* (*spect*)
expect*or*ate
exped*i*ent
exped*i*te
exped*i*tion
ex*pel* (*pell*)
ex*pend*
ex*pens*e
exper*i*ence
exper*i*ment
ex*pert*
exp*i*ate
ex*pire* (*spir*)
ex*plain* (*plan*)
*pl*etive
ex*plic*able
ex*plic*ate
ex*plic*it
ex*plode* (*plaud*)
ex*plore*
ex*plos*ion
  (*plaus*)
ex*pon*ent
ex*port*
ex*pose*
ex*posit*ion
ex*postul*ate
ex*pound* (*pon*)
ex*press*
ex*pugn*
ex*puls*ion
ex*punge*

ex*purg*ate
ex*quisit*e
ex*sicc*ant
ex*sicc*ate
ex*tant* (*stant*)
ex*tempor*ane-
  ous
ex*tempor*e
ex*tend*
ex*tens*ion
ex*tent*
ex*tenu*ate
ex*ter*ior
ex*termin*ate
ex*ter*nal
ex*tinct*
ex*tinguish*
ex*tirp*ate (*stirp*)
ex*tol* (*toll*)
ex*tort*
ex*tract*
ex*tradit*ion
extra*judic*ial
extra*mund*ane
*extra*neous
extra*vag*ant
extra*vas*ate
ex*treme*
ex*tric*ate
ex*trins*ic
ex*trude*
ex*trus*ion
ex*uber*ant
ex*ude* (*sud*)
ex*ult* (*salt*)

ex*ust*ion
*exu*viæ
*exu*viable

*fab*aceous
*fa*ble
*fab*ric
*fab*ricate
*fab*ulous
*fa*çade
*fa*cet
*facet*ious
*faci*al
facile
*facil*itate
*facil*ity
fac-*simil*e
fact
*fact*ion
*fact*ious
*fact*itious
*fact*or
*fact*ory
fac*to*tum
*facul*ty (*facil*)
*fæc*es
faint (*feint*)
*fal*chion
*falc*iform
*fal*con (faw'kn)
*fall*acy
*fall*ible
false
*fal*ter (*fall*)
*fa*me

familiar
family (*famili*)
famine
fanatic
fantasy (*phan*, *phain*)
farce
farina
farm (*firm*)
farrago
farrier (*ferr*)
fascinate
fascine
fascis
fashion (*faci*)
fastidious
fatal
fate
fatigue
fatuity
fauces
fault (*falt*)
faun
favor
feasible (*fac*)
feat (*fact*)
febrifuge
febrile
February
feculent
fecundity
federal
federation
feldspar
felicitate

felicity
feline
felon
female (*femell*)
feminine
femoral
fence (*fens*)
ferment (*ferv*)
ferocious
ferreous
ferriferous
ferruginous
ferrugo
fertile
ferule
fervent
fervid
fervor
festal
festive
fetich (*fact*)
fetid (*fact*)
fiber
fibrile
fictile
fiction
fictitious
fidelity
fiducial
fiduciary
figment (*fing*)
filament
file
filial
filigree

final
finance
fine
finis
finish
finite
firmament
fiscal
fissile
fissure
fistula
flaccid
flagellate
flagitious
flagrant
flatulent
flatus
flavor
flexible
flexile
flexion
flexuous
flexure
floccose
flocculent
flora
floral
floret
floriculture
florid
florin
florist
floscule
floss
flour (*flor*)

*flour*ish (*flor*)
flower (*flor*)
*fluctu*ate
*flu*ent
*flu*id
*flu*me
*flu*sh
*flut*e (*flat*)
*flu*vial
flux
*flux*ible
*flux*ion
*foc*us
*foli*aceous
*foli*age
*foli*ate
*foli*o
*foll*icle
*fo*ment (*fov*)
font
*for*amen
*foramin*ated
*foramin*iferous
*forc*eps (*form*)
*for*eclose
*for*eign
*for*est
for*feit* (*fact*)
formic
*formic*ate
*formid*able
*form*ula
fort
*fort*e (*fort*)
*fort*ify

*fort*itude
*fortu*itous
*fortu*ity
*fortun*e
*for*um
*foss*e
*foss*il
found (*fund*)
*found*er (*fund*)
*found*ery
   (*fund*)
*found*ry (*fund*)
*fount*ain (*font*)
fracas (*fracass*)
*fract*ion
*fract*ious
*fract*ure
*frag*ile (*frang*)
*frag*ment
   (*frang*)
*fragr*ant
*fra*il (*frang*)
*franch*ise
*frang*ible
frank (*franc*)
*frank*incense
   (*frank*)
*fran*tic (*phren*)
*frater*nal
*fratr*icide
fraud
*fren*zy (*phren*)
*frequ*ent
*fresc*o
*fri*able

*frict*ion
*frig*id
*frit*ter
*fri*volous
frond
front
*front*al
*front*ier
*frontispiec*e
   (*spec*)
*front*let
*fruct*ify
*frug*al
*frug*iferous
fruit (*fruct*)
*frustr*ate
frustum
*fuc*us
*fuc*oid
*fug*acious
*fugit*ive
*fulc*rum
*fulg*ent
*fulig*inous
*fulmin*ate
*fulv*ous
*fum*e
*fum*igate
fun*ambul*ist
*funct*ion
fund
*fund*ament
*fund*amental
*funer*al
*funer*eal

funiform
furcate
furious
furnace
furor
furtive
fuscous
fuse
fusee
fusible
fusil
fusion
futile (*fund*)
future

gable (*gabel*)
gainsay (*gegn*)
galaxy
gallinaceous
ganglion
gan**grene**
   (*grain*)
gantlet (*gat*)
garment (*garn*)
garner (*gran*)
garnish
garrulous
gastric
gastro**nom**y
gaudy
gelatine
gelid
gem (*gemm*)
geminous
gemmation

gender (*gener*)
genealogy
general
generate
generic
generous
genesis
genial
geniculate
genii
genitive
genius
genteel
Gentile
gentle
gentry
genu**flect**ion
genuine
genus
geocentric
geogony
geography
geology
geometry
georgic (*erg*)
geranium
germ
german
germane
germinal
germinate
gestation
gesticulate
gesture
gibbous

gigantic
glabrous
glacier
glacis
gladiator
gland
glebe
globe
glomerate
glory
gloss
glossary
glottis
glucose
glume
glut
gluten
glutinous
glutton
glycerine (*gluc*)
gnome
gnomon
gorge
gorgeous
gorget
go**spel**
govern (*gubern*)
grace (*grati*)
grade
gradual
graduate
graft (*graph*)
grain (*gran*)
grallatory
gramineous

*gramin*ivorous
grammar
*gram*pus
*gran*ary
grand
*grand*ee
grandi*loqu*ent
*gran*ge
*gran*ite
*gran*ule
*graph*ic
*grat*eful
*grat*ify
*grat*is
*grat*itude
*grat*uitous
*grat*uity
*grat*ulate
*grav*amen
*grav*e
*grav*itate
*grav*ity
*greg*arious
grief (*grav*)
*griev*e (*grav*)
*griev*ous (*grav*)
gross
*gubern*atorial
*guer*don
*guerr*illa
*gurg*le
gust
*gust*atory
*gutt*er
*guttur*al

*gymn*asium
*gymn*ast
*gymn*osper-
   *m*ous
*gymn*otus (*not*)
*gyn*archy
*gyr*e (*gur*)

*habil*iment
   (*habill*)
habit
*habit*ation
*habit*ude
*hallucin*ation
*hal*o
harmony
*haught*y (*haut*)
*haut*boy
   (ho'boy)
*haut*eur
   (ho tur')
*hears*e
*hebdomad*al
*hecatom*b
*hec*tic
*heder*aceous
hegemony
*hein*ous
heir
*heli*acal (*helio*)
*heli*cal
*heli*coid
*helio*centric
helix
*helminth*ic

helminthology
hemi**stich**
hemorrhage
   (*haim*)
hemorrhoids
   (*haim*)
hendecagon
hepatic
heptagon
hept**archy**
herb
hereditable
hereditament
hereditary
heresy (*hair*)
heritable
heritage
hermeneutics
hermeneutical
hermit (*eremi*)
hernia
hero
hesitate
hetero**dox**
hetero**gen**eous
hetero**mor-**
   phous
hexagon
hexa**hedr**on
hiatus
hibernal
hibernate
hierarchy
hiero**glyph**ic
hilarity

hippodrome
hippopotamus
hirsute
history
histrionic
holo**caus**t (*cai*)
homage
homicide (*cæd*)
homily
homocentric
hom**œopath**y
homo**gen**eous
homo**log**ous
hom**onym**ous
honest
honor
horizon
horologe (*leg*)
horoscope
horror
hortative
horticulture
hospitable
hospital
host (*hospit*)
host**age**
hostile
hostler (*hostel*)
hotel (*hospit*)
hulk
human (*hom*)
humble
humeral
humiliate
humility

humor
hydra
hydrant
hydraulic
hydrogen
hydrometer
hydropathy
hydrophobia
hydrostatics
hymn (*humn*)
hyper**bola** (*ball*)
hyper**bole**
  (*ball*)
hypnotic
hyper**borean**
  (*Boreas*)
hyp**hen**
hypo**chondr**ia
hypocrisy
hypo**gastr**ic
hypo**ten**use
  (*tein*)
hypothecate
hypo**thes**is
hysterical

iambic (*iapt*)
ibex
ichneumon
ichthyology
ichthyopha-
  gous
icono**clast**
  (*eicon*)
iconography

(*eicon*)
icosahedron
idea
identity (*idem*)
idiom
idiosyncrasy
idiot
idol
idyl
igneous
ignescent
igniferous
ignis-**fatu**us
ignite
ignominy
ignoramus
ignorant
ignore
iliac
il**laps**e
il**lat**ive
il**lud**e
il**lumin**e
il**lus**ion
il**lustr**ate
illustrious
image
imagine
imbecile
  (*imbecill*)
im**bib**e
imbricated
im**bru**e (*bever*)
im**bu**e (*bib*)
imitate

imm**macul* ate
im**man* ent
im**medi* ate
im**mens* e
im**merg* e
im**mers* e
im**migr* ate
im**min* ent
im**mol* ate
im**mun* ity
im**mur* e
im**mut* able
im**pact**
im**pair** (*peior*)
im**pal* e
im**part**
im**pass* ive
im**peach**
im**ped* e
im**pel** (*pell*)
im**pend**
im**perat* ive
im**peri* al
im**peri* ous
im**petu* ous
im**pet* us
im**ping* e (*pang*)
im**ple* ment
im**plic* ate
im**plic* it
im**plor* e
im**ply** (*pli*)
im**port**
im**port* ant
im**portun* e

im**pos* e
im**posit* ion
im**post** (*posit*)
im**post* or
im**pot* ent
im**precat* e
im**pregn* able
    (*prehend*)
im**prompt* u
im**prov* e
im**provis* e
im**pud* ent
im**pugn**
im**puls* e
im**pun* ity
im**put* e
in**an* e
in**an* ition
in**augur* ate
in**cand* escend
in**cant* ation
in**carcer* ate
in**carn* ate
in**carn* ation
in**cendi* ary
in**cens* e
in**cent* ive
in**cept* ion
in**cept* ive
in**cess* ant
in**cest** (*cast*)
in**cid* ent (*cad*)
in**ciner* ate
in**cipi* ent
in**cis* ion (*cæs*)

in**cis* ive (*cæs*)
in**cis* or (*cæs*)
in**cit* e
in**clin* e
in**clud* e
in**clus* ive
in**cognit* o
in**coher* ent
in**commod* e
in**compar* able
in**congru* ous
in**corpor* ate
in**corrig* ible
in**creas* e (*cusc*)
in**cub* ate
in**culc* ate (*calc*)
in**culp* ate
in**cumb* ent
in**cur** (*curr*)
in**curs* ion
inde**fatig* able
in**del* ible
in**demn* ity
in**dent**
in**dex**
in**dic* ate
in**dict**
in**dig* enous
in**dig* ent
in**dign* ant
in**dign* ity
indite (*indicat*)
in**divid* ual
in**dol* ent
in**dors* e

in**dubit**able
in**duc**e
in**duct**
in**duc**tion
indue (*endo*)
indulge
in**dur**ate
industry
    (*industri*)
ine**bri**ate
ine**ff**able
in**ept** (*apt*)
inert
inertia
ine**vit**able
ine**xor**able
in**fam**y
in**fant**
in**fant**ry
in**fatu**ate
in**fect** (*fact*)
in**fer**
inferior
infernal
in**fest**
in**fidel**
in**fin**ite
in**firm**
in**flat**e
in**flect**
in**flict**
in**flor**escence
in**flu**ence
in**flu**enza
in**flux**

in**form**
in**frac**tion
in**fring**e (*frang*)
in**fus**e
ingenious
ingenuous
in**grat**e
in**grati**ate
in**gred**ient
    (*grad*)
in**gress**
inguinal
in**habit**
in**hal**e
in**here** (*hær*)
in**herit**
in**hibit** (*habit*)
inimical
iniquity (*æqu*)
initial
initiate
initiative
in**ject**
in**junc**tion
in**jure**
in**nate**
in**noc**ent
in**noc**uous
in**nov**ate
in**nu**endo
in**numer**able
in**ocul**ate
in**opera**tive
in**quest**
    (*quæsit*)

in**quire** (*quær*)
in**quisit**ion
    (*quæsit*)
in**sati**able
in**sati**ate
in**scrib**e
in**scrip**tion
in**scrut**able
in**sect**
in**sert**
insidious
insignia
in**sinu**ate
in**sipid** (*sapid*)
in**sist**
in**sol**ent
in**solv**ent
in**spect**
in**spir**e
in**spiss**ate
in**stall**
in**stanc**e
    (*stand*)
in**stant**
instigate
in**still** (*still*)
in**stinct**
in**stitut**e
in**struct**
in**stru**ment
insular
insulate
in**sult** (*salt*)
in**super**able
in**sure** (*secur*)

insurgent
insurrection
intaglio
   (in tal'yo)
integer
integral
integrity
integument
intellect
intelligent
intend
intense
intent
inter (terr)
intercalate
intercede
intercept (capt)
intercession
intercostal
intercourse
   (curs)
interdict
interest
interfere
interim
interior
interjection
interlard
interlocutor
interloper
interlude
intermediate
interminable
intermission
intermit (mitt)

intermittent
intermural
internal
internecine
interpellation
interpolate
interpose
interposition
interpret
interregnum
interrogate
interrupt
intersect
intersperse
   (spars)
interstice (stat)
interval
intervene
intestate
intestine
intimate
intimidate
intoxicate
intrench
intrepid
intricate
intrigue (tric)
intrinsic (sequ)
introduce
intrude
intuition
inundate
inure (oper)
invade
invalid

invective
inveigh (veh)
invent
inverse
invert
investigate
inveterate
invidious
invincible
invite
invoice (envoi)
invoke (voc)
involve
invulnerable
irascible
ire
irony
irradiate
irrefragable
irreparable
irrevocable
irrigate
irriguous
irritate
irruption
isolate
isosceles
isothermal
issue
isthmus
item
iterate
itinerant
itinerate
itinerary

jaundice
jocose
jocular
jocund
journal
journey
jubilant
jubilee
judicatory
judicial
judiciary
jugular
junction
juncture
junior (juven)
junto
jurisdiction
jurisprudence
jurist
juror
jury
just
justice
juvenile
juxtaposition

kaleidoscope
kleptomania

labial
labor
laboratory
labyrinth
lacerate
lachrymal

lachrymose
lactation
lacteal
lactiferous
lactometer
laity
lambent
lamelliferous
lament
lamina
laminar
lamprey
    (lamb, peti)
lanated
lance
lancinate
land
language
    (lingu)
languid
languish
languor
lanigerous
lantern
lapidary
lapideous
lapse
larceny
lard
lardaceus
larder
largess
larva
laryngoscope
larynx

lascivious
lassitude
latent
lateral
latitude
lattice
laud
laudatory
laundress (lav)
laureate
lava
lave
laver
lavish
lax
laxative
laxity
lay
layman
league (lig)
lease (laiss)
leash (laiss)
leaven (lev)
lecture
legacy
legal
legate
legend
legerdemain
legible
legion
legislate
legitimate
leguminous
leisure (lic)

lemma
lemur
lenient
lenitive
lenity
lenticular
lentus
leonine
leopard
leper
lepidodendron
lepidoptera
leporine
lesion (*læs*)
lessee
lesson (*lect*)
lethal
lethargy
lethean
levant
levee
level (*libr*)
lever
leveret (*lepor*)
levigate
levity
levy
lexicon
liable
libation
libel
liberal
liberate
libertine
liberty

libidinous
library
librate
license
licentiate
licentious
lieu
lieutenant
ligament
ligature
ligneous
ligniferous
lignite
lignum-*vitæ*
limit
limpid
lineage
lineal
lineament
linear
linen
lingual
linguist
liniment
lining
linnet
linseed
linsey-*wool*sey
lintel (*limit*)
lion (*leon*)
liquefy
liquid
liquor
liquorice
    (*glucu, rhiz*)

litany
literal
literary
literati
literature
litharge
lithography
lithotomy
litigant
litigate
litigious
litter
littoral
liturgy
local
locate
locomotion
locomotive
logarithm
logic
longevity (*æv*)
longitude
loquacious
lotion
loyal (*leg*)
lubricate
lucent
lucid
lucifer
lucre
lucubration
ludicrous
lugubrious
lumbago
lumbar

*lumin*ary   *major*   *mar*ine
*lumin*ous   *major*-domo   *marit*al
*lun*ar   *mal*ady   *mar*itime
*lun*ate   mal*apert*   *mark*et (*merc*)
*lun*atic   *mal*aria   *marry* (*marit*)
*lun*e   male*dict*ion   mar*shal*
*lun*ette   male*fact*or   *marsupi*al
*lup*ine   male*vol*ent   *marti*al
lurid   *mal*ice   *martyr*
*lustr*ate   *mal*ign   *mar*vel (*mir*)
*lustr*ous   *malle*able   *mascul*ine
*lustr*um   *mall*et   *mass* (*miss*)
*lut*e   mal*vers*ation   *master*
*luxat*ion   *mamm*al   (*magister*)
*lux*ury   *mamm*illary   *mastic*ate
lymph   *mamm*oth   *mast*oid
*lyr*e   *man*acle   *materi*al
    *man*age   *mater*nal
*macer*ate   *mand*amus   *mathem*atics
*machin*ation   *mand*ate   *matin*ee
*machin*e   *mand*atory   (mat e na')
*macr*ocosm   *mand*ible   *matin*s
*macul*ate   *man*ger   *matr*icide
ma*dam*   *man*ia   *matr*iculate
Ma*donn*a   mani*fest*   *matr*imony
*madr*igal   *man*ipulate   *matr*on
*magister*ial   *man*ner   *matter* (*materi*)
*magistr*ate   *man*œuver   *matur*e
magn*anim*ous   *man*or   *matutin*al
*magn*ate   *man*sion   *maul*stick
*magn*ify   *man*ual   *maxill*ary
*magn*i*loqu*ence   manu*fact*ure   *maxim*
*magn*itude   *man*umit   *maxim*um
*main*tain   *man*uscript   *mayor* (*major*)
*majest*y   *margin*   *meagr*e

measure (*mens*)

mechanic

medal (*metall*)

mediate

medical

medicament

medicate

medicine

medieval

mediocre

meditate

medium

medley

medullary

meerschaum

megalornis

megalosaur

mega**theri**um

melancholy

melilot

meliorate

mellifluous

melodrama

melody

member

   (*membr*)

membrane

memento

memoir

   (*memor*)

memorandum

memorial

memory

menace

menagerie

(men azh'e ry)

mendacious

mendacity

mendicant

mendicity

menial

mensurable

mensuration

mental

mention

mercantile

mercenary

mercer

merchandise

merchant

mercy

mere

merge

meri**di**an

merit

mermaid

mesentery

meso**zo**ic

message (*miss*)

messuage

   (*mans*)

metal (*metall*)

metallurgy

meta**morph**ose

meta**morph**ous

meta**phor**

meta**phras**e

metaphysical

metem**psych**osis

met**eor** (*aeir*)

met**hod**

meto**nym**y

metre

metropolis

miasma

microphone

microscope

mid**riff** (*hrif*)

migrate

mildew (*mell*)

mile (*mill*)

militant

military

militate

militia

mill (*mol*)

millennium

million

mimic

mineral

miniature

minim

minimum

minister

minor

minority

minster

   (*monasteri*)

minstrel

mint (*monet*)

minuend

minuet

minus

minute

minutia

miocene
miracle
mirage
   (mi razh')
mirror
misanthrope
misanthropy
miscellaneous
mischief (chef)
mischievous
   (chief, chef)
miscreant
   (cred)
misdemeanor
   (men)
miser
miserable
misnomer
misogynist
missal
missile
mission
missionary
missive
mitigate
mnemonic
mnemonics
mob (mobil)
mobile
modal
moderate
moderator
modern
modest
modicum

modify
modulate
molar
molasses (mell)
mole
molecular
molecule
molest
mollient
mollify
mollusc
moment
momentum
monad
monarch
monastery
monetary
money (monet)
monition
monitor
monitory
monk
monocular
monody
monogamy
monogram
monograph
monolith
monologue
monomania
monopoly
monotheism
monotone
monsoon
   (musim)

monster
   (monstr)
monument
mood (mod)
moral
morbid
mordacity
morphia
morsel
mortal
mortgage
   (mor' gej)
mortify
mortuary
motion
motive
motor
motto
mountebank
   (banc)
move
mucilage
mucous
mulet
multifarious
multilateral
multiply (pli)
multitude
municipal
munificence
munition
mural
muriatic
muricated
murmur

*mus*cle
*mus*coid
*mut*able
*mut*ation
*mutil*ate
*mutin*y
myriad
*myrm*idon
*myst*ery
*mys*tic
myth

*na*iad
*narc*otic
*narr*ate
*nas*al
*nas*cent
*nat*al
*nat*atory
*nat*ion
*nat*ive
*nat*ure
*naus*ea
*naut*ical
*nautil*us
*nav*al
*nav*e
*nav*igate
*nav*y
*nebul*a
*necess*ary
*necro*logy
*necro*mancy
*necro*phagous
*necro*polis

ne*far*ious
*negat*ion
*negat*ive
neg*lect*
neg*lig*ent (*leg*)
*negoti*ate
neigh*bor*
neo*phyt*e
*ner*eid
*neur*al
*neur*algia
neuter
*neutr*al
*nid*us
*nigr*escent
*nihil*ism
*nobl*e (*nobil*)
noct*ambul*ist
*noct*ivagant
*noct*urnal
*noct*urne
*nod*e
*nod*ose
*nod*ule
*noi*some
*nom*ad
*nomen*clature
*nomin*al
*nomin*ate
*nomin*ative
non*ent*ity
non-*jur*or
non*pareil*
*norm*al
*nostr*um

*not*able
*not*ary
*not*ation
*not*ice
*not*ify
*not*ion
*not*orious
noun (*nomen*)
*nour*ish (*nutr*)
*nov*el
*Novem*ber
*nov*ice
*novi*tiate
*nox*ious
*nuc*leus
*nud*e
*nui*sance
nugatory
*null*ify
*null*ity
*numer*al
*numer*ation
*numer*ator
*numer*ical
*numer*ous
*numism*atic
*nunc*io
*nupti*al
*nurt*ure (*nutrit*)
*nut*ation
*nutr*iment
*nutr*ition
*nutr*itious
*nutr*itive
nymph

obdurate
obedient
obeisance
obelisk
obese
obfuscate
obituary
object
objurgate
oblate
oblation
obligate
obligation
oblige
oblique
obliterate
oblivion
oblong
obloquy
obnoxious
obscure
obsequies
obsolescent
obsolete
obstacle
obstinate
obstreperous
obstruct
obtain (ten)
obtrude
obtuse
obverse
obviate
obvious
occasion

occident
occiput
occult
occultation
occupation
  (cap)
occupy (cap)
occur
octagon
octahedron
octave
octavo
October
octopus
ocular
oculist
odious
odium
odontoid
offend
offer
official (fac)
officiate (fac)
officious (fac)
oil (ole)
ointment (unct)
oleaginous
oleaster
oleiferous
olfactory
oligarchy
ominous
omit
omnibus
omnipotent

omnipresent
omniscience
omnivorous
onerous
onion (un)
onomatopœia
oolite
opacity
opaque (opac)
opera
operate
ophicleide
  (cleid)
ophidian
ophiomorphous
ophthalmia
ophthalmic
ophthalmo-
  scope
opinion
oppidan
opponent
opportune
opportunity
oppose
opposite
oppress
opprobrious
opprobrium
oppugn
optative
optical
optician
optics
optimism

option
opulent
oracle
oracular
oration
orator
oratory
orb
orbit
orchestra
ordain (*ordin*)
or**deal**
ordinal
ordinance
ordinary
ordination
ordnance
   (*ordin*)
ordure
organ (*erg*)
oriel (*aur*)
orient
oriole (*aur*)
orifice
origin
orison
ormoly (*aur*)
ornament
ornate
ornithology
orotund
orphan
orpin
ortho**dox**
ortho**epy**

ortho**graphy**
oscillate
osculate
osseous
ossify
ostensible
ostentation
osteology
ostracism
outrage
outrageous
oval
ovarious
ovate
ovation
overt
overture
oviform
oviparous
ovoid
oxygen
oxymel
oxytone
oz**o**ne

pabulum
pace (*pass*)
pachy**derma**-
   tous
pacific
pacify
pact
paleology
   (*palæ*)
palestra

palimpsest
palindrome
   (*drom*)
palinode
palisade
pall
pallet
palliate
pallid
pallor
palpable
palpitate
pamper
pan**ace**a
pan**creas**
pan**egyr**ic
pannier
pan**oply**
pan**orama**
pan**the**ism
pan**the**on
panto**mime**
pantry
papaverous
papilionaceous
para**bola**
parachute
   (*shut*)
para**clet**e
parade
para**digm** (dim)
para**dox**
para**graph**
par**allax**
par**allel**

paralysis	passage	pedagogue
paralytic	passenger	pedal
paralyze	passerine	pedant
paramount	passion	pedestal
parapet	passive	pedestrian
parasite	passport	pediment
parasol	pastern	pedobaptism
paregoric	pastille	peel (pell)
parent	pastor	peer (par)
parenthesis	pasture	pellicle
parhelion	paternal	pellucid
parietal	pathetic	peltry
parity	pathology	pelvis
parlance	pathos	pen (penn)
parley	patience	penal
parliament	patient	penance
parlor	patriarch	pendant
parochial	patrician	pendent
parody	patrimony	pendulous
parole (parl)	patriot	pendulum
paronym	patron	penetrate
parotid	patronymic	peninsula
paroxysm	paucity	penitent
parricide (patr)	pauper	pennant
parry	pause	pennate
pars	pavilion	penny (penuri)
parterre	(papilion)	pensile
partial	peccable	pension
participate	peccadillo	pensive
participle	peccant	pentagon
particle	pectinal	pentahedron
partisan	pectoral	pentameter
partition	peculate	pentateuch
partner	peculiar	penult (ultim)
parvenue	pecuniary	penultimate

penumbra
people (*popul*)
pepper (*piper*)
perambulate
perceive (*cap*)
per cent
percipient
percolate
percussion
  (*quass*)
perdition
peregrinate
peremptorily
perennial (*ann*)
perfect (*fact*)
perfidy
perforate
perform
perfume
perfunctorily
pericardium
perigee
perihelion
perimeter
period
peripatetic
periphery
peristaltic
perjure
permanent
permeate
permit
pernicious
peroration
perpendicular

perpetrate
perpetual
perplex
perquisite
persecute
persevere
persist
person
perspective
perspicacious
perspicuous
perspire
persuade
persuasion
pertain (*ten*)
pertinacious
  (*ten*)
pertinent (*ten*)
perturb
peruse
pervade
pervasive
perverse
pervert
pervivacious
pervious
pessimist
pester (*past*)
pestiferous
pestilence
pestle (*pist*)
petal
petiole
petition
petrifaction

petrify
petroleum
petrous
petulant
phalanx
phantasm
phantasmago-
  ria
phantom
pharmaceutical
pharmacopœia
pharmacy
phase
phenomenon
philanthropy
philology
philosophy
philter
phlebotomy
phlegm
phocine
phonetic
phonograph
phospherous
photograph
photophobia
photosphere
phototype
phrase
phraseology
phrenetic
phrenology
phthisic
phthisis
phylactery

*phyll*oid
*phyll*ophagous
*phyll*ophorous
*phys*ic
*physi*ognomy
*physi*ology
*physi*que
*phyt*oid
*pi*acular
*piano*forte
*pict*orial
*pict*ure
pier (*petr*)
*pi*ety
*pig*ment
*pil*aster
*pil*e
*pilgr*im
   (*peregr*)
*pil*lage
*pil*lar
*pinn*ate
*pi*ous
*pir*ate
*pisc*atorial
*pisc*iculture
*pist*il
*pist*on
*plac*able
*plac*id
*plagi*ary
*plag*ue
plain (*plan*)
plane
*plan*et

*plan*isphere
*plan*k
plant
*plant*igrade
*plas*ter
*plas*tic
*plat*e
*plat*eau (pla to')
*plat*form
*plat*inum
*plat*itude
*plat*ter
*plaud*it
*plaus*ible
*pleb*eian
*ple*iades
pleisto*cene*
*plen*ary
pleni*potent*iary
*plen*itude
*plen*ty
*pleon*asm
*pleth*ora
*pleur*a
*pleur*isy
*pli*able
*pli*ant
*pli*cated
plinth
plio*cene*
   (*pleion*)
*plov*er (*pluvi*)
*plum*age
*plumb*ago
*plumb*eous

*plumb*er
*plumb*iferous
plume
*plumm*et
   (*plumb*)
plump (*plumb*)
plunge (*plump*)
*plur*al
*pluvi*al
ply (*pli*)
*pneumat*ic
*pneumat*ics
*pneumon*ia
poach
*poach*er
*po*em
*po*esy
*po*et
*poign*ant
*pois*e
*pois*on (*pot*)
*polem*ical
*pol*ice
*pol*icy
*pol*ish
*pol*ite
*polit*y
*poll*en
pol*lute*
poly*gamy*
poly*glot*
poly*gon*
poly*graph*
poly*hedr*on
poly*pus*

polytechnic
polytheism
pomaceous
pomade
pomegranate
pommel
pomology
pomp
pompous
ponder
ponderable
ponderous
pontiff
pontoon
populace
popular
populate
population
populous
porcelain
porch (port)
porcine
pore
pork (porc)
porphyry
porpoise (pisc)
porraceous
port
portable
portage
portal
portcullis (col)
porte-monnaie
portend
portent

porter
portfolio
port-hole
portico
portion (part)
portly
portmanteau
portrait
portray (trait)
pose
position
positive
posse
possess (port)
possible
post
post-diluvian
posterior
posterity
postern
posthumous
    (postum)
postillion
post-meridian
post-mortem
postpone
postprandial
postscript
postulant
postulate
posture (posit)
potable
potation
potent
potentate

potential
potion
poultry
poverty
    (pauper)
practical
practice
pragmatic
praise
praxis
prayer (precar)
preamble
    (ambul)
prebend
precarious
precede
precedence
precedent
precentor
    (cant)
precept (capt)
precession
precinct
precious
precipice
precipitate
precipitous
precise
preclude
precocious
    (præcoci)
precursor
predatory
predecessor
predial

predic**ament**
predic**ate**
predict
predilection
predominant
predominate
preface (*fat*)
prefatory
prefect (*fact*)
prefer
prefix
pregnable
prehensile
prejudice
prelate
preliminary
prelude
premature
premier
premise
premium
premonition
premonitory
prepare
prepense
preponderate
preposition
prepossess
preposterous
prerogative
presage
presbyter
presbyterian
prescience
prescribe

prescript
prescription
present
presentiment
preserve
preside
prestige
　　(*prestigi*)
presume
presumption
presumptuous
pretend
pretense
pretention
pretentious
preterit
pretermit
pretext
prevail (*val*)
prevaricate
prevent
previous
prey (*præd*)
price (*preci,
　　preti*)
priest
　　(*presbyter*)
prim
primal
primary
primate
prime
primer
primeval
primitive

primogeniture
primordial
　　(*ordin*)
prince (*princip*)
principal
principle
print (*prim*)
prior
priority
prism (*priz*)
prison
pristine
private
privation
privilege
probable
probate
probation
probe
probity
problem (*bol*)
proboscis
procedure
proceed
proceeds
process
procession
proclaim
proclivity
procrastinate
procumbent
procure
prodigal
prodigious
prodigy

(*prodigi*)
pro*duce*
pro*duct*
proem
pro*fane*
pro*fess*
prof*fer*
pro*fic*ient (*fac*)
pro*file*
pro*fit* (*fact*)
pro*flig*ate
pro*found*
(*fund*)
pro*fund*ity
pro*fuse*
pro*genit*or
pro*geny*
pro*gno*sis
pro*gno*sticate
pro*gramm*e
pro*gress*
pro*hibit*
pro*ject*
pro*ject*ile
pro*late*
*prol*etarian
*prol*ific
pro*lix*
pro*locut*or
pro*log*ue
pro*long*
*promen*ade
pro*min*ent
pro*misc*uous
pro*mise*

pro*mote*
prompt
*promul*gate
prone
pro*nomin*al
pro*nounce*
(*nunci*)
pro*nunci*ation
*propag*ate
pro*pel*
pro*pens*ity
pro*phe*t
*propinqu*ity
*propit*iate
*propit*ious
pro*portion*
pro*pose*
pro*posit*ion
pro*pound*
(*pon*)
*propri*etary
*propri*etor
*propri*ety
pro*puls*ion
pro*rog*ue
pro*scen*ium
pro*scribe*
pro*secut*e
*proselyt*e
pros*ody*
pro*spect*
pro*sper*
pro*strat*e
pro*tect*
pro*test*

proto*col*
proto*plas*m
proto*type*
proto*zo*a
pro*tract*
pro*trude*
pro*tuber*ance
pro*verb*
pro*vide*
pro*vince*
(*provinci*)
pro*vis*ion
*provis*o
pro*voke* (*voc*)
*proxim*ate
*proxim*ity
*prud*ent
prune
*prun*iferous
*prur*ient
*psal*m
pseudo*nym*
*psych*ical
*psych*ology
*puber*ty
*publ*ic (*popul*)
*publ*ish (*popul*)
*pud*ency
*puer*ile
*pugil*ist
*pugn*acious
*pul*let (*poul*)
*pulmon*ary
*pulmon*ic
*puls*e

*pulver*ize
*pum*ice (*spum*)
*punct*ate
*punct*ilious
*punct*ual
*punct*uate
*punct*ure
*pung*ent
*pun*ish
*pun*itive
punt (*pont*)
*pup*a
*pup*il
*pup*pet
pur*chas*e
*pur*e
*purg*ative
*purg*atory
*purg*e
*pur*ify
*Pur*itan
pur*lieu* (*all*)
pur*loin* (*long*)
pur*port*
pur*pos*e
*purs*e (*burs*)
pur*su*e
*pur*ulent
push (*pouls*)
*pusill*animous
*pustul*e
*put*ative
*putr*efy
*putr*escence
*putr*id

*pygm*y
*pyl*orus
*pyr*e
*pyr*otechnics
pyx

*quadr*angle
*quadr*ant
*quadr*ate
*quadr*atic
*quadr*ennial
*quadr*ille
*quadr*oon
*quadr*uped
*quadr*uple
*qual*ify
*qual*ity
*quant*ity
*quant*um
*quarant*ine
*quarr*el (*quer*)
*quarr*y (*quade*)
*quarr*y (*cor*)
*quart*an
*quart*er
*quart*ette
*quart*o
quash
*quatern*ary
*quatern*ion
*quatr*ain
*queri*monious
*queru*lous
*quer*y
*quest*ion

*quid*dity
*quid*nunc
*quies*ce
*quies*cent
quiet
*quiet*us
*quin*ary
*quin*quennia
*quint*essence
*quint*uple
quit
*quit*e
quoin (*cunc*)
quorum
*quot*a
*quot*e
*quot*ient
*quot*um

*rabbl*e
*rab*id
*rac*e (*radic*)
*radi*ant
*radi*ate
*radic*al
*radi*us
radix
*ram*al
*ram*ify
*ranc*id
*ranc*or
*rang*e
rank (*rang*)
rant
*ran*unculus

*rap*acious
*rap*id
*rap*ine
rapt
raptorial
rapture
*rar*e
*rar*efy
*ras*e
*ras*orial
*ras*ure
*rat*e
*rat*ify
*rat*io
*rat*ion
*rav*age
*rav*e (*rab*)
*rav*ine
*rav*ish
*re*al
reason (*ration*)
re*bat*e
re**bel**
*re*bus
rebut
re**calcitr**ant
re**cant**
re**capitul**ate
re*ced*e
re**ceipt** (*capt*)
re**ceiv**e (*cap*)
recent
recipe
recipient
reciprocal

reciprocate
reciprocity
re*cit*e
re**claim** (*clam*)
re*clin*e
re**clus**e (*claus*)
re**cognit**ion
re**cogniz**e
   (*cognosc*)
re**coil**
re**collect**
re**concile**
   (*concili*)
re**cond**ite
re**connoit**er
   (*cognosc*)
re**cord**
recover
   (*recuper*)
re**cre**ant (*cred*)
re**crimin**ate
re**cruit** (*cret*)
rectangle
rectify
rectilinear
rectitude
rector
re**cumb**ent
recuperation
recuperative
re**cur**
re**cus**ant
red**dit**ion (*dat*)
red**eem** (*em*)
re**dempt**ion

red**integr**ate
red**ol**ent
redoubt
   (*ridott*)
re**dress**
re**duc**e
re**duc**tion
red**und**ant
re**fect**ion (*fact*)
re**fect**ory (*fact*)
re**fer**
re**fin**e
re**flect**
re**flex**
re**flu**ent
re**flux**
re**form**
re**fract**
re**fract**ory
re**frag**able
re**frain** (*fren*)
re**frang**ible
re**friger**ate
re**fug**e
re**fulg**ent
re**fus**e
re**fut**e
re**gal**
regale
regalia
regatta
re**gener**ate
regent
regicide (*cæd*)
*reg*ime

(ra-zheem')
regimen
regiment
region
regi**ster** (*gest*)
re**gn**ant
re**gress**
regular
regulate
re**habil**itate
  (*habill*)
re**hears**e (*herc*)
reign (*regn*)
reim**burse**
re**iter**ate
re**ject**
re**juven**ate
re**laps**e
re**lat**e
re**lax**
re**leas**e (*laiss*)
re**leg**ate
re**lent**
re**lev**ant
re**lic** (*linqu*)
re**lict**
re**lief** (*lev*)
re**liev**e (*lev*)
religion
re**linqu**ish
reliquary
re**luct**ant
re**ly** (*lie*)
re**main** (*man*)
re**mand**

re**med**y
re**member**
  (*memor*)
reminiscence
re**mit**
remnant
  (*reman*)
re**monstr**ate
re**morse**
re**mot**e
re**muner**ate
renal
re**nasc**ent
ren**counter**
  (*contra*)
render
rendezvous
  (ren'de voo)
rendition
  (*reddit*)
renegade
re**nounce**
  (*nunci*)
re**pair** (*par*)
re**partee**
re**past**
re**peal** (*appell*)
re**peat** (*pet*)
re**pel** (*pell*)
re**pent** (*pœnit*)
repertory
re**plen**ish
re**plete**
re**plevy**
re**ply** (*pli*)

re**port**
re**pos**e
re**pos**itory
re**prehend**
re**prieve**
  (*reprov*)
reprimand
re**pris**al
re**proach**
  (*propi*)
re**prob**ate
re**prov**e
reptile (rep'til)
re**public**
re**pud**iate
re**pugn**ant
re**pulse**
re**put**e
re**quest**
  (*quæsit*)
requiem
re**quir**e (*quær*)
re**quisit**e
  (*quæsit*)
re**quit**e
re**scind**
re**script**
rescue (*rescon*)
re**semble**
re**sent**
re**serv**e
re**sid**e (*sed*)
residue
re**sign**
re**sil**ient (*sal*)

re*sist*
re*solut*e
re*solv*e
re*son*ant
  (rez'onant)
re*sort*
re*sourc*e
re*spect*
re*spir*e
*respit*e
  (*respect*)
re*spond*
re*st*
*restaur*ant
re*stitut*ion
  (*statut*)
*rest*ive
*rest*ore
  (*restaur*)
re*strain*
  (*string*)
re*strict*
re*sult* (*salt*)
re*sum*e
re*surrect*ion
resus*cit*ate
re*tail* (*taill*)
re*tain* (*ten*)
*retali*ate
re*tard*
*retic*ent
*retic*ule
*ret*ina
re*tin*ue (*ten*)
re*tir*e

re*tort*
re*tract*
re*treat* (*tract*)
re*trench*
re*tribut*ion
re*trieve* (*trov*)
retro*ced*e
retro*cess*ion
retro*grade*
retro*spect*
re*veal* (*vel*)
revel
re*veng*e
re*ven*ue
re*verber*ate
re*ver*e
re*vers*e
re*vert*
re*vis*e
re*viv*e
re*vok*e (*voc*)
re*volt* (*volut*)
re*volut*ion
re*volv*e
re*vuls*ion
*rhaps*odist
  (*rhapt*)
*rhetor*ic
*rhe*um
*rhe*umatism
*rhino*ceros
  (*ceras*)
*rhiz*ophagous
*rhod*odendron
rhomb

*ridd*le (*ræd*)
*rid*icule
*rig*id
*rig*or
*rip*arian
*ris*ible
*rit*e
*riv*al
*riv*ulet
robust
*rod*ent
*rog*ation
*rostr*al
*rostr*um
*rot*ary
*rot*e
rotund
*roug*e (roozh)
*rout*e (*rupt*)
*rout*ine
*roy*al
*rub*icund
*rubr*ic
*rub*y
*ruct*ate
*rud*e
*rud*iment
*rug*ate
*rug*ose
ruin
*rul*e (*regul*)
*rumin*ant
*rumin*ate
rumor
*rupt*ure

rural
ruse
russet
rustic
rut (*rupt*)

saccharine
sacerdotal
sack (*sacc*)
sacrament
sacred
sacrifice (*fac*)
sacrilege
sacristy
sagacious
sagittal
saint (*sanct*)
salad
salary
salient
saline
saliva
sally
salmon
   (*sam'un*)
saloon (*sall*)
salt
salt**peter**
salubrious
salutary
salute
salvage
salvation
salve (sav)
salver

salvo
sanatory
sanctify
sanctimony
sanction
sanctity
sanctuary
sanctum
sane
sanguinary
sanguine
sanguineous
sanitarium
sanitary
sapid
sapient
saponaceous
sapor
sarcasm
sarcophagus
satellite
satire
satisfy
saturate
sauce (*sal*)
sausage (*sal*)
savage (*sylv*)
save (*salv*)
savor (*sap*)
scale
scalene
scalpel
   (*scalpell*)
scan (*scand*)
scansion

scansorial
scapular
scene
sceptic
scepter
schedule
scheme
schism (sism)
   (*schiz*)
schist (*schiz*)
school (*schol*)
sciatic (*ischi*)
science
scintilla
scintillate
sciolist
scion
scission
sclerotic
scorbutic
scoria
scribble
scribe
script
scripture
scrivener
   (*scrib*)
scruple
   (*scrupul*)
scrutiny
sculpture
scurrilous
scutiform
sebaceous
secant

secede
secession
seclude
second (*sequ*)
secret
sect (*secut*)
section
sector
secular (*sæcul*)
secure
sedate
sedentary
sediment
sedition
seduce
sedulous
segment (*sec*)
segregate
seignior (*sen*)
select
selenography
seminal
seminary
senary
senate
senescence
seneschal
senile (se'nil)
senior
sense
sensible
sensitive
sensorium
sensual
sentence

sentient
sentiment
separate
September
septennial
septic
septilateral
sepulcher
  (*sepult*)
sepulture
sequacious
sequel
sequent
sequester
serenade
serene
serf (*serv*)
series
sermon
serpent
serrate
serried
serum
servant
servile (ser'vil)
servitude
sessile
session
setaceous
sever (*separ*)
several (*separ*)
severe
sexagenary
sextant
sibilant

siccative
sickle (*sec*)
sidereal
sign
signal
silent
silex
silicious
silvas
similar
simile
similitude
simious
simous
simulate
simultaneous
sine
sincere
sinecure
single (*singul*)
sinister
sinous
sinuate
sinuous
sinus
siphon
site
situate
skeleton
sober
social
society
sojourn (*diurn*)
solace
solar

solder (*solid*)
soldier (*solid*)
sole
solemn
solicit
solid
soliloquy
soliped (*solid*)
solitary
solitude
solo
solstice
soluble
solution
solve
solvent
sombre
somer**sault**
    (*salt*)
somer**set** (*salt*)
somnambulist
somniferous
somnific
somniloqu**ist**
sonata
sonnet
sonorous
sophist
soporiferous
soprano
sorcery (*sort*)
sordid
sororicid**e**
    (*cæd*)
sort

sortie
sound (*sund*)
sovereign
    (*superan*)
space (*spati*)
spasm
special
specie
species
specify
specimen
specious
spectacle
spectator
specter
specular
speculate
speculum
sperm
spermac**eti**
spice (*speci*)
spine
spiracle
spire
spirit
spite (*spect*)
splendid
splendor
spoil (*spoli*)
spoliation
spondee
    (*spend*)
sponsor
spontaneous
sporadic

spouse (*spous*)
sprite (*spirit*)
spume
spurious
squadron
squalid
squaloid
squalor
squamose
square (*quadr*)
stable
stagnate
stalactite
stalagmite
stamen
stamina
stannery
stanniferous
stanza (*stant*)
state
station
statue
stature
status
statute
steganopod
stellar
stenography
stereoscope
stereotype
sterile
sternutation
stertorous
stethoscope
stigma

*stil*etto
still
*stimul*ate
*stimul*us
stipend
  (*stipendi*)
*stipul*ate
stolid
*stom*ach
store (*staur*)
*strangl*e
  (*strangal*)
*strang*ury
*strat*a
*stratag*em
  (*strateg*)
*strateg*y
*strat*ify
*strenu*ous
strict
*strict*ure
*string*ent
*stroph*e
*struct*ure
*strychn*ine
*stud*ent
*stult*ify
*stup*endous
*stup*id
*stup*or
*styl*e (*stil*)
*styl*e (*stul*)
*styp*tic
*suas*ion
*suav*ity

sub*altern*
sub*aqu*eous
sub*due* (*due*)
sub*jac*ent
sub*ject*
sub*jug*ate
sub*junct*ive
sub*lim*e
sub*lun*ary
sub*marin*e
sub*merg*e
sub*miss*ion
sub*mit*
sub*ordin*ate
sub*orn*
sub*pœn*a
sub*scrib*e
sub*sequ*ent
sub*serv*e
sub*side* (*sed*)
sub*sidi*ary
sub*sidy*
  (*subsidi*)
sub*sist*
sub*stanc*e
  (*stant*)
sub*stitut*e
sub*structur*e
sub*tend*
sub*terfug*e
sub*terr*anean
sub*tl*e (*subtil*)
sub*tract*
sub*trah*end
sub*urbs*

sub*vert*
suc*ceed* (*ced*)
suc*cess*
suc*cinct*
suc*cor* (*curr*)
suc*cul*ent
suc*cumb*
*sud*atory
*sudor*ific
*su*e
suf*fer*
suf*fic*e (*fac*)
suf*foc*ate
suffrage
suf*fus*e
sug*gest*
*sui*cide (*cæd*)
*sui*t
*su*ite
*sulc*ate
sultan
*summ*ary
*summ*it
sum*mon* (*sub*)
*sumptu*ary
*sumptu*ous
*super*able
super*annu*ated
superb
*super*cil*ious*
*super*fic*ial*
*super*fic*ies*
super*flu*ous
super*incumb*-
  ent

super**intend**
superior
super**lative**
super**lun**ar
supernal
super**numer**ary
super**scribe**
super**sede**
superstit**ion
super**struct**ure
super**vene**
super**vise**
supine
sup**plant**
sup**ple** (*plic*)
sup**pli**ant
sup**plic**ate
sup**ply** (*pli*)
sup**port**
sup**pose**
sup**pur**ate
supra**mund**ane
supremacy
sur**cing**le
sur**face** (*faci*)
sur**feit** (*fact*)
surge
sur**mise**
sur**mount**
sur**name**
sur**pass**
sur**pl**ice (*pell*)
sur**plus**
sur**pris**e
sur**render**

sur**rept**itious
sur**rogate**
sur**tout** (*tot*)
surveillance
   (sur val'yans)
sur**vey**
sur**vive**
susceptible
sus**pect** (*sub*)
sus**pend**
sus**pense**
sus**pic**ion (*spec*)
sus**pir**ation
sus**tain** (*ten*)
sycamore
sycophant
syl**lab**le
syl**log**ism (*syn*)
sylph (*silph*)
sylvan
sym**bol** (*ball*)
sym**metry** (*syn*)
sym**pathy** (*syn*)
sym**phony** (*syn*)
symposium
sym**ptom** (*pipt*)
syn**ær**esis (*hair*)
syn**er**esis (*hair*)
syn**agog**ue
syn**chron**al
syn**chron**ism
syncopate
syncope
syn**dic**
syndicate

syn**od**
syn**onym**
syn**opsis**
syn**tax**
syn**the**sis
syringe
sy**stem** (*histe*)
sy**stol**e (*stell*)
sy**zygy** (siz'e je)

tabernacle
tabid
table (*tabul*)
tableau (tab'lo)
tabular
tabulate
tacit
taciturn
tactics
tailor (*taill*)
taint (*tinct*)
talent
tally
talon
tandem
tangent
tangible
tantamount
tapestry
tardy
taurine
tautology
tavern (*tabern*)
tax
taxidermy

technical
technology
tedious (*tædi*)
tegular
tegument
tele**gram**
   (*gramm*)
tele**graph**
tele**phone**
tele**scope**
tellurian
temerity
temper
tempest
temple
temple
   (*tempor*)
temporal
temporary
temporize
tempt
tenable
tenacious
tenant
tend
tender
tendon
tenebrous
tenement
tenet
tenon
tenor
tense
tense (*tempus*)
tension

tent
tentacle
tentative
tenter
tenuity
tenuous
tenure
tepe**fact**ion
tepid
tergiversation
term (*termin*)
terminal
terminate
terminology
terminus
ternary
terrace
terra cotta
   (*coci*)
terraqueous
terrene
terrestrial
terrible
terrier
terrify
territory
terror
terse
tertiary
tesselated
test
testaceous
testament
testator
testatrix

tester
testimonial
testimony
tetra**gon**
tetra**hedr**on
tetr**arch**
tetra**stich**
tetra**style**
text
textile
texture
theater
theism
theme
theocracy
   (*crati*)
theodolite (*od*)
theogony
theology
theorem
theory
theosophy
therapeutic
thermal
thermometer
thesaurus
thesis
theurgy (*erg*)
thorax
thurible
tile (*tegu*la)
till
tiller
timid
timorous

tincture
tint (*tinct*)
tirade
tissue
title (*titul*)
titular
tocsin
toga
toggery
toilet
tolerable
tomb
tome
tone
tonsil
tonsorial
tonsure
topic
topography
torment (*torqu*)
torn (*tourn*)
tornado
torpedo
torpid
torrent
torrid
torsion
torso
tortoise
tortuous
torture
total
tournament
toxicology
toxophilite

trace (*tract*)
trachea
tract
tractable
tradition
tra**duce** (*trans*)
tragedy (*od*)
trail (*trah*)
train (*trah*)
trait (*tract*)
traitor (*tradit*)
tranquil
trans**act**
trans**cend**
(*scand*)
trans**crib**e
(*trans*)
trans**sept** (*trans*)
trans**fer**
trans**figure**
trans**fix**
trans**form**
trans**fuse**
trans**gress**
trans**ient**
trans**it**
trans**it**ion
trans**it**ory
trans**lat**e
trans**luc**ent
trans**mar**ine
trans**migr**ate
trans**mit**
trans**mut**e
transom

trans**par**ent
trans**pire**
(*trans*)
trans**port**
trans**pose**
trans**vers**e
trap
trapezium
travail
tra**vers**e (*trans*)
tra**vest**y (*trans*)
treat (*trail*)
treble (*triplus*)
tre**foil** (*foli*)
trellis
tremble
(*tremul*)
trench
trend
trepidation
tres**pass**
tri**angle**
tribe
tribulation
tribunal
tribune
tributary
tribute
tri**cuspid**
tri**dent**
tri**enn**ial (*ann*)
tri**foli**ate
tri**furc**ate
trigonometry
trinity

*tri*o
*tripart*ite
triphthong
*tripli*cate
tripod
trisect
*trit*e
*tritur*ate
triumvir
triumph
triune
trivial
*troch*ee (*trech*)
troglodyte (*du*)
*tromb*one
*trop*e
trophy
*trop*ic
*trov*e
*trov*er
*truc*ulent
truncate
*trunc*heon
trunk (*trunc*)
tube
tuber
*tuber*cle
*tuit*ion
*tum*efy
*tum*id
*tum*or
*tum*ulous
*tum*ult
tunic
*turb*id

*turbin*ate
*turb*ulent
*tur*een (*terr*)
*turg*id
turn (*tourn*)
*turp*itude
*turr*et
*tutel*age
*tutel*ar
*tut*or
*twi*light
*twi*ll
*twi*n
*twi*ne
*twi*st
tympan
*tympan*um
*typ*e
*typh*us (*tuph*)
typo*graph*y
*tyran*t (*tyrann*)

*ubiqu*ity
ulcer
*ulm*aceous
*ulter*ior
*ultim*ate
*ultim*atum
*ultim*o
ultra*mar*ine
ultra*mont*ane
umbel (*umbell*)
*umbr*age
*umbr*ella
*umbr*iferous

*un*animous
(*anim*)
un*couth* (*cudh*)
*unct*ion
*unct*uous
*und*ulate
*ungu*ent
*ungul*ate
*uni*corn
*uni*form
unify (*fac*)
*uni*on
*uni*que
unison
*uni*t
*uni*te
*uni*ty
*univers*e
*urb*an
*urb*ane
*urg*e
*urs*ine
*us*e
*usu*al
usurp
*usur*y
*ut*ensil
*util*ize
*uv*eous
*uv*ula
*uxor*ious

*vac*ant
*vac*ate
*vacc*inate

vaccine
vacillate
vacuous
vacuum
vade-mecum
vagabond
vagary
vagrant
vague
vain (*van*)
valediction
   (*dict*)
valedictory
   (*dict*)
valetudinarian
valhalla
valiant
valid
vallation
valley
valor
value
valve
vandal
   (*wandel*)
vanish
vanquish (*vinc*)
vapid (*vapp*)
vapor
variegate (*ag*)
variety
variolus
varioloid
various
vary (*vari*)

vascular
vase
vast
vault (*volut*)
veer (*vir*)
vegetable
vegetate
vehement
vehicle
veil (*vel*)
vein (*ven*)
velocipede
velocity
venal
vend
vender
vendible
venerate
vengeance
venial
venison
venom (*venen*)
venous
ventilate
ventral
ventricle
ventriloquist
venture
   (*aventur*)
venue
veracious
veracity
verb
verbal
verbatim

verbiage
verbose
verdant
verdict (*dict*)
verdigris (*æris*)
verdure
verge
verify (*fac*)
verily
verjuice (*verd*)
vermicular
vermifuge
vermilion
   (*vermicul*)
vermin
vermivorous
vernal
versatile
verse
version
vertebra
vertex
vertical
vertigo
very
vesicate
vesicle
vesper
vespers
vessel (*vas*)
vest
vestibule
vestige
vestment
vestry

vesture
veteran
veterinary
veto
vex
viaduct
viand (*vivend*)
vibrate
vicar (*vicari*)
vicarious
vice (*viti*)
vicegerent
viceroy (*roy*)
vicinage
vicinity
vicious (*viti*)
victim
victor
victuals (vit'ls)
videlicet
vigil
vigilant
vignette
  (vin yet')
vigor
vile
villa
village
villain
villous
vinaceous
vincible
vindicate
vindictive
vine

vinegar (*aigr*)
vineyard
vinous
vintage
vintner
violate
violent
virago
virgin
virgo
viridity
virile
virtue
virulent
virus
visage
viscera
viscid
viscous
visible
vision
visit
visor
vista
visual
vital
vitiate
vitreous
vitrify (*fac*)
vitriol
vituline
vituperate (*viti*)
vivacious
vivacity
viva **voc**e

vivid
vivify (*fac*)
viviparous
vocable
vocabulary
vocal
vocation
vociferate
voice (*voc*)
volant
volatile
volition
volley
voluble
volume
voluminous
voluntary
voluptuous
volute
vomit
voracious
vortex (*vert*)
votary
vote
votive
vouch (*voc*)
vow (*vot*)
vowel (*vocal*)
voyage (*vi*)
vulgar
vulnerable
vulpine
vulture (*vuls*)

walnut

xanthic   **zeal** (*zel*)   **zoolit**e (*loth*)
xanthous   **zodi**ac   **zo**ology
xiphoid   **zon**e   **zoophyt**e
xylography   **zo**ography   **zymotic**
   (*xule*)   **zo**oid

ALPHABETICAL STEM LIST

A

Abb—father, religious leader; *abb*ott (the *governor* of a monastery). Syriac, *abb*a.

Abd—hide; *abd*omen (the lower cavity of the body in which the *entrails* are *concealed*). L. *abd*ere.

Abol—do away with; *abol*ish. L. *abol*ere.

Ac—needle; *ac*iform. L. *ac*us.

Acaleph—nettle; *acaleph*oid. G. *acalephe*.

Acanth—spine, thorn; *avanth*aceous, *acanth*us[1] (a *thorny* shrub). G. *acantha*.

Accip—seize; *accip*itres (an order of *rapacious* birds). L. *accip*ere. L. *ad*, to, unto; *cap*ere, to take.

Accoutr—dress, array; *accoutr*ement. F. *accoutr*er.

Acerb—bitter; *acerb*ity. L. *acerb*us.

Acerv—heap; *acerv*ate. L. *acerv*us.

Acid—sour. L. *acid*us.

Acinac—short sword; *acinac*iform. G. *acinac*es.

Acm—top, summit; *acm*e. G. *acm*e.

Acon—whetstone, sharp stone; *acon*ite (the herb monk's-hood, which grows on steep, *sharp rocks*). G. *acon*e.

Acro—pointed, upper, top, first; *acro*bat (an athlete, a contortionist, one who can *go* on the *points* of his toes), *acro*gen (a plant having its *growth* at the *top*), *acro*polis (a citadel, an *upper city*), *acro*stic (a word or sentence formed from the *first*, or last, letters of several successive *lines*). G. *acro*s.

Acu—sharpen; *acu*te, *acu*men (*sharpness*, or keenness of intellect). L. *acu*ere.

Adept—proficient. L. *adip*isci, *adept*us.

Adip—fat; *adip*ose. L. *adip*s, *adip*is.

Adjut—assist; *adjut*ant (a regimental staff officer, the colonel's *assistant*), co*adjut*or (one *assisting with*). L. *adjut*are.

Adolesc; adult—grow up; *adolesc*ence (the period of *growth*), *adult* (a *grown-up* person). L. *adolesc*ere, *adult*us.

Adul—flatter; *adul*ation. L. *adul*ari.

Adulter—corrupt; *adulter*ate, *adulter*y. L. *adulter*are.

Advanc (*avanc*)—go forward; *advance*. F. *avanc*er. F. *avant*. L. *ab*, from, *ante*, before.

Advant (*avant*)—before, ahead; *advant*age (profit, an *advance*). F. *avant*. L. *ab*, from, *ante*, before.

Advic; advis (*avis*)—opinion; *advic*e (an *opinion* of what *seems* best), *advis*e. L. *ab*, from, *ante*, before.

Æg—goat; *æg*is (a protecting power[2], recalling the *goat*-skin shield of Minerva[3]). G. *aix*, *aig*os.

Aer—air; *aer*ial (belonging to the upper *air*), *aer*iform, *aer*olite (a meteric stone, a *stone* from the upper *air*[4]), *aer*onaut (a balloonist, an *air sailor*). L. *aer*. G. *aer*.

Æsth (*aisth*)—perceive, feel; *æsth*etic (tasteful, *perceiving* the beautiful), *æsth*etics (the principles of *beauty*, that which awakens pleasurable *feeling*), an*æsth*etic (a drug that destroys *feeling*). G. *aisth*omai.

Ag; act—drive, urge, act; *ag*ent (that which *acts*, or causes an effect, also one *acting* in behalf of another), *ag*itate (continue to *urge*), ambi*g*uous (doubtful, *driving about*), co*ag*ulate (curdle, or *drive together*, as rennet does the milk), counter*act* (*act against*), ex*act* (complete, correct, *worked out*, also to compel, or *urge out*), ex*ig*ent (pressing, *urging out*), prod*ig*al (lavish, wasteful, *driving forth*), trans*act* (perform, *drive beyond*). L. *ag*ere, *act*us.

Agger—heap; ex*agger*ate (to overstate, make *out* a great *amount*). L. *agger*.

Agi—a saying; ad*age* (a wise *saying*). L. *agi*um.

Agog—leading, bringing; dem*agog*ue (a *leader* of the *people*), ped*agog*ue (a teacher, or *child leader*), syn*agog*ue (a congregation, a *bringing together*). G. *agog*os, *agog*ee. G. *ag*ein, to lead, bring.

Agon—contest, struggle; *agony* (great pain, causing a *struggle*), ant*agon*ist (an opponent, one *struggling against*). G. *agon*.

Agr—field, land; *agr*iculture, *agr*arian (relating to the holding of *lands*). L. *ager*, *agri*. (See Per*egr*ination, Pil*gr*im.)

Al—feed; *al*iment (*food*). L. *al*ere.

Al—wing; *al*iped (*wing-footed*), *aisl*e (the *wing* or side portion of a church). L. *al*a.

Alacr—swift; *alacr*ity. L. *alacer*.

Alb—white; *alb*umen (the *white* of an egg, the *white* part of wheat), *alb*urnum (the *white* ring of wood just under the bark), *alb* (a *white* vestment), *alb*um (a book with empty, and therefore *white*, or *blank*, pages), *Alb*ion (England, the land of the *white* chalk cliffs). L. *alb*us.

Ald (*eald*)—old; *ald*erman (a member of a city council, one of the City *Fathers*). A.S. *eald*.

Alesc—grow; co*alesc*e (form close union, *grow together*). L. *alesc*ere. L. *al*ere, to nourish.

Alg—pain; neur*alg*ia (*nerve pain*). G. *alg*os.

Ali—another; *ali*en (strange, from *another* land), *ali*as (*other*wise), *ali*bi (in *another* place), *ali*quot (being an exact part of *another*). L. *ali*us.

All—other; *all*opathy (a system of cure producing

symptoms *other* than those of the disease), *all*egory (a description of one thing under the image of *another*), par*all*el (beside each other). G. *all*os.

Allel—one another. G. *allel*on.

Ally (*ali*)—bind up; *all*y (bind together). O.F. *alier*[5]. L. *ad*, to, unto, *lig*are, to bind.

Almon (*almosn*)—alms; *almon*er (a distributor of *alms*). O.F. *almosne*. G. *eleemosyn*e.

Alphabet—a set of written characters to represent elementary sounds, like the Greek alphabet, whose first two letters are *alpha* and *beta*.

Alt—high; *alt*itude (*height*), *alt*ar (an *elevated* table for sacrifice, or religious service), ex*alt* (lift up, on *high*), *alt*o (the lowest female voice, formerly the *tenor*, or *high* male voice), contr*alt*o (an intermediate female voice, the counter-tenor, or *high* voice). L. *alt*us.

Alter—other; *alter*, *alter*nate (to succeed one *another* by regular turns), *alter*cation (a dispute, a bickering between one *another*). L. *alt*er.

Alve—cavity; *alve*olar. L. *alve*us.

Am—love; *am*atory, *am*ative (addicted to *love*). L. *am*are, *am*atus, to love.

Amator—lover; *am*atory. L. *amator*. L. *am*are, to love.

Ambassad—an embassy; *ambassad*or, *embassad*or (one sent on a mission, or *embassy*). F. *ambassade*.

Ambrosi; ambrot—immortal; *ambrosi*a (the food of the gods, which conferred *immortality* upon those who tasted of it), *Ambrose* (the *immortal* one), *ambrot*ype (an unfading, and therefore called *immortal, type*). G. *ambrosi*os. G. *ambrot*os. G. *brot*os, a mortal.

Ambul—walk; per*ambul*ate (*walk through*), somn-*ambul*ist (a *sleepwalker*), fun*ambul*ist (a tight-*rope-walker*), *ambul*ator (a *walking* carriage), *ambul*ance (a vehicle for the sick, moving at a *walking* pace), *amble* (to jog along at a brisk *walk*). L. *ambul*are.

Amen (*amœn*)—pleasant; *amen*ity (a delicate attention designed to give *pleasure*). L. *amœn*us.

Amic—friend; *amic*able (*friend*ly), *am*(*ic*)ity (*friend*ship), *ami*(*c*)able (*friend*ly). L. *amic*us. L. *am*are, to love.

Amic (*amict*)—a garment thrown round one; *amic*e (a pilgrim's *stole*). L. *amict*us.

Amnest—forgotten; *amnest*y (a general pardon, in which offenses are to be deemed as *forgotten*). G. *amnest*os.

Amor—love; *amor*ous (prone to *love*), *en*amor (to inspire with *love*). L. *amor*.

Ampl—spacious, large; *ampl*itude, *ampl*ify (enlarge upon), *ample*. L. *ampl*us.

Amyl—starch; *amyl*aceous. L. *amyl*um.

An—one; *any* (a one). A.S. *an*.

Ancien—old, belonging to a former time; *ancien*t. F. *ancien*. L. *ante*, before.

Anem—wind; *anem*one (the *wind*flower). G. *anem*os.

Angel—messenger; *angel* (God's *messenger*), *ev*ange*list* (the *messenger* of *good* tidings). G. *angel*os.

Angio (*angeio*)—vessel; *angio*sperm (a plant having *seed vessels*), hydr*angeia*. G. *angeio*n.

Ang; anx—choke, distress; *ang*uish, *ang*ina (*distressing* pain), *anx*ious (in *distressed* suspense). L. *ang*ere, *anx*us.

Anim—breath, life; *anim*al (a *living* and *breathing* creature), *anim*ate (having *life* or *breath*, also, to *enliven*). L. *anim*a.

Anim—mind, soul, spirit; un*anim*ous (of *one mind*), magn*anim*ous (*great soul*ed), pusill*anim*ous (*mean spirit*ed), equ*anim*ity (the state of having a well-balanced or *equal mind*), *anim*osity (fullness of *passion*, or excited *mind*). L. *anim*us.

Ann—year; *ann*als (*yearly* records), *ann*iversary (a *yearly return*), *ann*ual (*yearly*), *ann*uity (a sum paid *yearly*), bienn*ial* (occurring once in *two years*), centenn*ial* (occurring once in *hundred years*), perenn*ial* (everlasting, continuing *through* a long series of *years*), superann*uated* (having reached an *excess* of *years*). L. *ann*us.

Annul—a ring; *annul*ar (*ring*-like, as an *annul*ar eclipse). L. *annul*us. L. *ann*us, a year[6].

Anomal—uneven, irregular, unusual; *anomal*y (an exception, an *unusual* case). G. *anomal*os. G. *ana*, not; *homal*os, even.

Ante—before; *ante*rior, en*hance* (to *advance*). L. *ante*.

Antenn—sail-yard; *antenn*æ (the feelers of an insect standing out like a *sail-yard*). L. *antenn*a.

Anth—flower; *anth*ology (a *collection* of the *flowers* of poetry), peri*anth* (the entire set of petals *surrounding* the *flower*), ac*anth*us (the *flowering thorn*). G. *anth*os.

Anthrac—coal; *anthrac*ite (mineral, or hard, *coal*). G. *anthrax*, *anthrac*os.

Anthrop—man; *anthrop*ophagi (*man-eaters*), mis*anthrope* (a *man-hater*), phil*anthrop*y (benevolence, *love* of *man*). G. *anthrop*os.

Antiqu—ancient; *antiqu*ity, *antique* (old, belonging to an *ancient* period). L. *antiqu*us.

Anx—See *ang*.

Aor (*aeir*)—rise up; *aor*ta (the great artery that *rises up* from the heart), met*eor* (an aerolite, the *stone lifted high* in the air).[7] G. *aeir*esthai. G. *aeir*ein.

Ap—bee; *ap*iary (a place for *bees*). G. *ap*is.

Ap (*nap*)—a cloth; *ap*ron (a large *cloth* spread before the person). O.F. *nape*. L. *mappa*.

Aper; apert—open; *ape*rient, *aper*ture (an opening), *Ap*ril (the month of the *opening* buds), mal*apert* (saucy, badly experienced, or *opened*). L. *aper*ire, *apert*us.

Apex—summit; *apex* (the point, or *summit*, of an angle, cone, or pyramid). L. *apex*.

Api—bee; *api*ary. L. *apis*.

Appurten (*aparten*)—belong to; *appurten*ance (that which *belongs to*). O.F. *aparten*ir. L. *ad*, to; *pertin*ere, to belong. L. *per*, thoroughly; *ten*ere, to hold.

Aps; apsid—bow, turn; *aps*e (a *curved* recess in the east end of a church), *apsid*es (the *turning* points in a planet's orbit). L. *aps*is, *apsid*is. G. *aps*is. G. *apt*ein, to tie.

Apt—fit, join; ad*apt* (*fit* to), *apt*itude (*fit*ness). L. *ap*ere, *apt*us.

Aqu—water; *aqu*atic, *aqu*eous, *aqu*educt (a *water* pipe or *conductor*), *aqu*arium (a *water* vessel in which fishes and marine plants are kept). L. *aqu*a.

Aquil—eagle; *aquil*ine (like the beak of an *eagle*). L. *aquil*a.

Ar—plow; *ar*able (fit for *plowing*), *Ary*ans (the *agricultural* ancestors of the Indo-European races[8]). L. *ar*are.

Ar—be dry; *ar*id (*dry*), *ar*efaction (making *dry*). L. *ar*ere.

Arbiter; arbitr—witness, judge, umpire; *arbiter* (a *judge*), *arbitr*ary (*decisive*), *arbitr*ate (to adjust, settle). L. *arbiter*.

Arbor—tree; *arbor*eous, *arbor*iculture. L. *arbor*.

Arc—bow; *arc* (a *bow*-like section of a circumference), *arc*her (a *bow*man), *arch* (a vault having a curved roof[9]), *arc*ade (a succession of *arches*). L. *arc*us.

Arc—keep; *arc*ana (things *kept* secret). L. *arc*ere.

Arch—rule, govern; an*arch*y (the state of being without *government*), hept*arch*y (the *government* of *seven*[10]), hier*arch*y (the *governing* authorities of a church), mon*arch* (one *ruling alone*), olig*arch*y (the *government* of a *few*), patri*arch* (the *father-ruler* of a race), tetr*arch* (one of *four rulers*). G. *arch*ein.

Archæ (*archai*)—ancient; *archæ*ology (the study of *ancient* life), *archa*ic (primitive, belonging to *ancient* times), *archa*ism (an *old* form of expression). G. *archa*ios, old. G. *arch*e, the beginning.

Archi—chief; *archi*tect (the *chief builder*), *archi*pelago (a sea interspersed with islands, like the Ægean Sea, the *chief* sea of the ancient Greeks), *archi*trave (the lower part of the entablature, the *chief beam* resting on the columns). G. *archi*.

Arct—a bear; *arct*ic (in the region of the Great *Bear* of the north). G. *arct*os.

Ard; ars—burn; *ard*ent, *ard*or (*burning* zeal), *ars*on (the crime of house *burning*). L. *ard*ere, *ars*us.

Ardu—steep, difficult, high; *ardu*ous (very *difficult*). L. *ardu*us.

Are—open space; *are*a. L. *are*a.

Aren—sand; *aren*aceous, *aren*a (the *sanded* floor of the Roman amphitheater[11]). L. *aren*a.

Argent—silver; *argent*iferous (*silver-yielding*). L. *argent*um.[12]

Argill—clay; *argill*aceous. L. *argill*a.

Argu—prove by argument; *argu*e. L. *argu*ere.

Arist—best; *arist*ocracy (*government* by the *best* people). G. *arist*os.

Arithm—number; *arithm*etic (the science of *number*), log*arithm* (a *ratio number*). G. *arithm*os.

Arom—spice, sweet herb; *arom*a, *arom*atic. G. *arom*a.

Ars—See *ard*.

Art—skill; *art*. L. *ars*, *art*is.

Arteri—windpipe; *artery* (a blood vessel suggestive of the *windpipe*). G. *arteri*a.

Articul—joint; *articul*ate (supply with *joints*, divide by *joints*), *article* (a *joint* or item). L. *articul*us.

Artiller—equip, *artillery* (heavy guns, a war *equipment*). O.F. *artiller*. L. *ars*, *art*is.

Arundin—reed; *arundin*aceous. L. *arundo*, *arundin*is.

Aryten—ladle; *aryten*oid. G. *arutaine*.

Asc—work, exercise; *asc*etic (given to severe *exercise*, or self-discipline). G. *asc*ein.

Asin—ass; *asin*ine (*ass*-like). L. *asin*us.

Asper—rough; *asper*ity, ex*asper*ate. L. *asper*.

Ast—craft; *ast*ute (*craftily*). L. *ast*us.

Aster; astr—star; *aster*isk (a *little star* (*) used in reference to a footnote), *aster*oid (a smaller planet, having the *form* of a *star*), *astr*ology (the science of fortune-telling by the *stars*), *astr*onomy (the science of the *stars*), dis*aster* (an *ill-starred* accident), *aster* (the *star* flower). G. *astr*on.

Asthm—a panting; *asthma* (a disease that causes a *gasping* for breath). G. *asthma*. G. *aaz*ein, to breathe out. G. *a*ein, to breathe.

Astr—See *aster*.

Asyl—unharmed, safe from violence; *asyl*um (a place of *refuge*). G. *asul*os. G. *a*, without; *sule*, right of seizure.

Athl—contest; *athl*ete (a muscular *contestant* in physical games). G. *athl*os, a contest.

Atmo—vapor; *atmo*sphere.[13] G. *atmo*s.

Atorn—direct, prepare, transact; *atorn*ey (one who *transacts* business for another). O.F. *atorn*er. O.F. *torn*er, to turn.

Atroc—cruel; *atroc*ious, *atroc*ity. L. *atrox*, *atroc*is.

Attir (*atir*)—adorn; *attir*e (to *dress*). O.F. *atir*ier. O.F. *tire*, a row, file.

Auct—See *aug*.

Aud—hear, listen; *aud*ible (capable of being *heard*), *aud*ience (a *hearing*, also a body of *hearers*), *aud*it (to pass upon accounts after a due *hearing*), obedient (obeying, giving *ear* to). L. *aud*ire.

Audaci—bold; *audac*ious (extremely *bold*). L. *audac*, *audac*is. L. *aud*ere, to dare.

Aug; auct—increase; *aug*ment, *aug*ust (very *grand*), *auct*ion (a sale having *increasing* bids), *auth*or (a *producer*, one who causes a work to *grow* or *increase*). L. *aug*ere, *auct*us.

Aur—ear; *aur*icular (told in the *ear*). L. *auris*.

Aur—gold; *aur*iferous (*gold producing*), *aur*eate (*gilded*), *or*iole (the *golden* thrush), *or*iflamme (the standard of St. Denis of France, which consisted of a blood-red flag cut at the end into *flame*-like strips and attached to a *gilded* staff), *or*iel (a recess with a window, formerly ornamented with *gold*), *or*molu (a kind of brass resembling pounded *gold*), *or*piment (yellow sulphuret of arsenic, the *golden pigment*). L. *aur*um.

Auscult—listen; *auscult*ation (a method of distinguishing diseases of the chest by *listening*). L. *auscult*are. L. *auris*, the ear.

Auster—harsh, severe; *auster*e. L. *austerus*.

Austr—the south wind, south; *austr*al (*southerly*), *Austr*alia (the *Southern* Continent). L. *Auster*.

Authentic—vouched for, warranted. G. *authentic*os. G. *authentes* (one who does things with his own hand[14]).

Auxili—help; *auxili*ary (*helping*). L. *auxili*um. L. *aug*ere, to increase.

Av; au—bird; *av*iary (a place for *birds*), *au*spice (favor, patronage, a token of good things, as indicated by the flight of *birds*). L. *av*is.

Aval—downward; *aval*anche (a *downfall* of loosened snow from a mountain). F. *val*, vale, valley.

Avar—greedy; *avar*ice (*greediness* for gain). L. *avar*us.

Aven—oats; *aven*aceous. L. *aven*um.

Aver—have, possess; *aver*age (a proportional amount, like the proportion paid by the tenant for the use of his *possessions*[15]). O.F. *aver*. L. *habere*.

Avid—greedy, eager; *avid*ity (*eagerness*). L. *avid*us.

Avoir—to have; *avoir*dupois (*to have* some *weight*). F. *avoir*. L. *habere*.

Axi—axis; *axi*s (the line on which any thing rotates). L. *axi*s.

Axio—worthy; *axio*m (a self-evident truth, and therefore *worthy* of unquestioning acceptance). G. *axios*.

Azur (*lazur*)—a bluish stone (the *lapis lazuli*); *azur*e (*blue*). Low L. *lazur*. L. *lapis lazuli* (the *lazaward stone*).

NOTES

[1] The *acanthus* leaf is the conspicuous ornament of the beautiful Corinthian capital.

[2] An American laborer on the Panama Railroad at the time of its construction, was subjected to such brutal treatment by his immediate boss, or overseer, that in a fit of frenzy he killed the latter. The laborer was summarily tried and condemned by the local authorities, regardless of the interposition of the American Consul, who thought that due weight had not been given to the amount of provocation. When the condemned man was led out to be shot to death, the consul sprang to his side, and, throwing around him the American flag, defied the soldiers to shoot through that if they dared. The execution was prudently deferred, the man being under the protecting *ægis* of the American flag.

[3] A conspicuous ornament in the center of Minerva's shield was the head of Medusa, the Gorgon slain by Perseus.

[4] The *aerolites* are masses of planetary substance revolving around the sun in accordance with planetary laws. They are considered either the ruins of disrupted planets, or else fragments thrown off by extreme centrifugal motion. Such a moving body, when brought within the scope of the earth's attraction, is drawn from its orbit and caused to approach the earth with inconceivable velocity. Striking the earth's atmosphere with such velocity, it is heated to a white heat by friction, and thus becomes a "shooting star." The heat is generally sufficient to convert it into vapor; but occasionally a partly consumed stone reaches the surface of the earth, to be characterized as an *aerolite*. Frequently the earth encounters a multitude of these small bodies, causing a "meteor shower."

[5] Previous to the Norman Conquest, A.D. 1066, the language of England was Anglo-Saxon. That conquest placed in power a people who spoke the French language of that period (O.F., *Old French*) as it was spoken in the province of Normandy, and called, therefore, Norman French. For a time there were two languages in the island; pride holding the Normans aloof from the conquered race, and hate restraining the latter from using the speech of their conquerors. Communication between them, however, became a necessity, and it resulted not in giving up either language entirely, but in making out of both a new language—the *English*. Hence our present words are but changed forms, or corruptions, of Old French and Anglo-Saxon words. To the conquered masses were allotted toil and struggle for the material necessities of life, and they retained their language for the expression of such ideas as came within their range of experience. We still express in strong Anglo-Saxon monosyllables what we see and feel and otherwise perceive directly. It was found easier to accept the language of the masses for familiar things than to force them up to the use of a strange and foreign speech. Hence the Anglo-Saxon is still our vernacular, the language of childhood, the speech of direct experience independent of education. After the wholesale confiscations following the Conquest, the Normans possessed a monopoly of luxury, with all that pertained to it, including education and refinement; and they were hence enabled to retain their own vocabulary for the expression of things with which the conquered people had become practically unfamil-

iar. The English language is richer than either of its ancestors, for it has all the strength of the sturdy Anglo-Saxon, and with it the grace and flexibility of the French. There is, moreover, an interlapping of the two elements instead of a sharp line of division, and this has enriched the resulting language with synonyms admitting great range and variety of expression. In "Ivanhoe," Sir Walter Scott puts into the mouth of the clown, Wamba, a humorous lecture on this border-land between the two languages that coalesced to form the English.

[6] A ring is a *circuit*, like the *circuit* of the *year*.

[7] See *Aerolite*.

[8] The Aryans were a prehistoric tribe; that is, they are not mentioned in formal history, neither are they mentioned in tradition. What is known of them is learned entirely from the evidences of language, which has been found to be the most enduring monument of the human race. From these evidences it has been determined that the Aryans occupied the plains of Deccan, to the south-east of the Caspian Sea; that they were a bright, energetic race, advanced much beyond the state of savagery; that by successive migrations they contributed to the populating of Hindustan to the south-eastward, of Persia to the eastward, and of all Europe to the westward. Four great migrations of Aryans are traceable in the populations of Europe. The Celtic migration was the first, and under the pressure of successive migrations, it moved on the westward until it occupied the remote portion of the continent, embracing the regions now known as France, Spain, Portugal, and the British Islands. Then came a migration which divided at the Bosporus, sending one division into Greece, and another around the mountains into Italy, and was called, therefore, the Greco-Italian migration. A third migration bore to the northward, and occupied Central and North-western Europe. This was called the Teutonic migration, and supplied to Europe its Teutonic races, including the Germans, Dutch, English (or Anglo-Saxon), and Scandinavians. A fourth migration, bearing to the north of the Caspian Sea, contributed the great Slavonic race, occupying Russia, Servia, Montenegro, Bosnia, and other Balkan provinces. In consequence of the territory occupied by these various migrations, the

resulting races are called Indo-Europeans. They are all of one blood and one speech, but have toward each other varying degrees of relationship, and these are determined mainly by the evidences of language.

9 The arch has long been a conspicuous feature in architecture. As such it was introduced by the Romans, its use being unknown to the Greeks and other nations, who distinguished themselves early in architecture. The Roman arch consisted of a continuous curve, or semicircle. The later Gothic architecture recognized the usefulness and beauty of the arch, but gave it a point, to make it conform to the pointed style of this architecture. The Gothic arch consists of two curves, or arcs, intersecting so as to form a point, or apex. Architecture produces the most satisfactory effects where it exhibits fitness or adaptation, solidity or strength, and beauty, harmoniously combined. The arch contributes to these three elements. The Romans had such a high estimate of the properties of the arch that they employed it as an ornament in itself, apart from any other structure, as seen in their triumphal arches—the monuments or trophies of their conquests. The fine arch of Titus, still in existence, is a notable example. The arch, by introducing the curved line into ornamentation, was doubtless the inspiring suggestion and starting-point of all the tracery subsequently developed in Gothic architecture.

10 The term is especially applied to the government of England under the seven Saxon kings. The seven kingdoms were Kent, Sussex (South Saxons), Wessex (West Saxons), Essex (East Saxons), East Anglia, Mercia, and Northumberland. These were all united finally into one kingdom by Egbert, king of Wessex. He allowed the other kings to reign for a time, but in token of submission he compelled them to row his barge on the Thames with their own hands.

11 The Roman people became addicted to barbarous amusements; they rejoiced in the torture and destruction of men and beasts. Their amphitheaters were slaughter pens, in which men were supplied with arms and compelled to fight for their lives. As it was truly a fight to the death, nothing could be more desperate than a gladiatorial combat. Blood alone did not satisfy

that fierce audience; they often required murder in its most cowardly and shocking form. If a gladiator fell wounded and helpless, his antagonist was obliged to place the point of his sword at the throat of his fallen adversary and act as the people signaled. If the thumbs were down it was the signal to destroy; if up, the signal to spare. These gladiatorial contests were varied with the fights of wild beasts; and often human beings were thrust into the arena to struggle with the beasts. Many of the early Christians were martyred in the arena—torn to pieces for the amusement of the Roman populace. Strange to say, the front seats in those extraordinary places of amusement were reserved for the upper classes, assigned by law to those of knightly rank. The gladiators once rebelled against the brutal uses to which they were assigned; under the leadership of Spartacus, and with headquarters in the crater of Mt. Vesuvius, for three years they defied the power of Rome. In marked constrast to the bloody arena of Rome were the noble and elevating public games of Greece. There, too, were exhibitions of courage, strength, and endurance, but they took the harmless forms of racing, wrestling, guiding the flying chariot, hurling the weight, etc. But the people found their highest delight in listening to some great bard, musician, or historian, or in witnessing the latest productions of their artists.

12 The *Argent*ine Republic occupies a *silver* region.

13 The atmosphere of the earth is estimated to be about fifty miles in thickness. The weight of this mass produces a pressure at the level of the sea equivalent to fourteen pounds to the square inch of surface. Like all gases and liquid substances, its pressure is in all directions. Animal life depends upon this pressure; for the removal of the pressure causes the fluids of the body to burst outward. This is why people suffer distress, and are affected with bleeding in ascending to great heights on a mountain or in a balloon. The pressure of fourteen pounds to the square inch would be crushing if applied in but one direction, as the hand may be crushed by placing it over the opening of the receiver of an air-pump while the air is being exhausted. The atmosphere takes up moisture from the ocean by its capillary quality, and carries it to the mountains, to be there precipitated, and thus to form the great streams of the world. This moisture-

laden atmosphere also supplies the useful showers for the thirsty fields. The earth is thus rendered productive and capable of sustaining animal life. The atmosphere is, moreover, a shield or protection against dangerous missiles from above. But for the atmosphere each aerolite would reach the earth in solid form, and with a velocity incalculably greater than that of a cannon ball. (See *Aerolite*.) The hail-stones, the very drops of rain, would all be deadly missiles but for the elastic resistance of the several strata of the atmosphere. Another mechanical property of the air is its affording a medium for locomotion. Birds propel themselves through it by the oar-like movements of their wings, and men are learning to traverse it by means of the balloon or airship. These are among the mechanical effects and uses of the atmosphere. The chemical properties of air, as such, open another great chapter in the economy of nature.

[14] An *authentic* manuscript is as reliable as if written by the author's *own hand*.

[15] Under the feudal system the tenant owed his lord and master not only personal service, but also the use of his horses, cattle, etc. In time the use of these articles came to be waived on the payment of a sum of money, called *average*.

B

Bacc—berry; *bacc*ivorous, *bacc*alaureate (relating to graduates, or *bachelors*, the wearers of the *bayberry* wreaths). L. *bacc*a.

Badin—jest; *badin*age. F. *badin*er.

Bail (*baill*)—secure, keep in custody; *bail* (*security*), *baill*iff (a *custodian*), *bail*iwick (a territorial *jurisdiction*). F. *bail*ler.

Ball—dance; *ball*, *ball*et, *ball*ad (a *dancing* song). Low L. *ball*are.

Ball—throw, put; hyper*bole* (an exaggeration, a *throwing over* or *beyond*), sym*bol* (a sign, something *put with*), em*ble*m (a sign or representation, something *put on*, as an ornament), para*ble* (a comparison, a *casting beside*). G. *ball*ein.

Band—proscribe, outlaw; *band*it (a robber *outlaw*). It. *band*ire. Low L. *bann*ir, to proclaim. O.H. Ger. *bann*an, to summon. O.H. Ger. *ban*, a *ban*.

Band—ban, proclamation; contra*band* (subject to forfeiture for being *against* the *proclamation*). It. *band*o.

Bank (*banc*)—bench, table; *bank* (an institution dealing in money, originally the money-changer's *bench*), *bank*rupt (an insolvent person, like the mone-changers whose *bench* was *broken*), *ban*quet (a great feast, originally a *little table*),

Bany (*banij*)—merchant; *bany*an (a wide-spreading tree of India, under whose shade the *merchants* held their market). Skt. *banij*.

Bapt—dip; *bapt*ize. G. *bapt*ein.

Bar—weight; *bar*ometer (an instrument for indicating the *weight* of the atmosphere). G. *bar*os.

Barb—beard; *barb*er (the *beard* dresser), *barb* (a *beard*-like projection), *barb*el (a *bearded* fish). L. *barb*a.

Barbar—stammering; *barbar*ians (uncivilized, originally merely foreigners, whose language seemed to the Greeks nothing more than a *stammering*). G. *barbar*os.

Barr—a bar; *barr*el (a vessel made of staves or *bars*), *barr*ier (an obstruction, like a *bar*), em*bar*go (an arrest, a stoppage, as by putting a *bar in* the way). F. *barr*e.

Barric—barrel; *barric*ade (a street obstruction, sometimes made of *barrels* of sand). Sp. *barric*a. Sp. *bar*ea, a bar, stave.

Barrow (*beorh*)—a hill; *barrow* (a burial mound). A.S. *beorg, beorh*. A.S. *beorg*an, to hide, protect.

Bary—heavy; *bary*tone, *bary*tes. G. *bar*us.

Bas (*bass*)—low; *bas*e (low), a*bas*e (bring *low*), *bas*ement (the *lowest* part of a building), *bas*s (the *lowest* part in music), *bas*s-relief (*low* relief), *bas*soon (a *bas*s instrument), de*bas*e (make *low*). Low L. *bas*sus.

Basil—king; *basil*ica (a *royal* hall for the administration of justice, also a *great* church), *basil*isk (a fabled serpent, a serpent or lizard having a spot on its head resembling a *crown*). G. *basil*eus.

Bast—build; *bast*ion (a strong *building* in a fortification), *bast*ile (a strongly-*built* fortress). O.F. *bast*ir.

Bastin (*baston*)—stick; *bastin*ado (a beating with a *stick* upon the soles of the feet). Sp. *baston*.

Bat—beat; *bat*ter (*beat* down), *bat*tle (a fight, a *striking*, or *beating*), *bat*talion (a command organized for *bat*tle), a*bat*e (*beat* down), com*bat* (fight or *strike* *together*), de*bat*e (argue, *beat* one another *down*), re*bat*e (a return, *beat back*). L. *bat*ere. L. *bat*uere.

Bath—depth; *bath*os (a sinking to the *depths* of the ridiculous). G. *bath*os.

Baton—a cudgel, stick; *baton* (a wand, a *truncheon*), *batten* (a wooden *rod*), *Baton* Rouge (the city of the *Red Stick*). F. *baton*. Low L. *bast*o, *bast*onis.

Batrach—frog; *batrach*ian. G. *batrach*os.

Beat—blessed; *beat*ify (make *blessed*), *beat*itude, *beat*ific. L. *be*are, *beat*us.

Beau—fine; *beau* (a *finely* dressed person), *beau*ty. F. *beau*. O.F. *bel*. L. *bell*us, fair, fine.

Bel; bell—fair, fine; *bell*e (the reigning *fair* one), em*bell*ish (to *beautify*, adorn), *bell*adonna (the drug nightshade, formerly used by *ladies* to increase their *beauty*, on account of its dilating the pupil of the eye), *bel*dame (a disagreeable old woman, called ironically a *fair lady*), *Bel*vedere (*beautiful to see*), *Bel*mont (the *beautiful mountain*), Ma*bel* (*my fair* one). L. *bell*us.

Belemn—a dart; *belemn*ite (a fossil shaped like the head of a *dart*). G. *belemn*os. G. *ball*ein, to throw.

Bell—war; *bell*igerent, *bell*icose, re*bel* (make *war again*). L. *bell*um.

Bene—well; *bene*factor (a helper, a *well-doer*), *bene*fice (a church living, a grant, a *well-doing*), *bene*fit (a favor or advantage, something *well done*), *bene*volent (charitable, *well-wishing*). L. *bene*.

Benedict—blessed; *benedict*ion (a *blessing*), *benedict* (a newly-married man). L. *benedict*us. L. *bene*, well; *dic*ere, *dict*us, to say.

Benign—mild; *benign*. L. *benign*us.

Besti—beast; *besti*al. L. *besti*a.

Bever (*bevr*)—drink; *bever*age. O.F. *bevr*e. L. *bib*ere.

Bey (*be*)—gape, expect anxiously; a*bey*ance (a state of suspension, as if with some *expectancy* of resumption). O.F. *bee*r.

Bi—life; *bi*ography (an account of a *life*), *bi*ology (the science of the nature of *life*), amphi*bi*ous (having its *life both* on land and in water). G. *bi*os.

Bias (*biais*)—slant, inclination; *bias* (a preference, a *leaning* toward). F. *biais*.

Bib—drink; im*bib*e (*drink in*), *bib*ulous (given to *drink*), *bib* (a cloth for imbibing, or *drinking in*, moisture). G. *bib*ere.

Bibl—book; *bibl*iomania (an eye for *books*), *bibl*iography (an *account* of the *books* treating of a given subject). G. *bibl*os. G. *bubl*os, Egyptian papyrus (from which the ancient *books* were made).

Bil—bile; *bil*e. L. *bil*is.

Bill—log, stump, stick; *bill*et (a *little log*), *bill*iards (the game played with a *stick*). F. *bill*e.

Bill—a writing; *bill*, *bill*et. Low L. *bill*a.

Bin—twofold; *bin*ary (occurring in *twos*), com*bin*e (join or fold *two* or more together). L. *bin*us. L. *bi*, double.

Bit—bite; *bit*e, *bit* (a morsel, a *bite*), *bit* (a curb on which a horse *bites*), *bit*ter (a sharp *bit*ing flavor), *bait* (cause of *bite*), *beet*le (the *bit*ing insect), *beet*le (to project over like an upper *jaw*), a*bet* (to incite, instigate, *bait* on), *bet* (to wager, to a*bet*). A.S. *bit*an.

Blanc—white; *blanc*h (to *whiten*), *blank* (*white*, empty), *blank*et (a *white* bedspread), Mont *Blanc* (the *white* mountain). F. *blanc*.

Bland—mild; *bland*. L. *bland*us.

Blas (*blaps*)—damage, evil; *blas*pheme (to *speak ill* of sacred things). G. *blap*sis.

Blaz (*blas*)—blow; *blaz*on (to publish far and wide, as with a *trumpet*). M.E. *blas*en.

Blazon (*blason*)—a coat of arms; *blazon* (to *portray armorial bearings*). F. *blason*. Ger. *blasen*, to blow.[1]

Bleac (*blæc*)—shining, pale; *bleac*h (to make *pale*), *bleak*. A.S. *blæc, blac*.

Blem—wound, stain; *blem*ish (to *stain*, spoil). O.F. *blem*ir, *blesm*ir. O.F. *bleme, blesme*, wan, pale.

Blow—to bloom; *blow, blos*som, *bloo*m, *bloo*d (the sign of *blooming* life), *blee*d (to lose *blood*), *bless* (to consecrate, as by sacrifice or the sprinkling of *blood*). A.S. *blow*an.

Bodk (*bidog*)—dagger; *bodk*in (a *little dagger*). W. *bidog*.

Bol—See *ball*.

Bolt (*buret*)—sift through coarse cloth. O.F. *buret*. O.F. *buire*, coarse woolen cloth. Low L. *burra*, coarse red cloth. L. *burr*us, reddish. See *Bur*eau.

Bomb—a humming; *bomb* (the *humming* shell). L. *bomb*us. G. *bomb*os.

Bombard—cannon; *bombard* (to assail with *cannon*). F. *bombard*e (the *bomb* thrower).

Bombast (*bombax*)—cotton, wadding; *bombast* (inflated language, as if filled out with *cotton*-wadding). Low L. *bombax*. L. *bombyx*. G. *bombux*, silk, cotton.

Bon—good; *bon*us (a special allowance, a *good*), *boon*, *bon*ny, *boun*ty (goodness). L. *bon*us.

Bor (*bur*)—peasant, dweller; neigh*bor* (the *near dweller*), *boor*. A.S. *bur*.

Bord—edge, side; *bord*er (an *edge*), over*board* (over the *side* of a vessel), star*board* (the right-hand side, the *steering side*), lar*board* (the *lading side*), *board* (a plank, such as goes on the *side* of a vessel). A.S. *bord*.[2]

Borough (*beorg*)—protect; *borough* (a large town,[3] originally a *protecting* fort). A.S. *beorg*an.

Bosc—feed; pro*bosc*is (the elephant's trunk, or *feeder* in *front*). G. *bosc*ein.

Botan—herb; *botan*y (the science of *plants*). G. *botan*e.

Bouch—mouth; de*bouch* (to emerge, as *from* a *mouth*). F. *bouch*e. L. *bucc*a.

Bov—ox, cow; *bov*ine. L. *bos, bov*is.

Brac—the two arms; *brac*e, *brac*elet, em*brac*e. O.F. *brac*e. L. *brachi*um.

Brachi—arm; *brachi*opod. L. *brachi*um.

Brachy—short; *brachy*cephalous, amphi*brach*. G. *brachu*s.

Brack—vomit; *brack*ish (nauseous, causing to *vomit*). Du. *brack*en.

Bracte—thin plate of metal; *bract*. L. *bracte*a.

Branchi—gill; *branchi*al. G. *branchi*on.

Bras (*brais*)—live coals; *bras*ier. F. *brais*e.

Brev—short; *brev*ity, *brev*et (a *short* commission giving rank without command), *brev*e (the sign of the *short* sound, also formerly the *shortest* note in music), *brev*iary (a summary of *short* form of religious exercices), *brev*ier (a kind of type, such as was used in printing *brev*iaries), *brief*, ab*brev*iate (to *shorten*). L. *brev*is.

Brig—strive after, fight; *brig*ade (a body of soldiers, or *fighting* men). It. *brig*are.

Brigant—a robber; *brigant*ine (a *pirate* ship), *brigand* (a *robber* outlaw), *brig* (short for *brigant*ine). It. *brigant*e. It. *briga*, strife, quarrel, trouble.

Brill—glitter; *brill*iant. F. *brill*er. L. *beryll*us, a beryl.

Broch—pierce, stitch; *broch*ure (a brief treatise, as of a few leaves *stitched* together), *broch* (to set agoing, as in *piercing* a cask of liquor). F. *broch*er. F. *broch*e, a spit.

Bronch—wind-pipe; *bronch*ial. G. *bronch*os.

Brum—winter; *brum*al. L. *brum*a.

Brut—stupid, irrational; *brut*e. L. *brut*us.[4]

Bry—teem, sprout; *bry*ony (the plant of luxuriant *growth*), em*bry*o (the *sprouting* germ). G. *bru*ein.

Bu (*bou*)—cow, ox; *bu*colic (pastoral, relating to *coxherds*), *bu*ffalo (the wild *ox*), *bu*gle (the horn of an *ox*), *bu*tter (*cow-cheese*). G. *bou*s.

Bucc—check; *bucc*al. L. *bucc*a.

Bucol—cowherd; *bucol*ic (pastoral, relating to *cow-herds*). G. *boucol*os. G. *bou*s, ox, cow; *kell*ein, to drive.

Bul—stem, trunk; *bul*rush (the *stem* rush), *bul*wark (a defense, as if made of the *trunks* of trees). Dan. *bul*.

Bull—boil; *ebull*ition (a *boiling* up). L. *bull*ire. L. *bull*a, a bubble.

Burl—waggery, mockery, trick; *burl*esque (a *mock* performance). It. *burl*a.

Burs—purse; *burs*ar (the *purse*-bearer), dis*burs*e (pay out of the *purse*), reim*burs*e (pay back, put *into* the *purse again*). Low L. *burs*a.

Bust—trunk of human body. Low L. *bust*um.

Butyr—butter; *butyr*aceous. G. *butyr*on. G. *bou*s, cow; *tur*os, cheese.

Byss—bottom; a*byss* (a *bottomless* chasm). G. *byss*os.

NOTES

[1] Armorial bearings represent some achievement which has given fame to the family. A victor's fame was proclaimed by the *trumpet* of a herald.

[2] The Anglo-Saxon speech, which forms the basis of the English language, came into England in the fifth century A.D. The Roman Empire began to give way in the fifth century to the pressure of barbarian hordes from the North and East (composed principally of the Goths, Vandals, and Huns). One of the first regions abandoned by the distressed Romans was Britain—for two reasons: first, because it was a very remote province, and therefore guarded with difficulty, and second, because it was never fully subjugated. (See *Gaelic*.) On the withdrawal of the

Roman garrisons, the island lapsed back into the possession of its native Celts. Some of these living nearest the Roman strongholds had become partly Romanized; that is, they had acquired some Roman ideas, some Roman customs, and some Roman speech. They were, therefore, out of harmony with the fierce, untouched Celts of the remoter regions. This lack of harmony soon led to conflicts, especially with the Picts and Scots of the north, who had never made a truce with the Roman legions. The hard-pressed Southrons looked around for aid, and invited in the Angles and Saxons of North Germany to their assistance. The latter came, and after repelling the Picts and Scots, were so pleased with the genial climate and productive soil, so different from the cold and murky lowlands of the north, that they resolved to hold the country, even against their allies. This determination reunited the Celts in a brave struggle against the common enemy, a struggle to the death, in which neither party gave nor asked quarter, a struggle that continued during the unexampled period of over two hundred years. The termination of this struggle left the Saxons in exclusive possession of England proper, but unwilling to pursue their desperate foes within the highlands of Scotland and the border morasses of Wales. Saxon blood, Saxon thrift, and Saxon speech took full possession of the conquered region, slightly modified by the later incursion of the Danes, but practically undisturbed until the time of the Norman Conquest, in the eleventh century.

3 The names of many English *towns* have the termination *borough*; as, Marl*borough*, Scar*borough*, etc.

4 The elder *Brut*us obtained his name from an appearance of *idiocy*, which he deliberately assumed in his youth, in order to escape the tyranny of the Tarquins, who had put to death his father and brothers.

C

Cachinn—laugh; *cachinn*ation (*laughter*). L. *cachinn*are.

Cad; cas—fall; *cad*ence (a *falling* of the voice), *cadu*cous (*falling* early), *case* (an event, a circumstance, a be*fall*ing), *cas*ual (happening, or be*fall*ing, by *chance*), ac*cid*ent (a happening, a *falling toward*), de*cad*ence, de*cay* (*fall apart*), de*cid*uous (*falling* in autumn), oc*cid*ent (the west, the place of the *setting* sun), oc*cas*ion (an opportunity, or necessity, *falling* to one's lot). L. *cad*ere, *cas*us.

Cadaver—corpse; *cadaver*ous (pale, emaciated, *corpse*-like). L. *cadaver*.

Cæd; cæs—cut, kill, slay; *cæs*ura (a pause in the middle of a verse, *cutting* the latter in two), ex*cis*ion, in*cis*ion, in*cis*ive, *chis*el, *scis*sors, homi*cid*e (the *killing* of a man), matri*cid*e, parri*cid*e, frati*cid*e, regi*cid*e, sorori*cid*e, sui*cid*e, uxori*cid*e, con*cis*e (compact, brief, *cut* short), de*cid*e (settle, *cut* off further debate), pre*cis*e (exact, having all that is misleading *cut* off). L. *cæd*ere, *cæs*us.

Cal—proclaim; inter*cal*ate (insert by *proclamation*). L. *cal*are, to proclaim.

Cal—beautiful; *cal*igraphy, *cal*ligraphy, *cal*isthenics, *kal*eidoscope, *cal*omel. G. *cal*os.

Calam—reed; *calam*iferous. L. *calam*us.

Calamit—misfortune; *calam*ity. L. *calamit*as.

Calc—lime, stone; *calc*areous, *calc*ine (reduce to lime), *calc*ium, *calc*ulate (to reckon, as by means of *pebbles* as counters), *chalk*. L. *calx*, *calc*is.

Calc—tread, press; *calk* (*press* in), in*culc*ate (*impress*). L. *calc*are. L. *calx, calc*is, the heel.

Cald—hot; *cald*ron (a large *kettle*), s*cald*. L. *cald*us, *calid*us. L. *cal*ere, to be hot.

Calend—the first of the month; *calend*s, *calend*ar. L. *calend*æ.

Call—hard skin; *call*ous. L. *call*us.

Calm (*caum*)—heat; *calm* (still, as during the noontide *heat*). G. *caum*a. G. *cai*ein, to be hot.

Calor—heat; *calor*ic, *calor*ific. L. *calor*. L. *cal*ere, to be hot.

Calu—deceive, misrepresent; *calu*mny (malicious *misrepresentation*).

Calx—lime, stone. L. *calx*.

Calypt—cover; apo*calyps*e (a revelation, an un*cover*-ing). G. *calupt*ein.

Calyx—a covering, cup; *calyx* (the *cup* of the flower). L. *calyx*. G. *calux*.

Camer—chamber; *camer*ated, *camer*a (the dark *chambered* instrument of photography), *com*-rade (a *room*mate), *chamber*. L. *camer*a.

Camp—field; *camp* (a temporary abode in the open *field*), *camp*estral (growing in *fields*), *camp*aign (a season of *field* service), *champ*ion (a combatant in the *field*), *champ*aign (an open *country*), *Champ*-pagne (the open *plain*), de*camp* (depart, break up *camp*), s*camp* (a vagabond, like a deserter from a battle*field*). L. *camp*us.

Campan—bell; *campan*iform, *campan*ula (the *little bell*). L. *campan*a.

Can—dog; *can*ine, *Can*ary (the Islands of the *Dogs*), *ken*nel (the *dog*-house), Prairie du *Chien*, (the *Dog* Prairie). L. *can*is.

Can; cann—reed; *cane, cann*on (a large gun, long and

hollow, like a *reed*), *can*ister (a *reed* basket), *can*on (a rule, rod, *reed*). G. *can*ne.

Cancell—lattice, grating; *cancel* (to draw lines across, like a *grating* or lattice-work), *chancel* (the part of a church shut off by a screen or *lattice*-work), *chancell*or (a high officer of state, originally an officer who stood near the *screen* before the judgment seat), *chancery* (a court of equity, presided over by the *chancellor*). L. *cancell*us. L. *cancer*, a crab.

Cancer—crab, eating tumor; *cancer*, *canker*. L. *cancer*.

Cand—glow, burn; *cand*le, *cand*or (frankness, *clearness*), in*cand*escent. L. *cand*ere.

Candel—candle; *candel*abrum (a branching *candle*-stick), *chandel*ier, *chandl*er (a dealer in *candles*), *cannel* (burning brightly, like a *candle*), *kindl*e (to light, as a *candle*). L. *candel*a.

Candid—white, clear, sincere; *candid*, *candid*ate (a seeker after office, who in ancient Rome was obliged to wear a *white* robe). L. *candid*us. L. *cand*ere, to glow.

Cant—sing; *cant* (a *singing* whine), *cant*icle (a *little song*), *cant*o (a division of a *song*), *cant*ata (a *song* set to *music*), ac*cent* (stress on a syllable, as in *singing*), *chant*, des*cant*, en*chant*, in*cant*ation, in*cent*ive, pre*cent*or, re*cant*. L. *cant*are.

Cap—cloak, hood; *cape*, *cap*, *cap*arison (trappings of a horse, enveloping him as a *cloak*), *cap*uchin (a *hooded* friar), *cap*e, es*cap*e (to get away, to slip out of one's *cap*e). Low L. *cap*a.

Cap—head; *cap*e (a *headland*). It *cap*o. L. *cap*ut.

Cap; capt—take, seize, hold; *cap*able, *cap*acious, *cap*tive, *capt*or, *capt*ure, *capt*ious (fault-finding, *seizing* upon), cable (a *holding* rope), ac*cept*, con*cept*ion, de*cept*ion, in*cept*ion, in*cip*ient, inter*cept*, oc*cup*y, per*cept*ion, pre*cept* (a rule or maxim *taken before-hand* as a guide to conduct), re*cept*acle, re*cept*ion, re*cip*e (a prescription, this *receive thou*), re*cip*ient, anti*cip*ate[1] (*take beforehand*), *cait*iff (a wretch *taken* into custody), con*ceive*, con*ceit*, sus*cept*ible (ready to *receive* or *undertake*). L. *cap*ere, *capt*us.

Capill—hair; *capill*aceous, *capill*ary (occurring in fine, *hair*-like tubes). L. *capill*us.

Capit—head; *capit*al, *capit*ation (so much per *head*), de*capit*ate, *capt*ain (the *head* man), oc*ciput* (the back of the *head*), sin*ciput*[2] (the fore part or *half* of the *head*), pre*cipit*ate (send *head*-long). L. *caput*, *capit*is.

Capitul—chapter; *capitul*ar (relating to a *chapter*), *capitul*ate (to divide into *chapters*, to surrender on the terms mentioned in the several *chapters*), reca-*pitul*ate (to sum up again the several *chapters*), *chapter*. Low L. *capitul*um. L. *caput*, *capit*is, head.

Capno—smoke; *capno*mancy. G. *capnos*.

Capr—goat; *capr*ice (a sudden freak, like the frisk of a *goat*), *capr*icorn (the *horned goat*), *capr*id, *caper* (to frisk about as a *goat*), *cabr*iolet (a light carriage, that frisks about like a *goat*), *cab* (short for *cabr*iolet). L. *capr*a.

Caps—box, case; *caps*ule. L. *caps*a. L. *cap*ere, to hold.

Capt—See *cap*.

Car—dear; *car*ess (to embrace what is *dear*). L. *car*us.

Caracol—snail; *caracol*e (a half turn made by a horse, suggestive of the *spiral* of a *snail*-shell). Sp. *caracol*.

Carbon—a coal; *carbon* (pure char*coal*), *carb*uncle (a precious stone, resembling a glowing *coal*, also an *inflamed* sore). L. *carbo*, *carbon*is.

Carcer—prison; in*carcer*ate (to confine in a *prison*). L. *carcer*.

Cardi—heart; *cardi*ac, peri*cardi*um (the membrane *around* the *heart*). G. *cardi*a.

Cardin—hinge; *cardin*al (chief, that on which a matter *hinges*). L. *cardo*, *cardin*is.

Caric—load; *caric*ature (a ludicrous representation, an *overloaded* picture). It. *caric*are.

Carin—keel; *carin*ated, *careen* (to incline so as to show the *keel*). L. *carin*a.

Carm—song, enchantment; *charm*. L. *carm*en.

Carn—flesh; *carn*al, *carn*age, *carn*ation (*flesh* color), *carn*ival (a period of levity before Lent, a *lightening* to the *flesh*), *carn*elian (a *flesh*-colored stone), *carn*ivorous (*flesh-eating*), in*carn*ate (in the *flesh*), in*carn*adine (to dye of a *carn*ation color), *charn*el (containing corpses, decaying *flesh*), *carr*ion (putrid *flesh*). L. *caro*, *carn*is.

Caro—stupefy; *caro*tid (a term applied to one of the two great arteries of the neck, any change in which was supposed to cause *stupor*). G. *caro*s.

Carp—pluck; *carp*et (a floor covering, made of rags *pulled* to pieces). L. *carp*ere.

Carpent—carriage; *carpent*er. L. *carpent*um.

Cart—a paper; *cart*e (a *bill* of fare), *cart*e-blanche (*blank paper* signed), leaving the holder unlimited opportunity for filling in), *cart*el (an agreement for the exchange of prisoners, a *little paper*), *cart*oon (a painting on a *large paper*), *cart*ridge (a charge incased in *paper*), *cart*ouch (a *paper* case). It. *cart*a. L. *chart*a. G. *chart*e.

Cartilag—gristle; *cartilag*e. L. *cartilag*o.

Casc—fall; *casc*ade (a water-*fall*). It *casc*are. L. *cad*ere, *cas*us.

Case—cheese; *case*ous. L. *case*us.

Cash (*cass*)—annul, discharge; *cash*ier (to *dismiss* from service). L. *cass*are. L. *cass*us, null, void.

Cast—pure, chaste; *cast*e (a class, a *pure* breed), *cast*igate (punish, make *pure*), *chaste*, *chaste*n (to afflict, in order to *purify*), *chast*ise, in*cest*. L. *cast*us.

Caten—chain; con*caten*ation (a complete series, *linked together*), *chain*. L. *caten*a.

Cathar—pure; *cathar*tic (a *purifying* medicine). G. *cathar*os.

Cathedr—seat, chair, throne; *cathedr*al (a bishop's church, containing his *throne*). G. *cathedr*a.

Cathol—in general; *cathol*ic (universal, *in general*). G. *cathol*ou.

Catoptr—mirror; *catoptr*ic (relating to *reflection*). G. *catoptr*on. G. *cata*, down; *opt*omai, I see.

Cau—tail; *caud*al. L. *caud*a.

Caud—stem; *caul*iflower, *cole*wort. L. *caul*is.

Caul—burn; *caus*tic, holo*caust* (*burned* whole). G. *cai*ein, *caus*o.

Caus (*calx*)—lime, stone; *caus*e-way (a *stone* road). L. *calx*.

Cauteri—branding iron; *cauteri*ze (to sear, as with a *branding iron*). G. *cauteri*on. G. *cai*ein, to burn.

Cav—hollow; *cav*ity, *cav*e, con*cav*e (*hollowed* in), ex*cav*ate (*hollowed out*). L. *cav*us.

Cav; caut—beware; *caut*ion, *cav*eat (*let him beware*). L. *cav*ere, *caut*us.

Cavall—horse; *caval*ier (a *horse*man), *caval*ry (the *horse* soldiers), *caval*cade (a *mounted* procession). It. *cavall*o. Low L. *cavall*us.

Cavill—a jeering; *cavil* (to wrangle, *jeer* at). L. *cavill*a.

Ced; cess—go, yield; *ced*e (yield up), abs*cess* (a *discharging* sore), ac*ced*e (*come toward, yield to*), ac*cess* (approach, *go to*), an*ces*tor (one who has *gone before*), ante*ced*ent (*going before*), con*ced*e (*yield up*), de*cease* (death, departure, *going away*), ex*ceed* (*go out* of bounds), ex*cess* (a *going out* of bounds), intercede (plead for, *go between*), precede[3] (*go before*), proceed (*go forward*), recede (*go* back), retrocession (a *going backward*), secede (withdraw, *go aside*, apart), succeed (*go* next). L. *ced*ere, *cess*us.

Ceil—See *cel*.

Cel—hide; con*ceal*. L. *cel*are.

Cel (*cœl*)—heaven; *cel*estial, *ceil*ing (a canopy, covering over as the *heavens*). L. *cœl*um.

Celebr—solemnize, honor; *celebr*ate. L. *celebr*are. L. *celeber*, frequented, populous.

Celer—swift; *celer*ity, ac*celer*ate (to *quicken*). L. *celer*.

Celib (*cœlib*)—single, unmarried; *celib*acy. L. *cœleb*s, *cœlib*is.

Cem (*coim*)—sleep; *cem*etery (a burial place, a place where the dead *sleep*). G. *coim*ao.

Ceno—empty; *ceno*taph (an *empty tomb*). G. *ken*os.

Ceno (*coino*)—recent; *ceno*zoic (belonging to *recent life*). G. *coino*s.

Ceno (*coino*)—common; *ceno*bite (a monk who lives a *life* in *common* with others). G. *coino*s.

Cens—See *cand*.

Cens—give an opinion, appraise; *cens*or (an assessor, appraiser, hence a critic[4]), *cens*ure (severe *criticism*). L. *cens*ere.

Cent—hundred; *cent*ury (a *hundred* years), *cent*ennial (occurring once in a *hundred years*), *cent*enary (relating to one *hundred*), *cent*urion (the commander of a *hundred* men), *cent*igrade (divided into one *hundred degrees*), *cent*ipede (the insect with many, as of a *hundred, feet*), *cent*uple (a *hundred fold*), *cent* (the one *hundredth* part of a dollar), per *cent* (by the *hundred*). L. *cent*um.

Cephal—head; a*cephal*ous, bi*cephal*ous, *cephal*ic, *cephal*opod. G. *kephale*.[5]

Cept—See *capt*.

Cer—wax; *cer*ecloth, *cer*ement (a *waxed* cloth for dead bodies), *cer*acious, *cer*ate. L. *cer*a.

Cer; cerat—horn; rhino*cer*os (the beast with a *horn* on the *nose*), ortho*cer*atite (the fossil resembling a *straight horn*). G. *cer*as, *cerat*os.

Ceram—potter's earth; *ceram*ic (relating to *pottery*). G. *ceram*os.

Cere—corn, grain; *cere*al (one of the *grains*). L. *cere*s.[6]

Cerebr—brain; *cerebr*um (the upper *brain*). L. *cerebr*um.

Ceremoni—rite; *ceremoni*y. L. *ceremoni*a.

Cern; cret—separate, observe; con*cern* (*observe* with), dis*cern* (distinguish, *separate apart*), dis*creet* (prudent, seeing things *separately*), se*cret* (a matter kept private, or *separated apart*). L. *cern*ere, *cert*us.

Cert—sure; *cert*ain, as*cert*ain (make *sure*). L. *cert*us.

Cerule (*cœrule*)—blue; *cerule*an (like the *blue* sky). L. *cœrule*us.

Cerv—stag; *cerv*ine. L. *cerv*us.

Cervic—neck; *cervic*al. L. *cerv*ix, *cervic*is.

Cess—cease; *cess*ation, in*cess*ant (*ceaseless*). L. *cess*are.

Cess—See *ced*.

Cet—whale; *cet*aceous. L. *cet*us. G. *cet*os.

Cha—gape, yawn; *cha*sm (a *yawning* gulf), *cha*os (confusion, like that of the *yawning* abyss). G. *cha*ein.

Chagrin—melancholy; *chagrin* (mortification). F; *chagrin*.

Chame (*chamai*)—on the ground; *chame*leon (the *ground lion*), *cham*omile (the *ground apple*[7]). G. *chamai*.

Chant—sing; *chant*, *chant*er, *chant*icleer (the cock, the *clear singer*), en*chant* (to charm with a weird *song*). F. *chant*er. L. *cant*are.

Character—an engraved or stamped mark; *character* (a letter or *mark* used as a symbol, also peculiar qualities or *marks*). G. *character*. G. *charass*ein, to furrow, scratch, engrave.

Charl (*ciarl*)—prattle; *charl*atan (a pretentious *talker*). It. *ciarl*are.

Chart—a paper; *chart*, *chart*er. L. *chart*a.[8] G. *chart*e.

Chauf—to warm; *chafe* (to *warm* by friction). O.F. *chauf*er. L. *cale*facere. L. *cal*ere, to glow; *face*re, to make.

Che—pour out, mix; al*che*my (the old science of *melting* and *mixing* metals with a view to producing gold), *che*mist (the successor of the al*che*mist[9]). G. *che*ein.

Cheir—hand; *cheir*opter (the *hand-winged* bat), *chir*opodist (one who treats the *feet* and *hands*), *chir*ography (*hand-writing*). G. *cheir*.

Chen (*chain*)—gape, crack open; a*chen*e. G. *chain*ein.

Cher—dear, *cher*ish (hold *dear*), *char*ity (assistance, forbearance, as to those we hold *dear*). F. *cher*. L. *car*us.

Cheval—a horse; *cheval*ier (a knight, a *horse*man), *chivalr*y (the condition or characteristics of a knight, or *chevalier*[10]), *chival*rous (like a good knight, or *chevalier*), *cheval*-de-frise (an obstruction of pointed stakes inserted in a piece of timber, used to resist an assault, humorously called the "*horse of Friesland*").

Chicaner—to wrangle; *chicaner*y (trickery, like that of *wrangling* pettifoggers). F. *chicaner*.

Chief—head; *chief* (at the *head*), *chief*tain (the *head* man), mis*chief* (a bad result, or *head*), a*chiev*e (bring to a *head*, accomplish), ker*chief* (a square cloth often used as a cover for the *head*). O.F. chef, *chief*. L. *caput*.

Chilio—thousand, *chilio*meter, *kilo*meter, *chilo*gram, *kilo*gram. G. *chilio*n.

Chim—See *cymb*.

Chir—See *cheir*.

Chlor—pale, green; *chlor*ine (a *pale green* gas), *chlor*ophyl (the *green* coloring matter in the *leaves* of plants). G. *chlor*os.

Chol—bile; *chol*era (a *bilious* disease), *chol*er (sudden anger, supposed to be due to a disturbance of the *bile*), melan*choly* (depression of spirits, supposed to be due to the presence of *black bile*). G. *chole*.

Chondr—cartilage; hypo*chondr*ia (the condition of imagining disease, supposed to be due to disease of the spleen, which is situated *under* the *cartilage* of the breast-bone). G. *chondr*os.

Chor—dance, band of singers; *chor*us (*a band of singers*). G. *chor*os.

Chor—go; an*chor*et (a recluse, one who retires, or *goes back*, from the world). G. *chor*ein.

Chord—string of an instrument. G. *chord*e.

Chri—anoint; *chri*sm (ointment), *Chri*st (the Lord's *Anointed*). G. *chri*o, I anoint.

Chrom; chromat—color; *chrom*o (a *colored* print), *chrom*atic (relating to *color*), a*chrom*atic (without *color*). G. *chrom*a, *chromat*os.

Chron—time; *chron*icle (an account of the immediate *time*), *chron*ic (having continued a long *time*), *chron*ology (the fixing of the *times*, or dates, of a series of events), ana*chron*ism (a blunder as to *time* or date), syn*chron*ism (occurring in the same time). G. *chron*os.

Chrys—gold; *chrys*alis (the *golden* sheath of the butterfly), *chrys*anthemum (the *golden flower*), *chrys*olite (the *gold stone*), *chrys*elephantine (consisting of *gold* and *ivory*), *chrys*oprase (the *gold leek* stone). G. *chrus*os.

Chyl—juice; *chyl*e (a white *fluid* drawn from the food while in the intestines). G. *chul*os. G. *chu*o, I pour.

Chym—juice; *chym*e (digested food). G. *chym*os. G. *chu*o, I pour.

Cicatric—scar; *cicatrix*, *cicatrize*. L. *cicatrix*, *cicatric*is.

Cid—See *cad*.

Cid—See *cæd*.

Cili—eyelid; *cili*ary. L. *cili*um.

Ciner—dust, ashes; *ciner*ary (containing the *ashes* of a cremated body). L. *cin*is, *ciner*is.

Cing; cinct—bind; sur*cing*le (a girth *bound* over a saddle, or over the back of a horse), *cinct*ure (a girdle *bound* around), pre*cinct* (an inclosure *bound before* with a fence), suc*cinct* (compressed, like a person whose loose robes have been *bound* snugly *under* the arms). L. *cing*ere, *cinct*us.

Circ—ring, circle; *circ*le (a little *ring*), *circ*us (a performance in a *ring*), *search* (to explore all around in a complete *ring*). L. *circ*us.

Cirr—curl, curled hair; *cirr*us (fleecy, having the form of *curled hair*). L. *cirr*us.

Cist—chest, box; *cist*, *cist*ern (a *box*-like receptacle for water), *chest*. L. *cist*a.

Cit—arouse, summon; *cit*e (*summon*), ex*cit*e (*arouse*), in*cit*e (*stir up*). L. *cit*are. L. *cie*re, *cit*us.

Citad—city; *citad*el (the inner or strongly fortified *city*, a stronghold). It. *citta*de. L. *civit*as, *civitat*is. L. *civ*is, a citizen.

Civ—citizen; *civ*il (obliging, like a citizen of a civilized state). L. *civ*is.

Cla—break; icono*cla*st (an assailant of established opinions, an *image breaker*). G. *cla*ein.

Claim (*clam*)—call out; ac*claim*, *claim*, de*claim*, ex*claim*, pro*claim*, re*claim*. L. *clam*are.

Clam—clay; *clam*my. A.S. *clam*.

Clandestin—secret, close; *clandestin*e. L. *clandestin*us.

Clar—clear; *clar*ify, *clar*et (wine *clarified* by honey), *clar*ion (the *clear*-sounding horn), de*clar*e (make *fully clear*), chanti*cleer* (the *clear singer*), *glair* (the *white* on an egg). L. *clar*us.

Class—rank, order; *class*, *class*ic (of the highest *order*). F. *class*e. L. *class*is, a class, assembly, fleet.

Claus (*claud*)—shut, close; *claus*e (a passage somewhat *complete* in itself), *cloi*ster (a monastery, an *inclosure*), con*clud*e, ex*clud*e, in*clud*e, pre*clud*e, re*clus*e (a solitary, one *shut back* from the general public), se*clud*e. L. *claud*ere, *claus*us.

Clav—key; *clav*icle (the collarbone, the *little key* between the shoulder and breastbone), *clav*ier (the *key*board of an organ or piano), con*clav*e (a secret meeting, as if under lock and *key*). L. *clav*is.

Clef—key; *clef* (a *key* in music). F. *clef*. L. *clav*is.

Cleid—key; ophi*cleid*e. G. *cleis*, *cleid*os.

Clemat—twig, shoot; *clemat*is (a *creeping* plant). G. *clem*a, *clemat*os.

Cler—lot; *cler*gy (the ministers of religion, those whose *lot* is the Lord), *cler*k (a writer, formerly one of the *cler*gy). G. *cler*os.

Client—listening; *client* (a suitor at law, the employer of *counsel*[11]). L. *clien*s, *client*is.

Climat—slope; *climat*e (average temperature, etc., due to the *slope* or curvature of the earth). G. *clim*a, *climat*os. G. *clin*ein, to lean.

Climax; climact—ladder; *climax* (a gradual *ascent* of thought). G. *climax*, *climact*os.

Clin—lean, bend; de*clin*e (*lean from*, hence, to refuse; *bend down*,[12] hence, to give way), in*clin*e (*lean forward*), re*clin*e (*lean back*). L. *clin*are.

Clin—bed, couch; *clin*ical (pertaining to medical attendance at the *bedside*). G. *clin*e.

Cliv—slope; ac*cliv*ity, de*cliv*ity, pro*cliv*ity (a natural inclination or *leaning* toward). L. *cliv*us.

Clud; clus—close, shut. L. *claud*ere, *claus*us.

Clype—shield; *clype*ate (in the form of a *shield*). L. *clype*us.

Clys—dash; cata*clys*m (a *deluge*), *clys*ter (an *injection* for the bowels). G. *clus*ein.

Coagul—rennet; *coagul*ate (to curdle or form clots, as *rennet* does the milk). L. *coagul*um. L. *co*, together; *ag*ere, to drive.

Cocc—berry; *cocc*iferous, *cocc*olite, *cocc*hineal (*berry*-like insects for dyeing scarlet). G. *cocc*os.

Coccyx—cuckoo; *coccyx* (a small bone resembling the *cuckoo's* beak). L. *coccyx*.

Coct—cook, boil; de*coct*ion (a *boiling down*), con*coct* (*cook* up), bis*cuit* (*twice baked*, as was the bread of the Roman soldiers). L. *coqu*ere, *coct*us.

Cod; codic—table, book; *code*, *codic*il (an *addition* to a will). L. *cod*ex, *codic*is.

Cog—compel; *cog*ent (*compelling* acceptance). L. *cog*ere. L. *co*, with; *ag*ere, to urge.

Cogit—think; *cogit*ate. L. *cogit*are.

Cognit—know; *cognit*ion (the act of *knowing*), in*cog*-*nit*o (*unknown*), re*cognit*ion (a *knowing again*), ac*quaint* (make k*nown to*), *quaint* (odd, old, well *known*). L. *cognosc*ere, *cognit*us. L. *co*, fully; *gnosc*ere, to know.

Cogniz (*cognosc*)—know; *cogniz*ance (*knowledge*), re*cognize* (*know again*). L. *cognosc*ere.

Col—strain; per*col*ate (*strain through*), *col*ander (a *strainer*), *cul*vert (an arched passage through which the water *drains*). L. *col*are.

Col—slide; port*cul*lis (a *sliding door*, or gate). L. *col*are.

Cole—sheath; *cole*optera (*sheath-winged* insects). G. *cole*os.

Coll—neck; *coll*ar (a *neck*band), *coll*et (the *neck* around the stone of a ring), *col*porteur (a distributeur of religious books, who formerly *carried* them suspended from his *neck*), acco*lla*de (the tapping on the *neck* with a sword in the conferring of knighthood), de*coll*ette (low-*necked*). L. *coll*um.

Coll—glue; *coll*odion (a *glue-like* substance), proto*col* (a first draught, like a *first* leaf *glued* on to a manuscript). G. *coll*e.

Colon—a clause; *colon*. G. *colon*.

Colon—a husbandman; *colon*y (a settlement, as of *husbandmen*). L. *colon*us. L. *col*ere, to cultivate.

Colonn—column; *colonn*ade (a succession of *columns*), *colon*el (the commander of the *column*). It. *colonn*a. L. *column*a.

Columb—dove; *columb*ary (a *dove*-cote), *columb*ine (like the *dove's* bill). L. *columb*a.

Column—pillar. L. *column*a.

Com (*coim*)—sleep; *com*a (a *stupor*), *com*atose. G. *coim*ao, I sleep. See *cem*etery.

Com—banquet, revelry; *com*edy (an amusing play suited to a *banquet* or *revel*), *com*ic (ridiculous, like a *revel*), en*com*ium (high commendation, like the laudatory praise of a *banquet*). G. *com*os. G. *coim*ao, I sleep, recline.[13]

Com—friendly; *com*ity (exchange of courtesies). L. *com*is.

Comb (*cymb*)—hollow; cata*comb* (a great chamber *hollowed under*ground). G. *cumb*e, bowl, hollow vessel. See *cymb*al.

Comet—long-haired; *comet* (the star with *streaming hair*). G. *comet*es. G. *com*e, hair.

Comit—accompany; con*comit*ant (*accompanying with*). L. *comit*ari. L. *comes*, *comit*is, companion.

Comm—stamp, mark; *comm*a (a *mark* of punctuation). G. *comm*a. G. *copt*ein, to strike.

Commod—fit, suitable, convenient; *commod*ious (roomy and therefore *convenient*), *commod*ity (an article of commerce designed to meet the wants or *convenience* of people), *accommod*ate (adapt, supply, *fit* in), in*commod*e (trouble, cause *inconvenience*). L. *commod*us. L. *con*, with; *mod*us, measure.

Commun—common; *commun*ity (a people having life in *common*), *commun*ion (a mingling in *common*), *commun*icate (make known, make *common*), *commun*e (to talk with on an equal, or *common*, footing). L. *commun*is. L. *com* (*cum*), together; *mun*is, obliging.

Complic—confederate; ac*complic*e (a *confederate*), *complic*ity (the act of *confederating* with). F. *complic*e. L. *com*(*cum*), together; *plic*are, to fold, twine.

Con—peg; *con*e (a pointed *peg*). G. *con*os.

Conch—shell; *conch*ology. L. *conch*a.

Concili—bring together; *concili*ate, re*concil*e. L. *concili*are. L. *concili*um, a council. L. *con* (*cum*), together; *cal*ere, to call, summon.

Cond—hide; abs*cond* (flee, *hide* away), re*cond*ite (of very *hidden* meaning). L. *cond*ere.

Conditi (*condici*)—covenant, condition; *conditi*on. L. *condici*o. L. *con* (*cum*), together; *dic*ere, to speak.

Congru—agree, suit; *congru*ous (*agreeing* with). L. *congru*ere.

Conniv—close the eyes at, overlook; *conniv*e. L. *conniv*ere.

Contamin—contagion; *contamin*ate (pollute, as with *contagion*). L. *contamen*, *contamin*is. L. *con*, together; *tang*ere, to touch.

Contra—opposite; *contra*ry, *country* (the region *opposite*), *contra*st (*place opposite*). L. *contra*.

Contumac—stubborn; *contumac*y (a *stubborn* resistance to advice or direction). L. *contumax, contumac*is.

Contumeli—insult; *contumel*y (gross *insult*). L. *contumeli*a.

Convivi—feast; *convivi*al (*festive*). L. *convivi*um. L. *con*, together; *viv*ere, to live.

Cop—cut; *cop*pice (a small wood, frequently *cut* off), *cop*se (a bunch of brush, frequently *cut* off). O.F. *cop*er. O.F. *cop*, a stroke. Low L. *colp*us. G. *colaph*os, a blow.

Copi—abundance; *copi*ous (occurring in abundance), *copy* (a duplicate, which may be *abundantly* multiplies). L. *copi*a.

Copul—a band; *copul*a (the verb *to be*, which *unites* the subject and predicate), *couple* (a *united* pair). L. *copul*a.

Cor—See *cord*.

Cor; cord—heart; *cord*ial (a stimulant for the *heart*), *cord*ial (hearty), ac*cord* (agreement, as of *hearts* beating *together*), con*cord*, dis*cord* (disagreement, *hearts* or feelings *apart*), re*cord* (recall *again* to mind, or *heart*), *core* (the very *heart* of an object), courage (boldness of *heart*). L. *cor, cord*is.

Corb—basket; *corb*eil (a carved *basket* with flowers and fruits), *corb*el (a *basket*-like projection, supporting a superstructure), *corv*ette (a small ship of war, formerly a slow-sailing ship, a mere *basket*). L. *corb*is.

Cori—leather, skin; *cori*aceous, ex*cori*ate (to flay, strip *off* the *skin*), *cui*rass (a breast-plate, formerly made of *leather*), s*cour*ge (to ex*cori*ate, strip *off* the *skin*). L. *cori*um.

Corn—horn; uni*corn* (a fabulous beast with *one* straight *horn* in the forehead), capri*corn* (the *horned goat*), *corn*et (a brass instrument, the *little horn*), *corn*ucopia (the *horn* of *abundance*), *corn*er (a *horn*-like point), *corn*ea (the *horny* membrane of the eye), *corn*el (a shrub whose wood is very hard and tough, like *horn*), *corn* (a hard, *horny* substance growing on the foot). L. *corn*u.

Coron—crown; *coron*ation (a *crowning*), *coron*al (a *crown*-like top), *coron*et (a *little crown* worn by a duke), *coron*er (a *crown* officer who inquires after the cause of sudden or violent death), *corn*ice (the *crowning* part of an entablature, or architectural ornament), *cor(on)*olla (the *little* flower *crown*), *cor(on)*ollary (a gratuitous statement, thrown in like a garland, or *crown*). L. *coron*a.

Corpus; corpor—*corpus*cle (a *little body*), *corps*e (a dead *body*), *corps* (a *body* of troops), *corp*ulent (fat, having large *body*), *corpor*al (relating to the *body*), *corpor*eal (of a *bodily* or material nature), in*corpo*rate (to organize into a *body*). L. *corpus, corpor*is.

Corr—See *curr*.

Corrig—correct, control, manage; in*corrig*ible (*unmanageable*). L. *corrig*ere. L. *con*, with; *reg*ere, to rule.

Cors—body; *cors*e (a dead *body*), *cors*et (a stays closely fitting the *body*), *cors*elet (a piece of armor protecting the *body*). O.F. *cors*. L. *corpus*.

Cort—court; *cort*ege (a *court* procession). It. *cort*e. L. *cors, cort*is.

Corusc—glitter; *corusc*ate. L. *corusc*are.

Corv—crow; *corv*ine. L. *corv*us.

Cosm—order, ornament, universe, world; *cosm*ic (relating to the *world*), *cosm*opolite (a *citizen* of the *world*), macro*cosm* (the *universe*, the *great world*), micro*cosm* (the *small world* of little things), *cos-*

*m*etic (a wash, a means of personal *adornment*). G. *cosm*os.

Cost—rib, side; inter*costal* (situated between the *ribs*), *cost*al, ac*cost* (address, come to one's *side*), *coast* (the *side* of a country), cutlet (a *little rib*). L. *cost*a.

Cotyl—cup; *cotyl*edon (the *little cup* of a sprouting plant), *cotyl*e. G. *cotyl*e.

Cov—hatch, brood; *cov*ey (a *brood* or crowd, of birds). O.F. *cov*er. L. *cub*are.

Crai—chalk; *cray*on (a *chalk* pencil). F. *crai*e. L. *cret*a.

Cran—notch; *cran*ny. F. *cran*. L. *cren*a.

Crani—skull; *crani*um. G. *crani*on.

Cras—a mixing; idiosyn*cras*y (a personal peculiarity, a *peculiar* make up or *blending together*). G. *cras*is. G. *kerannu*mi, I mix.

Crass—thick, dense; *crass*. L. *crass*us.

Crastin—tomorrow; pro*crastin*ate (put off till *tomorrow*). L. *crastin*us. L. *cras*.

Crat—hurdle; *crat*e (a wicker-work *hurdle*). L. *crat*es.

Crat—govern; aristo*crac*y (the government of the *best*), auto*crac*y (the *government* of an individual's *self* alone), demo*crac*y (the *governement* by the *people*). G. *crat*ein.

Crater—bowl; *crater* (the *bowl* of a volcano). L. *crater*. G. *crater*.

Creas—flesh; pan*creas* (*all flesh*). G. *creas*.

Creas (*cresc*)—grow; in*creas*e, de*creas*e. L. *cresc*ere.

Creat—L. *cre*are, *creat*us.

Cred—believe, make trust; *cred*ible, *cred*ulous, *cred*ence, *cred*it, *creed*. L. *cred*ere.

Crem—burn; *crem*ation (the *burning* of the body of a dead person). L. *crem*are.

Cren—notch; *cren*ate, *cren*elate, *cran*ny. L. *cren*a.

Creo—flesh; *creo*sote (the *flesh*-preserver). G. *creo*s.

Crep; crepit—crackle, burst, make noise, sound; de*crep*it (very old, and consequently moving about *noiselessly*), dis*crep*ant (disagreeing, like *sounds* that are out of harmony), *crev*ice (a *rent* in the earth), *crev*asse (a *bursting* of the banks). L. *crep*are, *crepit*us.

Cresc; cret—grow, increase; *cresc*ent (the *increasing* moon), ac*cret*ion (a *growing* to), con*cret*e (*grown* together), ex*cresc*ence (a *growing* out). L. *cresc*ere.

Cret—chalk; *cret*aceous. L. *cret*a.[14]

Cret—See *cern*.

Crev—burst, rend; *crev*ice (a *rent* in the earth), *crev*asse (a *bursting* of a swollen river through its banks). O.F. *crev*er. L. *crep*are.

Crimin—crime; *crimin*al, *crimin*ate (fix *crime* upon), re*crimin*ate (to make charges, as of *crime*, *back* and forth). L. *crimen*, *crimin*is.

Crin—lily; *crin*oid (in the *form* of a *lily*). G. *crin*on.

Crin—hair; *crin*oline (an expansive skirt, formerly made of *hair*-cloth). F. *crin*. L. *crin*es, the hair.

Cris—a discerning; *cris*is (a moment of trial, or *discernment*). G. *cris*is. G. *crin*ein, to judge.

Crisp—wrinkled. L. *crisp*us.

Crit—a judge; *crit*ic, *crit*erion (a standard, or means of *judging*). G. *crit*es. G. *crin*ein, to judge.

Cruc—cross; *cruc*ify (to fasten upon a *cross*), *cruc*ial (severe, like a *cross*-incision in surgery), ex*cruc*iate (to torture, as on the *cross*), *crus*ade (an expedition in behalf of the *Cross*), *cruis*e (to *cross* the sea). L. *crux*, *cruc*is.

Crud—raw; *crud*e. L. *crud*us.

Crur—the leg; *crur*al (belonging to the *leg*). L. *crus*, *crur*is.

Crust—shell; *crust*acean. L. *crust*a.

Cryph (*crypt*)—hidden; Apo*crypha* (the unauthorized, and therefore *hidden* away, books of the Bible). G. *crupt*os. G. *crupt*ein, to hide.

Crypt—vault. G. *crupt*e. G. *crupt*os, hidden. G. *crupt*ein, to hide.

Crystall—ice; *crystal* (in the form of *ice*). G. *crustall*os.

Cub—to lie down, sit; in*cub*ate (to *sit* on eggs), in*cub*us (a nightmare, *sitting* heavily *on* one). L. *cub*are.

Cubit—elbow; cubit (the distance from the *elbow* to the end of the middle finger). L. *cubit*us.

Cucull—hood; *cucull*ate. L. *cucull*us.

Culc—See *calc*.

Culin—kitchen; *culin*ary (belonging to the *kitchen*), kiln. L. *culin*a.

Culmin—top, summit; *culmin*ate (reach the *highest point*). L. *culmen, culmin*is.

Culp—fault, offense; *culp*able (guilty of a *fault*), *cul*prit (one charged with an offense), in*culp*ate (to fasten an *offense* upon), ex*culp*ate (to free from the charge of an *offense*). L. *culp*a.

Cult—till; *cult*ivate, *cult*ure. L. *col*ere, *cult*us. (See *col*ony.)

Cumb—lie down, recline; in*cumb*ent (*reclining* or resting *upon*[15]), pro*cumb*ent (*reclining* forward), suc*cumb* (yield, *lie down* under). L. *cumb*ere.

Cumul—heap; ac*cumul*ate (*heap* up), *cumul*us (in the form of a *heap* or mass). L. *cumul*us.

Cune—wedge; cuneiform, *cune*ate, *coin* (a piece of money stamped with a *wedge*), *coigne* (a *wedge*-like projection). L. *cune*us.

Cup—cup; *cup*ola (a small dome, the *little* reversed *cup*). Low L. *cup*a. L. *cup*a, a tub.

Cup—desire, crave; cupidity (a *craving* for money). L. *cup*ere.

Cupr—copper; *cupr*eous. L. *cupr*um.[16]

Cur—care, attention; *cure* (to heal by due *attention* or *care*), ac*cur*ate (exact, on account of receiving sufficient *care*), *cur*ious (giving *attention* to), *cur*ate (a priest having the *care* of souls), pro*cur*e (manage, take *care* of), se*cur*e (safe, free from *care*), sine*cur*e (without a *care*). L. *cura*.

Curr; curs—run; *curr*ent (the *running*), *curs*ory (*running* along), dis*curs*ive (*running* about), ex*curs*ion (a *running out*), in*cur* (*run into*), in*curs*ion (an inroad, a *running into*), inter*course* (a *running between*), oc*cur* (*run* against), pre*curs*or (a fore-*runner*), re*cur* (happen again, *run back*), suc*cor* (help, *run under*), *coarse* (rough, of the common *run*), con*course* (a *running together*), *cour*ier (a messenger, a *runner*), *course* (the distance *run*), dis*course* (a *running* about), re*course* (something to *run back* to), suc*cor* (assistance, a *running under*), *corr*idor (a long passage *running* through a building). L. *curr*ere, *curs*us.

Curt—short; *curt*, *curt*ail (*shorten*). L. *curt*us.

Cusp; cuspid—point; bi*cuspid* (having *two points*). L. *cusp*is.

Custod—guardian; *custod*y (*restraint*, control). L. *custos*.

Cut—skin; *cut*is (the main *skin*), *cut*icle (the outside *skin*). L. *cut*is.

Cycl—circle; *cycl*e (a complete *circle* of time), *cycl*opœdia (the entire *round* of *instruction*), *cycl*orama (a circular view), bi*cycl*e (a *two-wheeled* vehicle), tri*cycl*e, *cycl*ops (the giant with the single *round eye*). G. *cucl*os.

Cylind—roll; *cylind*er (in the form of a *roll*), calender (a *roller*). G. *culind*ein.

Cymb—a cup, cavity; *cymb*al (a *cup*-shaped musical instrument), cata*comb* (an *underground* city of the dead), *chim*e (a concert of bells, suggestive of the ringing of *cymb*als). G. *cumb*e.

Cyn—dog; *cyn*ic (a snappish, *dog*-like person), *cyno*-sure (an attraction, like the polestar in the end of the *dog-tail* of the Little Bear). G. *cuon, cun*os.

Cyst—bag, pouch. G. *cust*is. G. *cu*ein, to contain.

NOTES

[1] *Anti* is for *ante*, before.

[2] *Sin* is for *semi*, half.

[3] Remote as well as present evil is guarded against by avoiding what would be an objectionable *precedent*. Under common law the decision of a competent court becomes a *precedent* having all the force of law. In devising our Constitution and polity of government, our forefathers had due regard to *precedents*, recommending this feature because it had been tried and found beneficial, and rejecting that because it had been tried and found injurious. A *precedent* for the establishment of two houses of legislation was found in the case of the two houses in the English Parliament, viz: the House of Lords and the House of Commons.

[4] The Roman *censor* was authorized by law to regulate the indulgences and expenditures of the people. *Censure* then was equivalent to prohibition.

[5] The famous horse of Alexander the Great, which could be ridden by no one but himself, was called Bu*cephal*us (the *cow-headed*).

[6] *Ceres* was the mythological goddess of agriculture. She was the mother of the famous Proserpine, who, while gathering wild flowers, was stolen by Pluto and carried to his regions below the earth. The afflicted mother sought her child everywhere, and, on learning of her situation, appealed to gods of Olympus to order her return. This petition was granted on condition that the

fair young captive eat nothing while in the infernal regions. The crafty Pluto, however, after failing to win her by blandishments, succeeded in inducing her to taste a pomegranate seed, and thereby gained an eternal claim to his queen. Again the distracted Ceres sought Olympus. The divinities could not recall their own solemn decree, but in pity for the suffering mother they ordered that the daughter be allowed to return to her for six months of the year. The story typifies the annual return of growth and bloom, springing up out of the earth.

[7] From its smell.

[8] *Magna Charta* (the *Great Charter*), wrested from King John of England at Runnymede in the beginning of the thirteenth century, was the first written constitution. The liberties then granted by the crown were never afterward surrendered by the people. That great document was a death-blow to absolutism in government.

[9] The old science failed to produce gold, but it called men's attention to the affinities of matter, and led to the development of the great modern science of chemistry.

[10] The knights of the Middle Ages were trained by long apprenticeship to the duties and virtues of their order. The candidate for knighthood began in youth as a page, and subsequently became a squire or attendant upon a knight. When of suitable age and found worthy, he was admitted to the rank of knighthood. To be worthy he must be found virtuous, honorable, gentle, and brave. His duties were to rescue the weak and oppressed, and especially to honor and protect woman. At the institution of knighthood the position of woman became reversed; she had been hitherto regarded as the inferior and slave of man; she now became his superior, the object of his homage and service. The perfect knight was the perfect *gentleman*; and when we use the terms *chivalry*, *chivalric*, and *chivalrous* we refer to the gentle courtesy and brave self-sacrifice of the knights of old.

[11] In the time of the Roman republic the *client* was a follower and adherent of some great man, to whom he looked up for

counsel and protection. It was the custom for all the clients of a patron to assemble at his house early in the morning to greet him on arising. (See *Levee* and *Matinee*.) At those meetings he would hear their grievances, if any, and give them directions for their conduct in the immediate future.

The idea of patron and client developed at a later time into that of master and man, and became the essential principle of the feudal system.

[12] The use of the term in grammar has reference to a device for presenting to the eye the six cases of the Latin noun. Six converging lines were employed, beginning with a vertical line for the nominative, called, hence, the *casus rectus*, or *upright case*. The other cases, the *genitive*, *dative*, *accusative*, *vocative*, and *ablative*, were represented by lines of progressively increasing inclination, and were called hence the *oblique cases*. Hence to *decline* is to give the cases in succession passing *down* the *leaning* lines.

[13] The ancients *reclined* at table on couches.

[14] So named after the island of *Crete*, from whence it came.

[15] The *incumbent* of an office has its duties *incumbent* on him, though he is often regarded as *reclining upon* a comfortable *berth*.

[16] Named after the island of *Cypress*, whence it was obtained.

D

Dactyl—finger; *dactyl* (having a long and two short syllables, like the long and two short joints of the *finger*), *date* (the fruit somewhat in the form of a *finger*). G. *dactul*os.

Dam—lady; *dame*, *dam*sel (a young *lady*), bel*dam* (a hag, formerly a fine *lady*). O.F. *dame*. L. *domin*a.

Dama—conquer; a*dam*ant (a very hard and *unconquerable* substance), *diam*ond. G. *dama*ein/

Damn—loss, penalty; *damn* (condemn to pay a *penalty*), con*demn* (sentence to pay a *penalty*), *dam*age (*loss*), in*demn*ify (make good, leave free from *loss*), in*demn*ity (freedom from *penalty*). L. *damn*um, *damn*are.

Dat—give; *date* (a *given* point of time), e*dit*ion (a publishing or *giving out*), per*dit*ion (utter loss, a complete *giving over*), re*dit*ion (a *giving back*), tra*dit*ion (a *giving across*). L. *dare*, *dat*us.

De—bind; dia*dem* (a fillet *bound around* the brows). G. *deo*.

De—god; *De*ity. L. *de*us.

Deal (*dæl*)—portion, share; *deal* (give out a *share*), *dole*, or*deal* (a trial,[1] a *dealing out* one's *portion*). A.S. *dæl*.

Deb; debit—owe; *deb*enture (an acknowledgment of what is *owed*), *debit*, *debt*. L. *debe*o, *debit*us.

Debil—weak; *debil*ity, *debil*itate. L. *debil*is.

Dec—become; *dec*ent. L. *dec*ere.

Deca—ten; *deca*de (a group of *ten*), *deca*logue (the *ten* commandments). G. *deca*.

Decant—tip a vessel on its edge. It. *decant*are. L. *de*, down; Ger. *kante*, corner, edge.

Decem—ten; *December* (the *tenth* month in the Roman year, which began with March). L. *decem*.

Decim—tenth; *decima*l (a *tenth*), *decim*ate (to kill every *tenth* man). L. *decim*us.

Decor—honor, ornament; *decor*ate. L. *decus*, *decor*is.

Decor—seemliness; *deor*um. L. *decus*, *decor*is.

Dect—receiving; pan*dect* (the code of Justinian, the *receive all*). G. *dect*es. G. *dech*omai, I receive.

Decuss—cross, put into the form of X. L. *decuss*are. L. *decuss*is, a coin worth ten (*decem*) *asses* (and consequently marked with an X).

Del—destroy; *del*eble, *del*ete. L. *del*ere.

Delect—delight; *delect*able, *delight*. L. *delect*are.

Deleter—destroyer; *deleter*ious. G. *deleter*. G. *dele*omai, I harm.

Delicat—luxurious; *delicat*e. L. *delicat*us.

Delici—delight, pleasure; *delici*ous (*delight*ful). L. *delici*a. L. *delic*ere, to amuse, allure. L. *de*, from, away; *lac*ere, to entice.

Delir—mad; *delir*ious (wandering in *mind*). L. *delir*us. L. *de*, from; *lir*a, furrow.[2]

Dem—the common people; *dem*agogue (a *leader* of the *common people*), *dem*ocracy (*government* by the *people*), epi*dem*ic (spreading among the *people*). G. *dem*os.

Dendr—tree; *dendr*ology (the science of *trees*), *dendr*oid (*tree-form*), *dendr*omys (the *tree mouse*), rhodo*dendr*on (the *rose tree*), lepido*dendr*on (the *scale tree* of the coal mines). G. *dendr*on.

Dens—thick; *dens*e (*thick*), con*dens*e (to compress, *thicken*). L. *dens*us.

Dent—tooth; *dent*ist, *dent*ine (the substance of the *tooth*), *dent*ifrice (a *tooth rub*), *dent*ate (*toothed*), in*dent* (*tooth* in like a saw). L. *dens*, *dent*is.

Derm—skin; epi*derm*is (the *outward skin*), pachy-*derm* (a thick-*skinned* animal), taxi*derm*y (the *arrangement* of the *skins* of animals so as to resemble life), hypo*derm*ic (*under* the *skin*). G. *derm*a.

Desider—desire; *desider*atum (a thing greatly to be *desired*). L. *desider*are. L. *de*, from; *sidus*, *sider*is, star.[3]

Despatch (*despech*)—to hasten (literally to "un-hinder"). O.F. *despech*er; *des* (*dis*), apart; *pesch*er, to hinder. L. *pedic*a, a fetter. L. *pes*, *ped*is, foot.

Despot—master; *despot* (an oppressive *master*). G. *despot*es.

Destin—ordain, establish; *destin*y (the *ordained* course). L. *destin*are. L. *destin*a, a prop.

Deterior—worse; *deterior*ate (becoming *worse*). L. *deterior*.

Deutero—second; *Deutero*nomy (the *second* book of Moses, the *second* giving of the *law*), *deutero*gamy (a *second marriage*). G. *deutero*s.

Devis—See *divis*.

Dexter—right hand; *dexter*ous (as skillful as the *right hand*), ambi*dextr*ous (using either hand, or both at once, as though *both* were *right hands*). L. *dexter*.

Di—day; *di*al (an indicator of the time of *day*), *di*urnal (*daily*), *di*ary (a *day*-book), meri*di*an (the mid*day* line). L. *di*es.

Diabol—devil; *diabol*ical (*devilish*). G. *diabol*os. G. *diaball*ein, to slander. G. *dia*, through; *ball*ein, to throw.

Dicat—declare; ab*dicat*e (give up by public *declaration*), de*dicat*e (devote, *declare* away), pre*dicat*e (make a *declaration*). L. *dicat*e, *dicat*us.

Dict—speak, say; contra*dict* (*speak against*), *dict*ion (manner of *speaking*), *dict*ionary, e*dict* (a proclamation, *outspoken*), inter*dict* (a prohibition, *spoken between*), pre*dict* (*say before-hand*), bene*dict*ion (a blessing, a *saying* that it may be *well* with thee), male*dict*ion (a *saying* that it may be *ill* with thee), vale*dict*ory (a *saying farewell*), ver*dict* (a report or *saying* of the *truth* of the mattre), *dict*ate (order, direct, continue to *say*), ad*dict*ed. L. *dic*ere, *dict*us.

Didact (*didasc*)—teach; *didact*ic (*teaching*). G. *didasc*ein.

Dieu—God; a*dieu* (I commend you to *God*). F. *dieu*. L. *deus*.

Digit—finger; *digit*ate (*finger*-shaped). L. *digit*us.[4]

Dign—worthy, merited; *dign*ity (respectable *worth*, honor), *dign*ify (make *worthy*), con*dign* (fully *merited*), in*dign*ant, *deign* (deem *worthy*), dis*dain*, (deem un*worthy*). L. *dign*us.

Dim (*dism*)—tenth; *dime* (the *tenth* part of a dollar). O.F. *disme*. L. *decim*us. See *dism*al.

Dioc (*dioic*)—dwell, govern; *dioc*ese (the district *governed* by a bishop). G. *dioic*eo, I dwell, govern. G. *dia*, throughout; *oic*eo, I dwell. G. *oic*os, a house.

Dioptr—an optical instrument for taking heights; *dioptr*ics (the science of the *refraction of light*). G. *dioptr*a. G. *dia*, through; *opt*omai, I see.

Diphther—leather; *diphther*ia (a disease of the *leathery* false membrane of the throat). G. *diphther*a. G. *der*ein, to prepare leather.

Dir—dreadful; *dire*. L. *dir*us.

Disc—quoit; *disc* (a round plate, resembling a *quoit*), *dish* (a *round* plate), *dais* (a raised floor in a hall, containing a high *round* table), *desk* (a sloping *table*). G. *disc*os.

Disc—learn; *disc*iple (a *learner*). L. *disc*ere.

Discrimin—separation; *discrimin*ate (to separate, distinguish). L. *discrimen*, *discrimin*is. L. *discer*nere, to distinguish.

Dispatch—See *despatch*.

Dissip—disperse; *dissip*ate. L. *dissip*are. L. *dis*, apart. O.L. *sup*are, to throw.

Dit—See *dat*.

Ditt (*dict*)—said; *ditt*o (the same, the *said*). L. *dic*ere, *dict*us.

Ditt (*dictat*)—dictated. *ditt*y (a song *dictated*). L. *dict*are, *dictat*us. L. *dic*ere, *dict*us.

Divid; divis—divide; *divid*e, *divid*end, *divis*or, *divi*sion, *devis*e (to plan, *divid*e up), in*divid*ual (single, *undivid*ed), *devic*e (a thing *devised*). L. *divid*ere.

Divin—divine. L. *divin*us.

Doc; doct—teach; *doc*ile (*teach*able), *doct*or (a *teacher*), *doct*rine (the matter *taught*), *docu*ment (an *instructive* paper). L. *doc*ere, *doct*us.

Dodeca—twelve. G. *dodeca*. G. *duo*, two; *deca*, ten.

Dogm; dogmat—opinion; *dogm*a (a statement of *opinion*), *dogm*atic (extremely *opinionated*). G. *dogm*a, *dogmat*os. G. *doc*eo, I show.

Dol—grieve, worry; *dol*eful, *dol*or, con*dol*e (*grieve* with), in*dol*ence (idleness, not *worrying*). L. *dol*ere.

Dom—house; *dom*estic (belonging to the *house*), *dom*icile (a habitation or *house*), *dom*e (a great cupola, a *house* in itself). L. *dom*us.

Domin—lord, master; *domin*ate (to *master*), *domin*eer (play the *master*), *domin*ion (the territory or jurisdiction of a *lord*), *domin*o (a disguise, the *master's* dress), pre*domin*ate (over*master*), *do*main (a*dominion* or territory of a*lord*). L. *domin*us.

Domit—tame; in*domit*able (*unconquerable*). L. *domit*are.

Don—gift, give; con*don*e (for*give*), *don*ation (a *gift*), *don*or (a *giver*), guer*don* (a recompensense or *give* back), par*don* (for*give*). L. *don*um.

Donna—lady; bella*donna*. It. *donna*. See *bell*.

Dorm—sleep; *dorm*ant (quiescent, *sleeping*), *dorm*itory (the *sleeping* quarters), *dorm*er (belonging to a *sleeping* room), *dorm*ouse (the *sleeping* mouse). L. *dorm*ire.

Dors—back; *dors*al (belonging to the *back*), in*dors*e (put on the *back*). L. *dors*um.

Dos—a giving; *dos*e (the quantity *given* to a patient). G. *dos*is. G. *did*omi, I give.

Dot—given; anti*dot*e (*given* against poison), anec*dot*e (a private story, *not* published or *given out*). G. *dot*os. G. *did*omi, I give.

Dox—opinion, glory, praise; ortho*dox* (of correct or current *opinion*), hetero*dox* (of *other* than current *opinion*), *dox*ology (the song of *praise*). G. *dox*a.

Dra—perform; *dra*stic (severe, *effective*), *dra*ma (a *performance*). G. *dra*o, I perform.

Drap—cloth; *drap*er (a *cloth* dealer), *drap*e, *drap*ery, *drab* (*cloth* color). F. *drap*.

Dress—direct, make right or straight; ad*dress* (*direct* to), *dress* (make *right*, or *straight*), re*dress* (make *right again*). F. *dress*er.

Droit (*direct*)—right, justice; a*droit* (skillful, proceeding *in* the *right* way). Low L. *direct*um. L. *dirig*ere, *direct*us, to direct. L. *di* (*dis*), apart; *reg*ere, *rect*us, to rule.

Drom—a running; hippo*drome* (a *race*-course for *horses*), *drom*edary (the *running* animal of the desert), palin*drome* (a word that *runs backward* in the same sense as forward). G. *drom*os. G. *dram*ein, to run.

Dry—tree; *dry*ad (a *tree* nymph), *dru*pe. G. *dru*s.

Du—two; *du*al (consisting of *two*), *du*el (a fight between *two*), *du*et (music for *two*), *deu*ce (the *two* of cards). L. *du*o.

Dubi—doubtful; *dubi*ous. L. *dubi*us.

Dubit—*doubt*; in*dubit*able (not to be *doubted*), *doubt*. L. *dubit*are.

Duc; duct—lead, bring; ab*duct*ion (a *leading* away), ad*duce* (*bring* forward), con*duce* (*lead* to), con*duct* (*lead* with), con*duit* (a *leader*, conductor), de*duce* (*bring* down), de*duct* (*bring* down), *doge* (the *duke* of Venice), *douche* (a shower-bath from a *conduit*), *duc*al (belonging to a *duke*), *duc*at (a coin of the *duchy* of Apulia), *duch*ess (the wife of a *duke*), *duch*y (the domain of a *duke*), *duct* (a conducting, or *leading*, pipe), *duct*ile (capable of being *led*, or drawn, out), *duke* (a military *leader*[5]), e*duc*ate (*bring* out), e*duce* (*bring* out), in*duce* (*bring* in), in*duct* (*bring* in), intro*duce* (*bring* within), pro*duce* (*bring* forward), pro*duct* (that which is *brought* forward), re*duce* (*bring* back), se*duce* (*lead* aside), tra*duce* (defame, *lead* over). L. *duc*ere, *duct*us.

Dulc—sweet; *dulc*et, *dulc*imer. L. *dulc*is.

Duodecim—twelve; *duodecim*al, *duodecim*o (a book having *twelve* leaves to a sheet of paper). L. *duodecim*. L. *duo*, two; *decem*, ten.

Duoden—twelve apiece; *duoden*um (the first of the smaller intestines, being in length about *twelve* finger-breadths). L. *duoden*i.

Dur—last; *dur*ation, en*dure*, *dur*ance (*lasting* captivity). L. *dur*are.

Dur—hard; in*dur*ate (to *harden*), ob*dur*ate (*hardened against*), *dur*ess (restraint, a *hardship*). L. *dur*us.

Dynam—power, force; *dynam*c (relating to *force*), *dynam*ite (a very *explosive* substance). G. *dunam*is. G. *dunami*.

Dynast—lord, ruler; *dynast*y (the *sovereigns* of a given family). G. *dunast*es. G. *dunami*.

NOTES

[1] The expression *fiery ordeal* resulted from a judicial procedure that once prevailed in England. A person arrested on suspicion was adjudged guilty unless he could prove his innocence by the *ordeal*. Persons of rank were subjected to the *ordeal by fire*, those of lower degree to the *ordeal by water*. In the *ordeal by fire* the accused was required either to take in his hand a piece of red-hot iron, or to walk barefoot and blindfold over nine red-hot plowshares laid lengthwise at unequal distances. If he escaped unharmed, he was adjudged innocent; otherwise he was condemned as guilty. The *ordeal by water* consisted in plunging the bare arm to the elbow into boiling-hot water, or by casting the accused into a river or pond. In the first place, an escape from injury was deemed an evidence of innocence. In the latter trial, if he floated he was deemed guilty, and if he sank he was acquitted. The chances in such procedure were rather against the accused. It was the practice of a barbarous age, in which the rack and other instruments of torture were employed in obtaining judicial evidence, and in which the *gauge of battle*, or trial by combat, was allowed. From the above forms of trial originated the expression, *passing through fire and water*.

[2] A *delirious* person is unmanageable, like a plow-horse that leaves the *furrow*.

[3] To desire is to miss, as if turning the eyes with regret from the *stars*.

[4] The nine *digits* are counted on the *fingers*.

[5] The great generals Marlborough and Wellington were created *dukes* in consequence of their great success as military *leaders*.

E

Ebri—drunken; in*ebri*ate. L. *ebri*us.

Eburn—ivory; *eburn*ean. L. *eburn*um.

Ecclesi—assembly, church; *ecclesi*astic (belonging to the *church*). G. *ecclesi*a. G. *ec*, out; *cale*o, I call.

Ech—sound; *ech*o, cate*chi*ze (to question, *din down* into one's mind). G. *ech*o, *ech*e.

Eclips—a failure; *eclips*e (an *obscuration* of the sun or moon by the interposition of the moon or earth). G. *ecleipsi*s. G. *ec*, out; *leip*ein, to leave.

Ecumen (*oicoumen*)—inhabited; *ecumen*ical (universal, including the whole *inhabited* globe). G. *oicoumen*os. G. *oic*eo, I inhabit. G. *oic*os, house.

Ed—eat; *ed*ible, *ed*acious (*greedy*). L. *ed*ere.

Ed (*æd*)—a building; *ed*ifice, *ed*ify (to instruct, *build*up). L. *æd*es.

Ego—I; *ego*tist (a conceited individual, having a great admiration for the *first person singular*), *ego*ism. L. *ego*.

Ela—drive; *ela*stic (*driving* back). G. *ela*o.

Electr—amber; *electr*ic (like the effects produced by the highly electric *amber*). G. *electr*on.

Eleemosyn—pity, charity; *eleemosyn*ary (devoted to *charity*), *alms* (*charity*, gifts), *almon*er (a distributer of *alms*). G. *eleemosun*e. G. *elee*in, to pity.

Eleg—a lament; *eleg*y. G. *eleg*os.

Element—first principle. L. *element*um.

Ellips—a defect; *ellips*e (an oval figure, deemed *defective* because its plane forms with the base of the cone a less angle than that of the parabola). G. *elleips*is. G. *en*, in; *leip*ein, to leave.

Em; empt—take, buy; ex*empt* (*take out*, free from liability), ex*amp*le (a specimen *taken* out), per*emp*tory (destroying, *taking* away *entirely*), pr*emium* (a reward, advance, or *taking before*), red*eem* (*buy back*). L. em*ere*, *empt*us.

Embroc—ferment, moisten; *embroc*ation (a *moistening* of a diseased part). G. *embroch*e. G. *en*, in; *brech*ein, to wet.

Empori—commerce; *empori*um (a mart, a *commercial* center). G. *empori*a. G. *empor*os, a traveler. G. *en*, in; *por*os, a way.

Emul (*æmul*)—striving to equal; *emul*ate. L. *æmul*us.

Enigm (*ainigm*)—riddle,[1] dark saying. G. *ainigm*a. G. *ainos*, a tale, story.

Enn—See *ann*.

Ent—being; *ent*ity, non*ent*ity. L. *ens*, *ent*is. L. *esse*, to be.

Enter—entrail; mes*enter*y (the membrane in the *middle* of the *entrails*), *enter*ic. G. *enter*on.

Entic—to coax, allure; *entic*e. O.F. *entic*er.

Entom—insect; *entom*ology (the science of *insects*). G. *entom*os. G. *en*, into; *temn*ein, to cut.[2]

Entr (*inter*)—within; *entr*ails (the *inward* parts). L. *inter*.

Ep—word; ortho*ep*y (the *correct* pronunciation of *words*). G. *ep*os.

Epact—added; *epact* (the *excess* of the solar month or year over the lunar). G. *epact*os. G. *epi*, upon; *ag*ein, to bring.

Epaul—shoulder; *epaul*ette (a *shoulder*-piece). F. *epaul*e.

Epic—narrative; *epic* (a great *narrative* poem[3]). G. *epic*os. G. *ep*os, a word.

Epiped—plane surface, base; parallelo(*e*)*piped*on (a solid having parallel *plane surfaces*). G. *epiped*on. G. *epiped*os, on the ground. G. *epi*, upon; *pedon*, the ground.

Episcop—overseer, bishop; *episcop*al (relating to a *bishop*). G. *episcop*os. G. *epi*, upon, over; *scop*os, seer.

Epoch—stop, pause; *epoch* (a great *arresting* and controlling event). G. *epoch*e. G. *epi*, upon; *ech*ein, to hold.

Equ (*æqu*)—equal; *equ*al, *equ*animity (*equal*ness, or evenness, of *mind*), *equ*ation (a statement of *equality*), *equ*ilibrium (*equal balancing*), *equ*inox (the time of *equal nights* and days), *equ*ity (*equal* justice), *equ*ivalent (of *equal value*), *equ*ivocal (of doubtful meaning, with *voice equally* one way and the other), ad*equ*ate (*equal* to). L. *æqu*us.

Equ—horse; *equ*ine, *equ*estrian (a rider on *horse*-back). L. *equ*us.

Erc (*arc*)—inclose; ex*erc*ise (set at work, as in driving cattle *out* of an *inclosure*). L. *arc*ere.

Eremi—the desert; *erem*ite (a hermit of the *desert*). G. *eremi*a. G. *erem*os, deserted, desolate.

Erg—work; en*erg*y (*work* within), *org*an (a *working* part). G. *erg*on.

Ero—love; *ero*tic (relating to *love*). G. *ero*s.

Err—wander; *err*ant, *err*or, ab*err*ation. L. *err*are.

Ert—erect; al*ert* (on the watch, in an *upright* posture). It. *ert*a. L. *erect*us.

Erysi (*eruther*)—red; *erysi*pelas (a disease characterized by a *red skin*). G. *eruthr*os.

Esc—eat; *esc*ulent (good to *eat*). L. *esc*are.

Escal—ladder; *escal*ade. Sp. *escal*a. L. *scal*a.

Eso (*oiso*)—carry; *eso*phagus (the gullet which *carries* to the stomach what is eaten). G. *phero*, *oiso*.

Esoter—inner, within; *esoter*ic (addressed to an *inner* circle of disciples). G. *esoter*. G. *eso*, within.

Ess—to be; *ess*ence (the *existing* substance, the real quality). L. *esse*.

Esth—See *æsth*.

Estim (*æstim*)—value; *estim*ate, *esteem*. L. *æstim*are.

Estu (*æstu*)—heat, surge, tide; *estu*ary (a river mouth receiving *tide* water). L. *æstus*.

Etern (*ætern*)—lasting for an age; *etern*al. L. *ætern*us.

Ethic—moral; *ethic*s (the science of *morals*). G. *ethic*os. G. *eth*os, custom.

Ethn—nation; *ethn*ic, *ethn*ology. G. *ethn*os.

Etymo—true; *etymo*logy (the science of the *true* sources of words). G. *etumo*s.

Eureka—I have found.[4] G. *eureka*.

Ev (*æv*)—life, age; long*ev*ity (long *life*), prim*ev*al, medi*ev*al. L. *ævum*.

Examin—tongue of a balance; *examin*e (test, as with a *balance*). L. *examin*, *examin*is.

Exampl—See *exempl*.

Excel—raise, surpass. L. *excell*ere. L. *ex*, out; *cell*ere, to drive.

Excels—lofty, high; *excels*ior (*higher*). G. *excels*us.

Excerpt—extract. L. *excerpt*um. L. *ex*, out; *carp*ere, to cull.

Exempl—sample, pattern, model; *exempl*ary (fit for a *model*), *exempl*ify (illustrate by an *example*), *example*. L. *exempl*um. L. *exim*ere, to select a sample. L. *ex*, out; *em*ere, to take.

Exerc—drive out of an enclosure; *exerc*ise (to put at work, like *driving* oxen *out of an enclosure*). L. *exerc*ere. L. *ex*, out; *arc*ere, to enclose.

Exili—banishment; *exil*e. L. *exili*um, *exsili*um. L. *exsul*, a banished man. L. *ex*, out of; *sol*um, the soil, ground.

Exo—outward; *exo*teric (of a popular nature, delivered to the *outside* public, or people at large), *exo*tic (belonging to a foreign, or *outside*, country, not native to a place). G. *exo*. G. *ex*, out.

Exordi—begin; *exordi*um (the *beginning* of an oration). L. *exordi*ri. L. *ex*, out; *ordi*ri, to begin, to weave.[5]

Expati—wander; *expati*ate (*wander* at large on a subject). L. *expati*ari. L. *ex*, out; *spati*ari, to roam. L. *spati*um, space.

Exped—to set free, facilitate; *exped*ite (to *hasten*, as if to take the *foot out* of a snare), *exped*ition (*hurry*, preparation), *exped*ient (desirable, because *facilitating* desired ends). L. *exped*ire. L. *ex*, out; *pes*, *pedis*, foot.

Exter—outward; *exter*ior, *exter*nal. L. *exter*, *exter*us.

Extra—beyond; *extra*neous (*beyond* what applies), *extr*eme. L. *extra*.

NOTES

[1] The famous enigma of the sphinx was a current story among the ancients, and gave rise to a great deal of poetry. The sphinx was a female monster who captured unwary travelers in the mountains, and propounded to them the following riddle: "What animal is it that begins life on four legs, passes to the use of two, and ends on three?" If the captive failed to solve the enigma he was strangled. The word *sphinx* means *"the strangler."* The victims were so numerous that the land groaned in distress until the arrival of Œdipus, who solved the riddle, slew the sphinx, and was made king by the grateful people. The answer to the riddle was: "Man, who crawls on hands and feet (*all fours*) in childhood, walks upright on two legs in mature life, and descends to the use of a staff (*third leg*) in old age."

[2] The insect's body is *divided into* three *sections*.

[3] To be an *epic*, the poem needs to be great in length, in quality, and in popularity. The early epics, by detailing the deeds of the heroes of a nation, became intensely popular among the people of that nation. So, an epic is a long narrative poem stirring the feelings of a people by portraying their past glories. But the term has been extended to include well-sustained narrative poetry, even though the theme be not national, but human, as in the case of Milton's "Paradise Lost." Among the great epics are Homer's "Iliad" and "Odyssey," Virgil's "Æneid," Dante's "Divina Comedia," and Milton's "Paradise Lost."

[4] A word originating in the expression of the great philosopher Archimedes when he discovered the principle of specific gravity. Hiero, king of Syracuse, had supplied a goldsmith with a quantity of pure gold to be made into a crown. Having some doubts as to the honesty of the goldsmith, he submitted the crown to Archimedes to determine whether it were made of pure gold. The philosopher pondered long over the problem, till at last a means of testing the crown came to him as an inspiration while he was in the bath. He noticed that the water partly supported his body, that he had lost weight by entering it; he also noticed that a quantity of water was displaced by his body and flowed over the edge of the bath. His quick philosophic intelligence connected the two facts, and deduced the principle that the loss of weight is equal to that of the amount of water displaced. He had the great principle of specific gravity by which to compare substances with water as a unit. He was so wrought up by the great discovery that he ran naked into the street, shouting *"Eureka!"* (*"I have found"* it.)

[5] The language of the oration is called the *text*, or what is *woven*.

F

Fa—speak; af*fa*ble (of easy manners, easy to be *spoken* to), con*fa*bulate (*talk with*), *fa*ble (a story, *told*), *fa*iry (a little *fay*, or elf), *fay* (a little *fate*, or goddess of destiny), *fate* (destiny, that which has been *pronounced*), inef*fa*ble (*unspeakable*), in*fa*nt (a babe, *unable* to *speak*), in*fa*ntry (foot-soldiers, the *infants*), ne*fa*rious (impious, not to be *spoken*), pre*fa*ce (an introduction, *spoken* before-hand). L. *fa*ri, *fa*tus.

Fabr—a workman; *fabr*ic (a product of *work*). L. *faber, fabr*i.

Fabul—fable. L. *fabul*a. L. *fa*ri, to speak.

Fac; fact—make, form, act, do; *fac*ile (ready to *do*), *fac*-simile (*make alike*), *fac*tion (an *active* section of a party), *fact*itious (artificial, *done* for effect), *fac*tor (that which *makes* a result, also one who *acts* for another), *fac*tory (a place where things are *made*), *fac*totum (a person of general usefulness, a *do-all*), *fac*ulty (a power to *do*), *fact* (a reality, something *done*), af*fect* (*act* upon, aim at), con*fect* (*make* up), de*fect* (a fault, *not made*), de*fic*ient (failing, *not making*), diffi*c*ult (*not* easy to *do*), ef*fect* (*work out, worked out*), effi*c*acious (capable of producing ef*fect*), in*fect* (taint, *put into*), per*fect* (*thoroughly made*), profi*c*ient (progressing, *making ahead*), re*fec*tion (refreshment, a *remaking* of the strength), suf*fic*e (to uphold, *make under*), af*fa*ir (a business, something to *do*), com*fit* (a preparation, or *make up*, of fruit with sugar), counterfeit (*made* like, or *opposite*), defeat (overthrow, *undo*), fashion (shape, *make* up), feasible (capable of being *done*), fetich (an idol *made* by hand), feat (a *deed*), feature (a *form*), profit (advantage, a *making forward*), surfeit (excess, an *overdoing*). L. facere, factus.

Fac—face, figure, form; deface (to *disfigure*), efface (to blot *out*, remove the *form* entirely), face, façade (a *front view* of a building), surface (the outside part, the upper *face*). F. face. L. facies.

Faceti—wit; facetious. L. facetia. L. facetus, courteous.

Faci—face, form; facial, superficial (being *over*, or outside, the form). L. facies.

Falc—sickle; falcon (a hawk, having a beak hooked like a *sickle*), falchion (a sword, curved like a *sickle*), defalcate (to take *away* trust funds, compared to cutting *down* grain with a *sickle*). L. falx, falcis.

Fall; fals—err, beguile, deceive; fallible, fallacy (a *deceiving* argument), false, falter, fail, fault, default. L. fallere, falsus.

Fam—hunger; famine, famish. L. fames.

Fam—report; fame, defame, infamy (not good *fame*). L. fama. L. fari, to speak.

Famili—household; familiar. L. familia.

Fan—temple; fane, profane (unholy, *outside the temple*), fanatic (an unreasoning enthusiast, like one *religiously* insane). L. fanum.

Fant—See *phant*.

Far—grain, spelt; farrago (a medley, like mixed *grains* for cattle), farina (ground *corn*). L. far.

Farc—stuff; farce (a play *stuffed* with jokes). L. farcire.

Farin—meal; farinaceous. L. farina. L. far, grain.

Fasci—bundle; fasciate, fasicular, fascis (the *bundle* of rods carried by a lictor), fascine. L. fascis.

Fascin—enchant; *fascin*ate. L. *fascin*are.

Fastidi—loathing; *fastidi*ous (overnice, particular, *squeamish*). L. *fastidi*um.

Fatig—to weary; *fatig*ue, inde*fatig*able (*unwearying*). L. *fatig*are.

Fatu—silly, feeble; *fatu*ous, *fatu*ity, in*fatu*ate (to make *foolishly* impressed). L. *fatu*us.

Fauc—throat; *fauc*es, suf*foc*ate (to stifle as by what chokes the *throat*). L. *fauc*es.

Febr—fever; *febr*ile. L. *febr*is.

Febru—expiate, cleanse; *Febru*ary (the month of *expiation* at Rome). L. *februare.

Fec (*fæc*)—dregs; *fec*ulent (full of *dregs*). L. *fæc*es.

Fecund—fruitful; *fecund*ity. L. *fecund*us.

Feder (*fœder*)—treaty, league; *feder*al, con*feder*ate. L. *fœd*us, *fœder*is.

Fel—cat; *fel*ine. L. *fel*is.

Felic—happy; *felic*ity. L. *felix, felic*is.

Felon—traitor, rebel; *felon* (one guilty of a great crime, like *treason*). Low L. *felo, felon*is.

Femell—young woman; *femell*e. L. *femell*a. L. *femin*a, a woman.

Femin—woman; *femin*ine, ef*femin*ate (*thoroughly womanish*). L. *femin*a.

Femur; femor—thigh; *femur* (the *thigh* bone), *femor*al. L. *femur, femor*is.

Fend; fens—strike; de*fend* (*strike down*), *fenc*e (that which protects, or *defends*), *fend* (ward off, *defend*), of*fend* (*dash against*), of*fens*e. L. *fend*ere, *fens*us.

Fenestr—window; *fenestr*al. L. *fenestr*um.

Fer—strike; *fer*ule (a *striking* rod of punishment), inter*fere* (*strike* among, as when one heel *strikes* against the other). L. *fer*ire.

Fer—wild, fierce; *fer*ocity. L. *fer*us.

Ferr—carry, bear, bring; *fer*tile (*bearing* crops), circum*fer*ence (the line *bearing around* a circle), con*fer* (*bring* together), de*fer* (*bear* apart, delay), de*fer* (submit, *bring* one's self *down*), dif*fer* (*bear* apart), in*fer* (*bring* in), of*fer* (*bring* near), pre*fer* (*bring* forward), re*fer* (*bear* back), suf*fer* (undergo, *bear* under), trans*fer* (*carry* across). L. *ferre*.

Ferr—iron; *ferr*eous, *farr*ier (a blacksmith, a worker in *iron*). L. *ferr*um.

Ferv—boil; *ferv*ent, ef*ferv*esce, *ferv*or, *ferv*id. L. *ferv*ere.

Fess—acknowledge; con*fess* (*acknowledge* fully), pro*fess* (*acknowledge* publicly). L. *fat*eri, *fess*us. L. *fari*, *fat*us, to speak.

Fest—feast; *fest*al, *fest*ive, *fest*ival. L. *fest*um.

Fest—strike; in*fest* (attack, *strike against*), mani*fest* (apparent, as if *struck* with the hand). L. *fend*ere, *fest*us.

Fi—become; *fi*at (let it *come* to pass). L. *fio*, I become.

Fict—fashion, feign; *fict*ion (a story of *feigned* characters and occurrences), *fict*ile, *fict*itious. L. *fing*ere, *fict*us.

Fid—faith, trust; con*fid*e (*trust* fully), dif*fid*ent (*distrusting* one's self), *fid*elity (*faithfulness*), in*fid*el (an unbeliever, one not of the *faithful*), per*fid*ious (treacherous, *faithless*), af*fid*avit (a written oath, or pledge of *faith*), af*fi*ance (a marriage *contract*, a plighting of *faith*). L. *fid*es.

Fig (*fing*)—make, form, feign; *fig*ment (a *feigned* story), *fig*ure (a *form*), ef*fig*y (an image *made* to represent an individual). L. *fing*ere.

Fil—thread, line; *fil*ament (a *thread*-like part), *fil*let (a *thread*-like band for the hair), *fil*e (a *line*, as of soldiers), en*fil*ade (a long *line*), *fil*igree (having a texture wrought out of *thread*-like wire), pro*fil*e (the front *line* of the face). L. *fil*um.

Fili—son, daughter; *fili*al. L. *filius, filia.*

Fin—end, limit; *fin*al, *fin*ish, *fin*ite (having an *end*), *fin*e (well-finished, or *ended*), *fin*e (a penalty that *ends* the case), con*fin*e (put within *limits*), de*fin*e (to *limit*), af*fin*ity (relationship, having *limits* bordering on each other). L. *fin*is.

Firm—steadfast, firm, strong; *firm*, *firm*ament (the *firmly* supported heavens), af*firm* (assert positively, fasten, or make *firm*, to), con*firm* (make thoroughly *firm*), in*firm* (not *strong*), *farm* (a property paying a *fixed* rent). L. *firm*us.

Fisc—basket of rushes, money-basket, purse; *fisc*al (relating to money matters, the *purse*), con*fisc*ate (turn into the public treasury, or *purse*). L. *fisc*us.

Fiss—split, rend; *fiss*ure. L. *find*ere, *fiss*us.

Fistul—pipe; *fistul*a. L. *fistul*a.

Fix—fixed, fastened; af*fix* (a part *fastened* to), pre*fix* (a part *fastened* before), suf*fix* (a part *fastened* after). L. *fing*ere, *fix*us.

Flacc—soft; *flacc*id (flabby, *soft*). L. *flacc*us.

Flagell—scourge, whip; *flagell*ate (to scourge with a whip). L. *flagell*um.

Flagiti—disgraceful act; *flagiti*ous. L. *flagiti*um. L. *flagit*are, to act with violence.

Flagr—burn; *flagr*ant (*glaring*), con*flagr*ation (a great *burning* up). L. *flagr*are.

Flat—blow; in*flat*e (*blow* into), *flut*e (a *wind* instrument). L. *fla*re, *flat*us.

Flav—yellow; *flav*or.[1] L. *flav*us.

Flect; flex—bend; de*flect* (*bend from*), *flect*ion, *flex*or, circum*flex*, *flex*ible, in*flect* (to modulate, *bend in*), re*flect* (*bend back*), re*flex*.[2] L. *flect*ere, *flex*us.

Flig; flict—strike to the ground, dash; af*flict*, con*flict*, in*flict*, pro*flig*ate (abandoned, *dashed headlong*). L. *flig*ere, *flict*us.

Flos; flor—flower; *flor*al, *flor*ist, *flor*id (red, like a blooming *flower*), *flos*cule, in*flor*escence, ef*flor*escence, *flour*ish. L. *flos*, *flor*is.

Flu—flow; *flu*ent (*flowing*), *flu*id, af*flu*ent (abounding, *flowing* to), con*flu*ent (*flowing* together), ef*flu*ence (*flowing* out), in*flu*ence (*flow* into), super*flu*ous (*overflowing*), *flu*x (a *flowing*), in*flu*x (a *flowing* in), re*flu*ent. L. *flu*ere.

Fluctu—a wave; *fluctu*ate (to be as changeful as a *wave*). L. *fluctu*s. L. *flu*ere, *fluct*us.

Foc—hearth, fire-place; *foc*us.[3] L. *foc*us.

Foli—leaf; *foli*age (the *leaves*), *foli*o (a volume made of a single *leaf*, or sheet, of paper), port*foli*o (an appartus for carrying writing materials, *leaves* of paper, etc.), tre*foil* (having three *leaves*). L. *foli*um.

Foll—bag; *foll*icle. L. *foll*is.

Foment—a warm application; *foment* (to *warm* up, stir up). L. *foment*um. L. *fov*ere, to warm.

Font—fountain. L. *fons*, *font*is.

For—outside, beyond; *for*eign (belonging to *outside* lands), *for*est (the wild tree land *outside* of the clearing), *fore*close (to close *out*), *for*feit (a thing lost by a misdeed, as for trespass, or going *beyond* one's lawful limits). L. *for*as, *for*is.

For—bore; per*for*ate, *for*amen. L. *for*are.

Form—shape; *form*, *form*ula (a little *form*), con*form*, de*form*, in*form* (tell, put *into form*), re*form*,[4] trans*form*. L. *form*a.

Formic—ant. L. *formic*a.

Formid—fear. L. *formid*o.

Fort—strong; *fort* (a *stronghold*), *fort*itude (*strength* to bear trial), com*fort* (to *strengthen*), piano-*forte* (the loud, or *strong*, sounding instrument). L. *fort*is.

Fortuit—casual; *fortuit*ous. L. *fortuit*us.

Fortun—chance; *fortun*e (that which *chances*). L. *fortun*a.

Foss—dug; *foss*e (a *ditch*), *foss*il (a petrified form *dug* out of the earth). L. *fod*ere, *foss*us.

Frag—See *frang*.

Fragr—emit odor; *fragr*ant. L. *fragr*are.

Franc—free; *franc*hise (a privilege, an exercise of *liberty*), *frank*incense, *frank*, *frank*lin (a *freeholder*), *France* (the land of the *Franks*,[5] or Free Men), *franc* (a coin of *France*). Low L. *franc*us.

Frang; fract—break; *frag*ile (easily *broken*), *frag*ment (a *broken* piece), *fract*ion (a part *broken* off), *fract*ure (a *break*), in*fract*ion (a *breaking* into), irre*frag*ible (not to be opposed or *broken* back), re*fract* (*break* back), re*frain* (the repetition, or *breaking* back, in a song). L. *frang*ere, *fract*us.

Frater; fratr—brother; *frater*nal, *frater*nity, *fratri*cide (the killing of a *brother*), *friar* (a *brother* of a religious order). L. *frater*, *fratr*is.

Fraud—deceit; *fraud*. L. *fraus*, *fraud*is.

Frequ—crowd, press; *frequ*ent. L. *frequ*ere.

Fresc—fresh; *fresc*o (a painting on *fresh* plaster[6]). It. *fresc*o.

Fri—rub; *fri*able (capable of being *rubbed* into powder), *fri*volous (silly, worthless, like *broken* potsherds). L. *fri*are.

Frict—rub; *frict*ion. L. *fric*are, *frict*us.

Frond—leafy branch. L. *frons*, *frond*is.

Front—forehead, face; *front*al, *front*, af*front* (an offense to the very *face*), con*front* (bring *face* to *face*), ef*front*ery (impudence, a *facing* a matter out). L. *frons*, *front*is.

Fruct—fruit; *fruct*ify (bear *fruit*). L. *fruct*us.

Frug—fruits of the earth, thrift; *frug*al (thrifty, careful, *fruitful*). L. *frux*, *frug*is.

Fruit—enjoy; *fruit*ion (*enjoyment* of what has been struggled for). L. *frui*, *fruit*us.

Frustr—in vain; *frustr*ate (make *vain*). L. *frustr*a.

Fug—flee; *fug*itive, re*fug*e, subter*fug*e (a cover, something to *flee* under when pressed in argument). L. *fug*ere.

Fulc—prop; *fulc*rum (the *prop* of the lever). L. *fulc*ere.

Fulg—shine; ef*fulg*ence, re*fulg*ent. L. *fulg*ere.

Fulmin—thunder; *fulmin*ate (*thunder* forth[7]). L. *fulmen*, *fulmin*is.

Fum—smoke; *fum*e, per*fum*e (*smoke* thoroughly), *fum*igate (drive *smoke* around), *fum*itory (a plant that smells like the *smoke* of the earth). L. *fum*us.

Fun—rope; *fun*ambulist (a *rope*-walker). L. *fun*is.

Funct—perform, finish; *funct*ion (that which any thing *performs*), de*funct* (dead, having *finished* the course of life). L. *fung*i, *funct*us.

Fund—bottom; *fund*amental (at the basis or *bottom*), *fund* (capital, the basis, or *bottom*, of a business), *found*er (to go to the *bottom*), *found* (establish, lay the foundation, or *bottom*), pro*found* (deep, reaching toward the *bottom*). L. *fund*us.

Fund; fus—pour, melt; *fus*ible (easily *melted*), *fus*ion (a union, a *melting* together), con*found* (*pour* together), con*fuse* (*pour* together), dif*fuse* (shed, or *pour*, abroad), ef*fus*ion (an *outpouring*), *found* (cast, or *pour* metals), *fut*ile (*pouring* forth in vain), in*fuse* (*pour* into), pro*fuse* (*poured* forth), re*fund* (*pour* back), re*fuse* (*pour* back), re*fut*e (to answer effectively, *pour* back), suf*fus*ion (a *pouring* over), trans*fuse* (*pour* across[8]). L. *fundere*, *fusus*.

Funer—a funeral; *funer*al, *funer*eal. L. *fun*us, *funer*is.

Fur—to rage; *fur*y. L. *fur*ire.

Fur—steal; *fur*tive (*stolen*). L. *fur*ari. L. *fur*, thief.

Furc—fork; bi*furc*ate (two-*forked*). L. *furc*a.

Furn (*forn*)—oven; *furn*ace (a great *oven*). L. *forn*us.

Fus—spindle; *fus*ee (the *spindle* in a watch). L. *fus*us.

Fusc—brown, dark; ob*fusc*ate (*darken*). L. *fusc*us.

Fust—cudgel; *fust*igate. L. *fust*is.

Fut—water-vessel to pour from; con*fute* (to prove to be wrong, *pour cold water upon*), *fut*le (in vain, easily *pouring* forth), re*fute* (to disprove, *pour back*). L. *fut*is.

Futur—about to be; *futur*e. L. *esse*, *futur*us.

NOTES

[1] It will be noticed that all primary words are for objects of sense or simple sensations. Ideas of thought and reflection are expressed by a figurative use of primary words. But the present word indicates an order in the use or education of the senses—sight before taste—and an attempt to express the experience of one sense in terms of another. Some resemblance was thought to be detected between the pleasures of taste and that of the attractive *golden* (*yellow*) color.

[2] All involuntary movements of the body are examples of *reflex action*. A sensor nerve carries to a nerve center (such as the brain or one of the ganglia) an intimation of some disturbance at the surface of the body, as, for example, contact with a hot substance. This is the *direct* action on the nerve center. The center thus affected immediately reacts by transmitting over a motor nerve to the muscles a message to remove the exposed member from danger. This is the backward or *reflex* action.

[3] The rays meet in the *focus*, as the rays diverge from a fire-place.

[4] Public education is based largely on the principle that it is easier to *form* than to *reform*—that it is easier to take children and make responsible citizens of them than to restore them after they have become profligate.

[5] The *Franks* were a Germanic tribe who conquered and occupied *France* (till then called *Gaul*) at the time of the downfall of the Roman Empire. The name was given them on account of the *free*, independent spirit which prevailed among them, and from them the name was applied to the country. The

people of France are mainly of Celtic origin, and up to the time of the Roman Conquest, they spoke the Celtic language. The Roman (*Latin*) language took almost entire possession of the country, though its Roman inhabitants were greatly in the minority. After the Frankish conquest, the reverse effect occurred; the Franks, being in a minority, gradually lost their language and adopted that of the country; so the French language today is substantially Latin, with slight intermixtures from German and other sources. In England, the struggle of languages resulted in a most remarkable compromise; the English language is neither German (Anglo-Saxon) nor Latin (Norman French), but both in a well-balanced adjustment. "Westward the course of empire moves;" all European tendencies seem to have focused themselves and formed a perfect union in the far western island. See *Romance*.

Franklin. Frank, free; *lin*, little. The *little freeman*; the holder of a *small* estate in *fee* as distinguished from the *serfs* or *villains* who occupied the estates of superior lords.

6 Many of the paintings of the great masters are *frescoes* in the mediæval churches, and as such are in a condition to be preserved to the enjoyment of many generations. The great painting of Michael Angelo, "The Last Judgment," is a *fresco* in the dome of St. Peter's at Rome. Some interesting specimens of ancient painting have been recovered as frescoes in the buried buildings of Pompeii.

7 In the old mythology, Jupiter was represented as the ruler of the universe; and his decrees were always accompanied by a peal of *thunder*, thus striking terror and securing obedience. He was called the *"Thunderer,"* and was represented with a thunderbolt in his hand ready to be hurled upon his enemies. His other accompanying symbol was the eagle (the *bird of Jove*), the imperial bird which alone of animals can face the thunder. One of the seven wonders of the ancient world was a statue of Jupiter erected at Olympia, in Elis, where were celebrated the famous Olympian games. This statue was executed by the renowned sculptor Phidias, and marked the highest point to which sculpture has ever attained. Like other objects of moderate dimensions, it disappeared amidst the convulsions of thousands of

years, the massive Parthenon alone being fitted to carry down to our day the handiwork of the great master.

[8] The progress of disease is often arrested by the introduction of healthy blood into the veins of the invalid. Hence, in arousing in another a noble desire, or passion, we are said to *transfuse* our spirit into him.

G

Gabl (*gabel*)—fork; *gable* (the place where the roof *forks*). Ger. *gabel*.

Gain (*gegen*)—against; *gain*say, *again*st. A.S. *gegen*.

Galax (*galact*)—milk; *galax*y (the *milk*y-way, hence a group of bright stars). G. *gala*, *galact*os.

Gale—helmet; *gale*ate. L. *gale*a.

Gallin—hen; *gallin*aceous. L. *gallin*a.

Gam—marriage; big*am*y, polyg*am*y, monog*am*y, cryptog*am* (a plant without visible organs of fructification, and therefore whose *marriage* is *concealed*), oheno*gam* (a plant whose *marriage*, or mode of fructification, is *apparent*), amal*gam*ate (to form a close *union*). G. *gam*os.

Gamb—leg; *gamb*rel, *gamb*ol. It. *gamb*a.

Gangli—a swelling, unch; *gangli*on (a nerve *bunch*[1]). G. *gangli*on.

Gangren—eating sore; *gangren*e. G. *gangrain*a. G. *grain*ein, to eat.

Gant—glove; *gant*let. O.F. *gant*.

Gant (*gat*)—lane; *gant*let (a *lane* of men with clubs). Sw. *gat*a.

Garn—warn, avert, protect, supply, adorn; *garn*ish (to cover over, *protect*), *gar(n)*ment (a robe of *protection*), *garn*iture (*adornment*), *garr(n)*ison (a *supply* of men in a fortress). O.F. *garn*ir, *warn*ir.

Garr—chatter; *garr*ulous, au*gur* (the personage who observed the flight and *chaterrings of birds*). L. *garr*ire.

Gaster; gastr—stomach; *gastr*ic (belonging to the

stomach), *gaster*opod (a reptile, like the snail, that uses the *stomach* as a *foot*). G. *gaster*.

Gaud—rejoice; *gaudy*. L. *gaud*ere.

Ge—the earth; *ge*ography (a description of the *earth's* surface), *ge*ology (the science of the *earth's* crust), *ge*ometry (the science used in surveying, or *measuring* the *earth*), georgic (relating to husbandry, or *working* the *earth*), *Ge*orge (a farmer, a tiller of the *earth*), apo*gee* (the point in the moon's orbit at greatest distance *from* the *earth*), peri*gee* (the point in the moon's orbit *nearest* to the *earth*). G. *ge*.

Gel—frost; *gel*d (*frosty*), con*geal* (to *freeze*), *gel*atine (an apparently *frozen* substance), *jelly* (an apparently *frozen* substance). L. *gel*er.

Gem (*gemm*)—a bud. L. *gemm*a.

Gen—knee; *gen*uflection (a *bending* of the *knee*), *gen*iculate (jointed, having *little knees*). L. *gen*u.

Gen; gener—kin, kind, race, class; *gen*us (a *class*), *gener*al (belonging to a whole *class*), *gener*ate (to produce, bring forth *kind*), *gener*ous (having good impulses, as if belonging to a noble *class*), de*gener*ate (to let *down* the *race*), *gender* (*kind*), *gender* (produce, bring forth *kind*), *gen*uine (of the true *kind*), pro*gen*y (*kin* brought forth). L. *gen*us, *gener*is.

Genea—birth; *genea*logy. G. *genea*.

Gener—kind, class, race; *gener*al, *gener*ate (bring forth *kind*), de*gener*ate (having the *race* let *down*), re*gener*ate, en*gender*, *gender*. L. *gen*us, *gener*is.

Genes—origin; *genes*is. G. *genes*is.

Geni—tutelary spirit, wit; *geni*us,[2] *geni*al. L. *geni*us.

Genit—born, begot; con*genit*al (existing at *birth*), pro*genit*or (an ancestor, one who has *begotten* offspring), primo*genit*ure (the system of the estate passing to the *first-born*[3]), *genit*ive (the case which contains the full stem, from which the noun has its *birth*). L. *gign*ere, *genit*us.

Gent—clan, tribe; *gent*ile (an unbeliever, like the members of a heathen *tribe*), *gent*le (carefully bred, after the manner of a good *clan* or family[4]), *gent*eel. L. *gens*, *gent*is.

Ger—bear, carry, rule; belli*ger*ent (*carrying* on war), corni*ger*ous, lani*ger*ous, vice*ger*ent (one *ruling in the place* of another). L. *ger*ere.

Geran—crane; *gern*ium (the plant having a seed-pod like a *crane's* bill). G. *geran*os.

Germ; germin—seed; *germ*, *germin*ate. L. *germ*en, *germin*is.

German—fully akin; *german*e (*related to*, bearing upon), cousin-*german*. L. *german*us.

Gest—carry, bring; con*gest*ion (a *bringing* together), di*gest* (separate, *carry* apart), *gest*ure (a movement, a *carrying* on), *jest* (a joke or trick perpetrated, *carried on*), re*gist*er (a record that *brings* back matters to mind), sug*gest* (*bring under* consideration). L. *ger*ere, *gest*us.

Gibb—hump, hunch; *gibb*ous. L. *gibb*a.

Gigant—giant; *gigant*ic. G. *gig*as, *gigant*os.

Glabr—smooth; *glabr*ous. L. *glaber*.

Glaci—ice; *glaci*er (a field or strem of *ice*), *glaci*al, *glaci*s (a smooth slope, as if covered with *ice*). L. *glaci*es.

Gladi—sword; *gladi*ator (one of the *swordsmen* of the Roman arena). L. *gladi*us.

Gland—acorn; *gland* (a bunch resembling an *acorn*). L. *glans*, *gland*is.

Gleb—soil; *gleb*e (a tract of *land* belonging to a church). L. *gleb*a.

Glob—ball; *glob*e. L. *glob*us.

Glomer—ball or clew of yarn; con*glomer*ate (rolled together like a *ball*). L. *glom*us, *glomer*is.

Glori—glory. L. *glori*a.

Gloss—tongue, language, word; *gloss*ary (a series of explanations of difficult *words*). G. *gloss*a.

Glott—tongue, language; *glott*is (situated near the *tongue*), poly*glot* (given in many *tongues*). G. *glott*a, *gloss*a.

Gluc—sweet; *gluc*ose. G. *gluc*us.

Glum—ball, busk; *glum*e. L. *gluma, glub*ere, to peel.

Glut—swallow, devour; *glut* (*swallow* greedily), de*glut*ition (*swallowing* down), *glut*ton (an excessive *eater*). L. *glut*ire.

Glutin—glue; *glutin*ous, ag*glutin*ate. L. *gluten, glutin*is.

Glyc—sweet; *glyc*erine (a *sweet* syrup-like substance), *gluc*ose (the *sugar* of grapes and other fruits), *lico*rice (the *root* of a plant from which a *sweet* juice is extracted). G. *gluc*us.

Glyph—carve; hiero*glyph*ic (a *sacred carving* of a word picture on an Egyptian temple). G. *glyph*ein.

Gno—know; prog*no*stic (a *knowing* beforehand), prog*no*sis (a *knowing* beforehand of the course of a disease), diag*no*sis (a thorough *knowing* of a case of disease), ag*no*stic (one that does *not know*), *gno*mon (an index, that makes *known*), *gno*me (a sprite, an *intelligence*). G. *gno*nai.

Gnomen; gnomin—name, fame; cog*nomen* (an additional *name*[5]), ig*nomin*y (disgrace, not having good *name*). L. *gnomen, gnomin*is.

Gon (*goni*)—corner, angle; poly*gon*. G. *goni*a.

Gorg—fearful; *gorg*on. G. *gorg*os.

Gorg—throat; *gorg*e, *gorg*et (*throat* armor), *gorg*eous (showy, causing a swelling of the *throat* with pride), *garg*le (to wash the *throat*). O.F. *gorg*e (the *throat* or *gullet*, which is as voracious as a *whirlpool*). L. *gurg*es, a whirlpool.

Grad; gress—step, go; *grad*e (a *step*), *grad*ual (*step* by *step*), *grad*uate (divide into degrees, or *steps*, as to graduate a scale), de*grad*e (cause to *step* down), in*gred*ient (that which *goes* into a composition), retro*grade* (*go* backward), ag*gress* (*go* against), con-*gress* (an assembly, a *going* together), di*gress* (*go* aside), e*gress* (an *outgo*), in*gress* (a *going* in), pro*gress* (*go* forward), trans*gress* (*go* beyond what is one's right[6]). L. *gradi, gress*us.

Grall—stilts; *grall*atory (long-legged, as if going on *stills*). L. *grallæ.* L. *gradus,* a step.

Gramin—grass; *gramin*eous, *gramini*vorous. L. *gramin, gramin*is.

Gramm—a letter, written character; *gramm*ar (the study of language, especially that which is *written*), ana*gram* (a change in a word due to the rearrangement of its *letters*), dia*gram* (a figure or plan, *written* out), epi*gram* (a terse utterance, like an inscription *written* upon a monument), mono-*gram* (a combination of several letters into a *single character*), pro*gramme* (*written* out beforehand). G. *gramma.* G. *graphein,* to write.

Gran—grain; *gran*ary (a store-house for *grain*), *gran*ge (a farm-house, originally a barn, or *grain* house), *gran*ule (a little *grain*), *gran*ite (the stone composed of small *grains*), pome*gran*ate (the fruit with many seeds or *grains*), *garn*er (to put into the *gran*ary), *garn*et (resembling the seed of the pome*gran*ate). L. *gran*um.

Grand—great. L. *grand*is.

Graph—write; auto*graph* (a *writing* by an individual's self), bio*graphy* (a *written* account of a person's *life*), geo*graphy* (a *written* description of the *earth's* surface), litho*graph* (*written* or drawn on *stone*), photo*graph* (*written* or drawn by *light*), stenogra-*phy* (close or short *writing*), *graph*ite (the mineral in lead-pencils with which we *write*), *graph*ic (vivid, as if drawn or *written* with a pencil or brush), *graf*t (to insert a scion pointed like a *writing*-pencil). G. *graph*ein.

Grat—pleasing; *grat*eful (*pleasing* to the senses), *grat*ify (to *please*), *grat*is (with free grace, or *pleasure*), *grat*uitous (given freely, or with *pleasure*), congra*tul*ate (to wish joy, or *pleasure*), grace, (favor, *pleasure*). L. *grat*us.

Grati—favor; in*grati*ate (work into *favor*), grace (*favor*). L. *grati*a. L. *grat*us, pleased.

Grav—heavy; *grav*e (*heavy*), *grav*ity (*weight*), *grav*itation[7] (attraction of *weight*), ag*grav*ate (increase the *weight*), *grief*, *griev*e. L. *grav*is.

Greg—herd, flock; *greg*arious (tending to *flock* together), con*greg*ate (*herd* together), ag*greg*ate (*herd* together), e*greg*ious (conspicuous, taken *out* of the *flock*), se*greg*ate (to separate, put *apart* from the *flock*). L. *greg*, *greg*is.

Gress—See *grad*.

Gross—fat, thick, great; *gross* (coarse, *fat*), *gross* (wholesale, *large* quantities), en*gross* (to write in *large* letters, also to take one's *entire* attention), *groc*er (a dealer in provision, originally a *wholesaler*). L. *gross*us.

Gubern—govern; *gubern*atorial (relating to a *governor*), *govern*. L. *gubern*are.

Guer (*widar*)—back, again; *guer*don (a reward, a *give back*). O.H.Ger. *widar*.

Guerr—war; *guerr*illa (carrying on irregular *war* on a small scale). Sp. *guerr*a.

Gurg—whirlpool; *gurg*le (to purl or bubble, like a *whirlpool*). L. *gurg*es.

Gust—a tasting; *gust* (relish, gratified *taste*), dis*gust* (offended *taste*). L. *gust*us.

Gutt—drop; *gutt*er (a trough or channel for catching the *drops* from the eaves), *gout* (a disease supposed to be due to a *dropping* of the humors of the body). L. *gutt*a.

Guttur—the throat; *guttur*al (formed in the *throat*). L. *guttur*.

Gymn—naked; *gymn*asium (a place where men exercise more or less *naked*). G. *gymn*os.

Gyn—woman; *gyn*archy. G. *gyn*e.

Gyr—ring, circle; *gyr*e. G. *gyr*os.

NOTES

[1] The brain and ganglia are called *nerve-centers*; and their function is to initiate action in the use of the body. The *sensor* nerves are the messengers inward carrying notice to the brain and ganglia of pleasurable or painful contact or excitement at the surface; the *motor* nerves, on the contrary, carry back to the muscles the mandate of action suited to the nature of the sensation. In voluntary movements of the muscles, the impulse comes from the brain along the motor nerves; but in involuntary movements, the impulse originates in the ganglia.

[2] From Homer downward, the great poets have been said to be endowed with genius, with Homer or Shakespeare, or both, at the head of all. Genius is also accredited to great authors in other departments; historians, scientists, orators, essayists, writers of fiction. Indeed, the term is applied to surpassing intellectual greatness exhibited in any line of private or public activity. Great sculptors, architects, painters, musicians, etc., have left us the *creations* of their *genius*; so also have great statesmen, great engineers, etc. The industrious and useful millions to whom the term *genius* is denied are said to have reached the stage of *mediocrity*.

[3] In the United States, all the children inherit equal shares of their father's estate. But in England the system of primogeniture prevails. In that country the father's estate descends to the eldest

son, including also his title, if he has any. The crown descends in like manner, according to the law of *primogeniture*, to the eldest son. The motive to primogeniture seems to have been to prevent the extinction of noble families by keeping in the hands of the head of the house the estate necessary to uphold its dignity. The extinction of ancient houses is also guarded against by the law of entail, which puts it out of the power of the hold to alienate, or dispose of, his real estate. An improvident or malicious holder may lay waste his lands, as did the grandfather of Lord Byron with regard to Newstead Abbey; but the land itself inevitably reaches the heirs under the law of entail. In all societies there are laws encouraging the accumulation of wealth; but in many countries, notably in the United States and France, there are laws looking to the redistribution of great fortunes. Among these is the law of equal inheritance among children.

[4] The noble families have usually maintained a refined state of society in which courtesy and *gentle* manners have prevailed. They have been stimulated to personal improvement by the high standards of their order; and they have had sufficient wealth to enable them to reach the standards set before them. The education of a *gentleman* (literally a *man of noble family*) has ever included, besides matters of practical utility, the graces of manner and the power to please in every way; it has also included the strengthening and training of the body and the elevation of the spirit, fitting both for enterprises of a daring and arduous nature. It has, also, at all times included the ideas of honor, truthfulness, fairness, and other traits of noble character. At times it has included temperance, chastity, and almost every moral virtue. (See *chivalry*.) These standards were not reached in every case by any means; but the effect of having such standards was to make gentlemen common in the nobility, and to make the nobility respected on account of its many respectable men. The education of manners and character is not now restricted to rank; in modern times it is conceded that any *man* may become a *gentleman*, no matter how humble may have been his birth.

[5] At a time when the Romans were hard pressed during the second Punic War, the elder Scipio led an army into Africa, boldly changing the scene of hostilities. He so confounded the

plans and expectations of the Carthagenians, and pressed them so hard on exposed points, that they were compelled to make terms of peace highly favorable to Rome. The exploit immortalized Scipio with the added name of *Africanus* (he whose deeds in *Africa* won glory and triumph to Rome). It also gave rise to a proverb. Any attempt to transfer the seat of war into an enemy's country is called *carrying the war into Africa*. Such an attempt was made in the American Civil War by the Confederate invasion of Pennsylvania. The attempt was brought to naught by the defeat at Gettysburg. Coriolanus, Britannicus, Germanicus, and Atticus are other examples of Roman *agnomens*.

^{6} A proper freedom is liberty to do right, to act our will in what is not wrong. Liberty to do wrong is license. Every government worthy of the name seeks to repress license; a despotism would shackle the human will in all things; a beneficent government represses only license, while it seeks to enlarge the boundaries of personal freedom in the attainment of proper ends. A government is a means, not an end; though the terms are often reversed by bad rulers. It is a means of promoting the happiness of the governed. Happiness is to be at liberty to follow one's bend, and to make the most of one's powers and the opportunities of life. It may promote happiness to increase the opportunities of life and to facilitate the attainment of proper ends. Hence, a government feels at liberty to assist as well as protect its people. But as there is always danger of harm from even individual assistance, so the danger is tenfold greater when the assistance is rendered by a government. Good government, therefore, throws the people as far as possible upon their own resources, and helps them only when absolutely necessary, or clearly expedient. Liberty is the right to our rights, the right to go to their limits in the attainment of our own good; when we pass beyond them we *transgress*; when we are beyond them we are immediately *trespassing* on the domain of some one else's rights.

^{7} The attraction of the sun and all other masses of matter is called gravity or weight, because the amount of attraction is exactly proportioned to the weight. The discovery of this principle threw such a flood of light upon the field of astronomy, that it is regarded as an epoch in the history of science. The planetary orbits were known, but the cause of their adherence to these circular pathways was a mystery until gravitation supplied the key. It is now clear that the circular movement is due to centrifugal force modified by the powerful attraction of the sun. Gravity also accounts for various disturbances in planetary revolution which were formerly a mystery. It also accounts for the noticeable phenomena of the tides, which are now attributed to the joint attraction of the moon and the sun. A very simple occurrence led to the discovery of this great principle. As Sir Isaac Newton lay in an orchard, an apple fell upon his face. He immediately queried as to what gave the apple motion, and he reached the great conclusion that the earth pulled the apple down after it was released from its stem. The little apple thus led him to the formative principle of the universe; for this principle acts at all distances, though its force varies as the square of the distance; and the position of all bodies in space, or, in other words, the structure of the universe, is a balancing of gravitation and centrifugal force.

H

Habill—dress, clothe; *habil*iment (*clothing*), dis*habill*e (carelessly *dressed*). F *habill*er. F. *habil*e, ready. L. *habil*is, having active power. L. *hab*ere, to have.

Habit—dress, condition, practive. L. *habit*us. L. *hab*ere, *habit*us, to have.

Habit—dwell, abide; *habit*able, *habit*ant (a *resident*), *habit*at (the nature *abode* of a plant), *habit*ation, in*habit*. L. *habit*are. L. *hab*ere, *habit*us, to have, hold.

Hair—take, choose; *her*esy (error in doctrine, a *taking* up what is not authorized), ap*hær*esis (a *taking away* of a letter or syllable from the beginning of a word), di*ær*esis (a mark indicating a *taking apart* of two vowels), syn*ær*esis (a coalescence of two vowels into a diphthong, a *taking together*). G. *hair*ein.

Hal—breathe; ex*hal*e (*breathe* out), in*hal*e (*breathe* in). L. *hal*are.

Hallucin—wander in mind; *hallucin*ation. L. *hallucin*ari.

Halo—a threshing floor; *halo* (a bright circular light, suggesting the white chaff of a *threshing-floor*). G. *halo*s.

Harm—a joining, fitting; *harm*ony (concord, a perfect *fitting*, or *joining* together). G. *harmo*s.

Haught (*haut*)—high; *haught*y (*lofty* in manner). O.F. *haut*.

Haust—to draw water; ex*haust* (to empty, *draw out*). G. *haust*ire, *haust*us.

Heal (*hál*)—whole, sound; *heal* (to make *whole*). A.S. *hál*.

Hears (*herc*)—harrow; re*hearse* (to repeat, like *harrowing* ground over *again*), *hearse* (originally a triangular, *harrow*-like, frame for holding candles at a funeral service). O.F. *herc*. L. *hirpex*, *hirpic*is.

Hebdomad—a week; *hebdomad*al (weekly). G. *hebdom*as, *hebdomad*os. G. *hepta*, seven.

Hecatom (*hecaton*)—hundred; *hecatom*b (a great sacrifice, as of a *hundred oxen*). G. *hecaton*.

Hectic—consumptive. G. *hectic*os. G. *hech*ein, to have.

Hedr—seat, base; poly*hedr*on, cat*hedr*al. G. *hedra*.

Hegemon—a guide, leader; *hegemon*y (the *leadership* among confederate states[1]). G. *hegemon*.

Hein (*hain*)—odious; *hein*ous. O.F. *hain*ous. O.F. *hai*r, to hate.

Helio—the sun; ap*helio*n (the earth's greatest distance from the *sun*), *helio*centric (having the *sun* as the center), *helio*trope (a flower that *turns* constantly to the *sun*), peri*helio*n (the earth's position when nearest to the *sun*). G. *helio*s.

Helix—a spiral; G. *helix*. G. *heliss*ein, to turn around.

Helminth—worm; *helminth*ology (the science of *worms*). G. *helmins*, *helminth*os.

Hem; hemat—blood; *hem*orrhage (the bursting of a *blood*-vessel), *hem*atite (the *blood*stone). G. *haim*a, *haimat*os.

Hemer—day; ep*hemer*al (continuing for but a *day*). G. *hemer*a.

Hendecca—eleven; *hendeca*gon. G. *hendeca*. G. *hen*, one; *deca*, ten.

Hepat—the liver; *hepat*ic (pertaining to the *liver*). G. *hepar*, *hepat*os.

Hepta—seven. G. *hepta*.

Her (*hær*)—stick; ad*here* (*stick* to), co*here* (*stick* together), in*here* (*stick* within). L. *hær*ere.

Herb—grass, fodder, herb. L. *herb*a.

Heredit—inherit; *heredit*ary, *heredit*ament. L. *heredit*are. L. *heres*, *heredis*, an heir.

Hermeneut—interpreter; *hermeneut*ic. G. *hermeneutos*.

Hermi (*eremi*)—desert; *hermit* (a dweller in the *desert*). G. *eremia*. G. *eremos*, deserted, desolate.

Hes (*hæs*)—stick; ad*hes*ion, ad*hes*ive, co*hes*ion, *hes*itate (to halt, as if the tongue *stuck* fast). L. *hær*ere, *hæsit*us.

Hesit (*hæsit*)—stick fast; *hesit*ate. L. *hæsit*are. L. *hæs*ere, *hæsit*us, to stick.

Hetero—another; *hetero*geneous (of various or *other kinds*), *hetero*dox (of *other* than established opinion). G. *hetero*dox.

Hex—six. G. *hex*.

Hiat—gape; *hiat*us (a *gap*). L. *hia*re, *hiat*us.

Hibern—wintry; *hibern*al, hibernate (pass the *winter* in sleep). L. *hibern*us.

Hibit (*habit*)—have, hold; ex*hibit* (*hold* out), pro*hibit* (*hold* forth). L. *hab*ere, *habit*us.

Hier—sacred, holy; *hier*archy (the government priests or *holy* men), *hier*oglyphic (a *sacred carving* on ancient Egyptian monuments[2]). G. *hieros*.

Hilar—cheerful; *hilar*ity (noisy, *mirth*). L. *hilar*is.

Hippo—horse; *hippo*drome (a race-course for *horses*), *hippo*potamus (the *river horse*). G. *hippos*.

Hirsut—bristly, rough. L. *hirsut*us.

Hisc—gape; de*hisc*ent (splitting, or *gaping* open). L. *hisc*ere.

Histor—knowing; *histor*y (*knowledge* of events). G. *histor*. G. *eid*enai, to know.

Histrion—actor; *histrion*ical (pertaining to *acting*). G. *histrio*, *histrionis*.

Hod—way, road; me*thod* (a mode of procedure, a *way after*), *od*ometer, peri*od* (a circuit, a *way around*), syn*od* (an assemblage, a *coming together*). G. *hodos*.

Holo—whole; *holo*caust (a sacrifice of victims *burnt whole*). G. *holo*s.

Hom—man; *hom*icide (the *killing* of a *man*), *hom*age (the service of *man* to master), *hum*an (belonging to *man*).

Homeo—See *homœo*.

Homil—throng, concourse; *homil*y (an address to an assembled *concourse*). G. *homil*os. G. *hom*os, same, together.

Homo—same; *homo*geneous (of the *same* kind). G. *homo*s.

Homœo—like; *homœo*pathy (a treatment with remedies that produce symptoms like those of the disease). G. *homoi*os.

Honest—honrable. L. *honest*us.

Hor—hour; *hor*ologue (a time-keeper, *hour*-teller), *hor*oscope (a *view* of the planets at the *hour* of birth). G. *hora*.

Horiz—limit, bound; *horiz*on, ap*horis*m (a definition, or *limitation*), ao*rist* (the indefinite, or *unlimited*, past tense). G. *horiz*on. G. *hor*os, a boundary.

Horr—shiver, dread. L. *horr*ere.

Hort—encourage; ex*hort* (*encourage* forth), *hort*atory (in the nature of *exhortations*). L. *hort*are.

Hort—garden; *hort*iculture (the culture of *gardens*). L. *hort*us.

Hospit—host, guest; *hospit*able (kind to stranger *guests*), *hospit*al (a retreat for the sick and infirm), *hospit*ality (entertainments of *guests*), hospice (a house for *guests*), *host*, *host*ess, *host*el (an inn, a place for *guests*), *host*ler, *ost*ler (the stableman, formerly the keeper of the *hostel* himself), *hot*el (a *hostel*, or inn). L. *hosp*es, *hospit*is.

Host (*obsid*)—one who remains behind with an enemy; *host*age (a person *given to an enemy* as a pledge for the fulfillment of an agreement[3]). L.

*obs*es, *obsid*is. L. *obsid*ere, to stay. L. *ob*, at, on, near; *sid*ere, to sit.

Host—an enemy; *host*, *host*ile. L. *host*is.

Host (*hosti*)—victim in a sacrifice. L. *hosti*a.

Hulk (*holk*)—a ship that is towed. G. *holk*os. G. *holk*ein, to draw, drag.

Hum—the ground; ex*hume* (take out of the *ground*), in*hume* (put into the *ground*), *hum*ble (lowly, toward the *ground*), *hum*ility (*lowliness*). L. *hum*us.

Hum—be moist; *hum*id, *hum*or. L. *hum*ere.

Humer—shoulder; *humer*al. L. *humer*us.

Humil—humble; *humil*iate (to *humble*), *humil*ity (*humbleness*), *humbl*e. L. *humil*is. L. *hum*us, the ground.

Hydr—water; *hydr*a (a *water*-snake), *hydr*aulics (the science of *liquids* in motion, as *water* through a pipe), *hydr*ogen (the *water-producer*), *hydr*ophobia (the *fear* of *water*), *hydr*ostatics (the science of *liquids* at *rest*). G. *hudr*os.

Hymn—a song. G. *humn*os.

Hypn—sleep; *hypn*otic (a medicine causing sleep). G. *hupn*os.

Hypocris—the acting of a part; *hypocris*y (pretense, *the acting of a part*). G. *hupocris*is. G. *hupocrin*omai, I reply, play a part. G. *hupo*, under; *crin*omai, I contend. G. *crin*o, I judge.

Hypoten (*hypotein*)—subtend; *hypoten*use (the line *subtending* the right angle). G. *hupotein*ain. G. *hupo*, under; *tein*ain, to stretch.

Hypothec—mortgage, security; *hypothec*ate (use as *security*). G. *hupothec*. G. *hupo*, under; ti*the*mi, I place.

Hyster—womb; *hyster*ics (a nervous affection having its origin in the *womb*). G. *huster*a.

NOTES

[1] Among the ancient Greek states there was usually a recognized hegemony. It was held alternately by Athens and Sparta, and led to many wars between those powerful states. Philip of Macedon claimed to have established the *hegemony* of Macedon; but he effected only a Macedonian *domination*.

The *hegemony* proper was a recognized institution to which the states submitted within certain limits without any sense of degradation. At the time of the great Persian invasion, Gelon, tyrant of Syracuse, offered to bring to the defense of Greece more boats and men than any other state on condition that the *hegemony* should pass to Syracuse. His proposition was rejected with scorn, the Greeks being unwilling, even in their last extremity, to buy assistance with humiliating conditions. Under the *hegemony* of Athens were fought the battles of Thermopylæ, Salamis, and Platæa, resulting in the expulsion of the Persians, and in victory and renown for the patriots.

[2] Much of the hieroglyphic writing is still preserved on the obelisks, the mummy cases, and the ruins of the gigantic temples and tombs of ancient Egypt. It originated, doubtless, like the picture language of the Indians, though it developed into a complete and settled language in which each picture or symbol came to have a conventional or permanent value. Matters pertaining to the king and inscribed by his order were accompanied with the royal cartouch or oval which was sacred to the king himself. The obelisk brought to America by Commander Gorringe and set up in Central Park, New York, contains the cartouch of the greatest Pharaoh, the conquering Sesostris or Ramses II, noted in Scriptural history as the oppressor of the Israelites. He did not erect this obelisk; he but carved the record of his exploits on a monument already venerable with age. It was seen by Abraham five hundred years earlier, pointing to the cloudless sky of Egypt, proclaiming the glory of that other Pharaoh, who admired the beauty of Sarah and sought the friendship of the patriarch. The absence of moisture and frost in the valley of the Nile left the stone nearly as fresh and well-preserved in the latter part of the Nineteenth Century as when first beheld by the Father of the Faithful nineteen centuries before the Christian Era.

The hieroglyphic writing was the forerunner and the germ of alphabetic writing; by dividing the symbols for words and phrases the ingenious Phœnicians invented an alphabet for the representation of elementary sounds.

After the conquest of Egypt by Alexander the Great, the country was ruled by the Ptolemies, a line of Grecian kings. The Ptolemies made use of both the hieroglyphic language and the written characters of the Greeks. Royal edicts were at times published in both forms engraved on stone. The discovery of one of those stones at Rosetta at the beginning of the Nineteen Century afforded a key to the hieroglyphic inscriptions, which had hitherto defied all attempts at deciphering or interpreting. Since the discovery of the *Rosetta stone* the hieroglyphic inscriptions are the most legible of all the ancient writings.

[3] In ancient times it was customary to take hostages as pledges for the fulfilling of the conditions of treaties between nations. Especially did the victors exact hostages from the vanquished to secure the fulfillment of conditions that were often harsh. In one instance, the giving of hostages led directly to the conquest of the world. The first people to attain to any thing like universal dominion were the Persians; the second were the Greeks. The second conquest came about in this way. Philip of Macedon was sent in early youth as a hostage to Thebes. Macedon had hitherto ranked low as a nation; in fact, it was treated as a region inhabited by aliens and barbarians, forming no part of the Greek race. Thebes was then at the head of Greek affairs, holding, for the first and only time, the hegemony so long disputed by Athens and Sparta. To this pinnacle of renown Thebes was elevated by her great soldier and statesman, Epaminondas, who found her at the lowest depths of subjugation, with foreign garrisons in her citadels. This man was noted for his spotless integrity, as well as for his penetrating wisdom and unrivaled ability. He remained so poor, that he was able to own but one cloak; whereas Lucullus, a Roman general, was able to give away three thousand to supply the wardrobe of the Roman stage. Yet Epaminondas contrived to have in his house capable tutors for his son, and was resolved that the boy should have a *sound* education whatever else failed. Philip's mother, the queen of Macedon, grieved deeply over the loss of her

boy departing into captivity; and, as an intelligent lady, she especially bewailed the interruption of his studies at that important age. The good Epaminondas told the mother to take no grief on that account; that he would take the boy into his own household and let him share the training of his own son. The queen was comforted, and declared that the boy would be the gainer by leaving home under such conditions. Philip's mind rapidly expanded under severe training and daily contact with a towering intellect. Especially did he absorb and study the military science of the great commander. He returned to Macedon with the intellectual penetration and military judgment of his illustrious master, but lacking his character. He immediately plotted the subjection of the Greek states, and, despite the immortal *philippics* of Demosthenes, he steadily accomplished it. He had learned from Epaminondas how to train an Alexander; and this youth, at the early age of twenty-two, started out to conquer the world.

I

I—go; amb*i*ent (embracing, *going* around). L. *i*re.

Iamb (*iapt*)—throw, cast, attack; *iamb*ic (a meter used in *satirical* poetry, and consisting of a short and a long syllable). G. *iapt*ein.

Ichn—track; *ichn*eumon (the chameleon, the *tracker* of crocodile's eggs). G. *ichn*os.

Ichthy—fish; *ichthy*ology (the science of *fishes*). G. *ichthu*s.

Icon (*eicon*)—image; *icono*clast (an assailant of established opinions, an *image breaker*). G. *eicon*.

Icos (*eicos*)—twenty; *icos*ahedron (a regular solid with *twenty faces*). G. *eicos*i.

Id—see; *id*ea (an image *seen* in the mind). G. *id*ein.

Id (*eid*)—appear; *id*ol (an image, form, *appearance*). G. *eid*omai, I appear. G. *id*ein, to see.

Id (*eid*)—form, shape; *id*yl (a short descriptive poem, *formed* by the poet's art). G. *eid*os. G. *eid*omai, I appear. G. *id*ein, to see.

Iden (*idem*)—the same; *iden*tical, *iden*tify, *iden*tity. L. *idem*.

Idio—one's own, peculiar; *idi*om (a form or turn of speech *peculiar* to a language), *idio*syncrasy (a *peculiar* habit or characteristic of an individual), *idio*t (a person *peculiar* by lack of mental power). G. *idio*s.

Ig—See *ag*.

Ign—fire; *ign*ite (set on *fire*). L. *ign*is.

Ili—the flanks; *ili*ac. L. *ili*a.

Illustri—bright, brilliant; *illustri*ous. L. *illustri*s.

Imag; imagin—image. L. *imag*o, *imagin*is.

Imbecill—feeble; *imbecil*e (*feeble*), em*bezzl*e (to make use of trust funds, and thus *weaken* the amount). L. *imbecill*is.

Imbric—tile; *imbric*ate (formed like a gutter-*tile*). L. *imbres, imbric*is.

Imit—imitate; *imit*ate. L. *imit*ari.

Impeach (*empech*)—hinder, stop; *impeach* (bring to trial for crimes or misdemeanors in office with a view to *checking* them). O.F. *empech*er.

Imperat—command; *imperat*ive (commanding), *emperor*. L. *imper*are, *imperat*us.

Imperi—command, empire; *imperi*al (belonging to an *empire*, fitted for high *command*), *imperi*-ous (haughty, disposed to assume *command*). L. *imperi*um. L. *in*, in; *par*are, to prepare.

Imping—strike against. L. *imping*ere. L. *in*, upon; *pang*ere, to fasten.

Importun—unfit, troublesome; *importune* (to press a *troublesome* request). L. *importun*us, troublesome, not easy of *access*. L. *in*, not; *port*us, access.

Improvis—unforeseen; *improvise* (to prepare on the spur of the moment for an *unforeseen* contingency). L. *improvis*us. L. *in*, not; *vid*ere, *vis*us, seen; *pro*, before.

Inan—void, empty; *inan*e (stupid, *empty*-minded), *inan*ition (exhaustion, prostration, *emptiness*). L. *inan*is.

Incend—set on fire; *incend*iary (*setting on fire*). L. *incend*ere. L. *in*, upon; *cand*ere, to burn.

Incent—sound an instrument, incite; *incent*ive (that which *incites*, like the *tones of an instrument*). L. *incen*ere, *incent*us. L. *in*, into; *can*ere, to sing.

Incip; incept—begin; *incip*ient (*beginning*), *incep-tion* (a *beginning*). L. *incip*ere, *incept*us. L. *in*, upon; *cap*ere, to seize, lay hold of.

Indemn—unharmed; *indemn*ity (compensation for damage, designed to leave the sufferer *unharmed*). L. *indemn*is. L. *in*, not; *damn*um, loss.

Index—a pointer. L. *index*. L. *indic*are, to point out.

Indic—point out; *indic*ate. L. *indic*are.

Indict—point out; *indict* (*single out* for trial). Low L. *indict*are. L. *indic*are, *indic*atus.

Indig—be in want; *indig*ent. L. *indig*ere. L. *ind*, within; *eg*ere, to want.

Indit (*indict*)—point out, make known; *indit*e (to write and *make known* one's thoughts). Low L. *indict*are. L. *indic*are, *indic*tus.

Indu—See *endu*.

Indulg—be courteous to; *indulg*e. L. *indulg*ere.

Industri—diligent; *industri*ous. L. *industri*us.

Inert—inactive; *inert* (*inactive*), *inert*ia (*inactivity*). L. *iners*, *inert*is. L. *in*, not; *ars*, skill.

Infer—low, nether; *infer*ior (*lower*), *infer*nal (belonging to the *lower* regions). L. *infer*us.

Infest—attacking, hostile; *infest* (*attack*). L. *infect*us.

Ingeni—natural capacity, invention; *ingeni*ous (*inventive*). L. *ingeni*um. L. *in*, in; *geni*us, tutelary spirit, wit.

Ingenu—inborn, free-born, frank; *ingenu*ous (*frank, free* to speak, guileless). L. *ingenu*us. L. *in*, in; *gign*ere, *genui*, to beget.

Inguin—groin; *inguin*al. L. *inguen*, *inguin*is.

Inimic—hostile; *inimic*al (*hostile*). L. *inimic*us. L. *in*, not; *amic*us, friend. L. *am*are, to love.

Iniquit—injustice; *iniquit*y (a gross *injustice*). L. *iniquit*as. L. *in*, not; *æquit*as, equity. L. *æquis*, equal.

Initi—beginning; *initi*al, *initi*ate. L. *initi*um. L. *in*, in; *ire*, *it*us, to go.

Insign—remarkable, noticeable; *insign*ia (the conspicuous or *noticeable marks* of office). L. *insign*is.

Instig—goad on; *instig*ate (stir up to do, *goad on*). L. *instig*are.

Instinct—impulse. L. *instinct*us. L. *instig*ere, to goad on.

Insul—island; *insul*ar (belonging to an *island*), *insu*late (to cut off, separate, as an *island*), peninsula (*almost* an *island*). L. *insul*a.

Integer; integr—entire, whole; *integer* (a *whole* number), *integr*al (consisting of an undivided *whole*), *integr*ity (perfection, or *wholeness*, of honor), red*integr*ation (making *entire* again). L. *integer, integr*i. L. *in*, not; *tang*ere, to touch (or harm).

Intellig; intellect—perceive, discern; *intellig*ible (*discernible*), *intellig*ence (mental *discernment*), *intellect* (the *discerning* power of the mind). L. *intellig*ere, *intellect*us.

Inter—within; *inter*ior, *inter*nal. L. *inter*us.

Interess—concern, engage attention; *interest* (to *concern*, or engage one's attention). L. *interess*e.

Interest—it is profitable; *interest* (the *profit* on money loaned). L. *interest*. L. *interess*e, to concern. L. *inter*, among; *ess*e, to be.

Interpret—an interpreter; *interpret* (act as *interpreter*). L. *interpres, interpret*is.

Intestin—inward; *intestine* (a bowel, or *inward* part). L. *intestin*us.

Intim—inmost; *intim*ate (to announce, bring *within*), *intim*ate (familiar, as if dear to the *inmost* affections). L. *intim*us.

Invidi—envy; *invidi*ous (inspired by *envy*, or malice). L. *invidi*ia, envy, a *looking upon* with jealousy. L. *in*, upon; *vid*ere, to see, look.

Invit—ask; *invit*e. L. *invit*are.

Invoi (*envoi*)—a sending; *invoi*ce (a bill of goods *sent*). F. *envoi*. O.F. *envoi*ce, to send.

Ir—anger; *ir*e, *ir*ascible (quickly aroused to *anger*). L. *ir*a.

Iron (*eiron*)—a dissembler; *iron*y (a *disguised* sarcasm or cutting criticism). G. *eiron*.

Irr—snarl as a dog; *irr*itate (tease, arouse, as in causing a *dog to snarl*). L. *irr*ire.

Irrig—flood; *irrig*ate (to moisten with an artificial *flood*). L. *irrig*are. L. *rig*are, to wet, to moisten.

Iso—equal; *iso*celes (having two *equal* legs, or sides). G. *iso*s.

Isol—island; *isol*ate (to separate, cut off, as an *island*). It. *isol*a. L. *insul*a.

Iss—depart, go forth; *iss*ue (to *go forth*). F. *iss*ir. L. *exi*re. L. *ex*, out; *i*re, to go.

Isthm—narrow passage; *isthm*us. G. *isthm*os.

It—go; circu*it* (a *going* completely around), ex*it* (a *going* out), amb*it*ion (a seeking after preferment, as when one *goes* around soliciting votes), trans*it* (a *going* across), preter*it* (*gone* by), sed*it*ion (dissension, a *going* aside). L. *i*re, *it*us.

Iter—again; *iter*ate (repeat, say *again*). L. *iter*.

Itiner—journey; *itiner*ant (*journeying* about). L. *iter*, *itiner*is.

J

Jac—lie; ad*jac*ent (*lying* against). L. *jac*ere.

Jacul—javelin; e*jacul*ate (express suddenly, like *hurling* forth a *javelin*). L. *jacul*um. L. *jac*ere, to cast, hurl.

Jaun—yellow; *jaun*dice (a disease which gives the skin and eyes a *yellow* color). F. *jaun*e. L. *galb*us.

Ject—cast, hurl; ab*ject* (base, as if *cast* away), ad*ject*ive (a modifying word *thrown* with a noun), con*ject*ure (a *throwing* or putting together, an inference, a guess), de*ject* (*cast* down), e*ject* (*cast* out), in*ject* (*cast* into), inter*ject*ion (a word of emotion or surprise *thrown* loosely in *among* the other words of a sentence), *jet*sam (goods *thrown* overboard), *jet*ty (a kind of pier *thrown* up to deepen a channel), *jut* (to project or *throw* forward), ob*ject* (something perceived, as *thrown* directly before the attention), pro*ject* (*cast* forward), pro*ject* (a plan *thrown* forth), re*ject* (*throw* back), sub*ject* (*cast* under). L. *jac*ere, *ject*us.

Jejun—hungry, meager; *jejun*e (*empty*). L. *jejun*us.

Journ (*diurn*)—daily; *journ*al (a *daily* record), *journ*ey (a *day's* travel), ad*journ* (put off to another *day*), so*journ* (a *day to day* stay), so*journ* (to dwell, stay from *day to day*). L. *diurn*us. L. *di*es, a day.

Jubil—shout of joy; *jubil*ation (rejoicing wildly, making *shouts of joy*). L. *jubil*um.

Jubil (*yóbel*)—shout of joy, blast of trumpet; *jubil*ee (a time of *great rejoicing*). Heb. *yóbel*.

Judic—judge; *judic*iary (the *judges* as a body), *judi*-

*c*ial (pertaining to a court or *judge*), *judic*ature (the office of a *judge*), *judic*ious (using careful *judgment*), ad*judic*ate (to determine as a *judge*), pre*judice* (an opinion or *judgment* formed in advance of investigation). L. *judex*, *judic*is.

Jug—yoke; con*jug*al (relating to husband and wife, those *yoked* together in the bonds of matrimony), con*jug*ate (to give a connected, or *yoked* together, view of the parts of a verb), sub*jug*ate (bring under the *yoke* of a conqueror). L. *jug*um.

Jugul—collar-bone; *jugul*ar (at the side of the neck, near the *collar-bone*). L. *jugul*um (the collar-bone, the little *yoke* that unites the breast and the shoulder). L. *jug*um, a yoke.

Jun (*juven*)—young; *jun*ior (*younger*), *jun*iper (an evergreen, and therefore ever-young, plant). L. *juven*is.

Junet—join; ad*junct* (an appendage, *joined* to), con*junct*ion (a *joining* together), in*junct*ion (a command, ordained, or *joined* into), *junct*ion (a *joining*), *junct*ure (a critical moment, like the *union* of the planets), sub*junct*ive (expressing a condition subjoined, or *joined* under). L. *jung*ere, *junct*us.

Jur—swear; ab*jure* (*swear* away), ad*jure* (address with *solemn invocation*), con*jure* (*swear* together), *jury* (a *sworn* body of men), per*jure* (to *swear* falsely, to *forswear*). L. *jur*are.

Jur—law, right; in*jure* (to harm, to do what is not *right*), *jur*idical (relating to *courts* of justice that *declare* the *law*), *jur*isdiction (the power of a court in pronouncing what is *law*), *jur*ist (a person well versed in the *law*). L. *jus*, *jur*is.

Juven—young; *juven*ile (*youthful*), re*juven*ate (restore *youth*). L. *juven*is.

L

La—the people; *la*ity (the *people* as distinguished from the clergy), *lay*man. G. *la*os.

Lab (*lamban*)—seize, take; syl*lab*le (a group of letters *taken together*). G. *lamban*ein.

Labi—lip; *labi*al (a *lip* letter). L. *labi*um.

Labor—work; col*labor*ate (*work* together), e*labor*ate (*work* out), *labor*, *labor*atory. L. *labor*.

Labyrinth—a maze; *labyrinth* (a place full of lanes intersecting[1]). G. *labyrinth*os.

Lacer—mangled, torn; *lacer*ate. L. *lacer*.

Lachrym—tears; *lachrym*ose, *lachrym*al. L. *lachrym*a.

Lact—milk; *lact*eal, *lett*uce. L. *lac*, *lact*is.

Lamb—lick; *lamb*ent, *lamp*rey (an eel-like fish that clings to, or *licks* the rocks). L. *lamb*ere.

Lament—mournful cry. L. *lament*um.

Lamin—thin plates of metal; *lamin*a, *lamin*ar. L. *lamin*a.

Lamp—shine; *lamp*. G. *lamp*ein.

Lan—wool; *lan*iferous. L. *lan*a.

Lanc—plate, dish; ba*lanc*e (a scale having two *plates* or *dishes*). L. *lanx*, *lanc*is.

Lance—lance; *lance*, *lance*t, *lance*olate (*lance-shaped*), *launc*h (to slide into the water, to hurl forth as a *lance*). L. *lance*a.

Langu—be weak; *langu*id, *langu*ish, *langu*or. L. *langu*ere.

Lantern. L. *lantern*a.

Lapid—stone; *lapid*ary (a carver of gems, or precious *stones*), di*lapid*ated (ruines, with the *stones* torn apart). L. *lapis*, *lapid*is.

Laps—slip; col*laps*e, e*laps*e, *laps*e, *laps*us linguae (a *slip* of the tongue). L. *labi, lapsus.*

Lar (*latr*)—robber; *larc*eny (*robbery*), burg*lar* (a house-breaker, a *town-robber*). L. *latro.*

Lard—fat of bacon; *lard,* inter*lard.* L. *lardus.*

Larg—large, liberal; *larg*e, *larg*ess (a *liberal* gift). L. *larg*us.

Larv—ghost, mask; *larv*a (the insect in its *masked* form). L. *larva.*

Larynx; laryng—the throat. G. *larynx, laryngos.*

Lasciv—lustful; *lasciv*ious. L. *lascivus.*

Lass—weary; *lass*itude, a*las!* (ah) I am *weary!*). L. *lass*us.

Lat—wide; *lat*itude. L. *latus.*

Lat—lie hid; *lat*ent. L. *latere.*

Lat—carry, lift, bring; col*lat*e, di*lat*e, e*lat*e (*uplift*), il*lat*ive (making an inference, a *carrying* in), ob*lat*e (compressed along the axis, having the poles *carried* together), pre*lat*e (a bishop, one *elevated* over a charge), pro*lat*e (extended along the axis, having the poles *carried forward*), re*lat*e (report, *bring back*), super*lat*ive (*elevated over* all others, the *highest*), trans*lat*e, legis*lat*e (*bring* forward and enact *laws*), ab*lat*ive (expressing deprivation, a *carrying away*). L. *toll*ere, *latus.*

Later—side; col*later*al (*side* by side), equi*later*al, *later*al, quadri*later*al. L. *latus, later*is.

Latr—servant, worshiper; ido*latr*y (the *worship* of idols). G. *latr*is. G. *latr*on, hire.

Latt—lath, thin plate; *latt*ice (a frame-work of crossed *laths*), *latt*en (sheet tin). Ger. *latte.*

Laud—praise; *laud,* *laud*ation. L. *laus, laud*is.

Lav; lau—wash; *lav*e, *lav*er (a *wash*-bowl), *lav*e (molten *wash* from a volcano), *lav*ender (a plant placed in freshly-*washed* linen), *lav*atory, *lau*ndress (the *washer*-woman). L. *lav*are, *lau*are.

Lav—bale out water; *lav*ish (profuse, as if throwing away, like *baled* water). A.S. *lave*.

Lax—loose; *lax*, re*lax*, *lax*ative. L. *lax*us.

Leaguer (*leger*)—a camp; be*leaguer* (to besiege with an army *encamped* about). Du. *leger*.

Lec (*leg*)—speak; dia*lect* (a variety of *speech*). G. *leg*ein.

Lect—*leg*.

Leg—appoint, send, bring; *leg*ate (an *ambassador*), *leg*acy (a sum *bequeathed*), al*leg*e (declare, *bring* forward), colleague (an associate, one *sent* with), de*leg*ate (to *appoint*, send as a representative), re*leg*ate (to banish, *send* away). L. *leg*are. L. *lex*, *leg*is, law.

Leg; lect—gather, choose; col*lect*, e*lect*, ec*lect*ic (selected, *picked out*), ec*leg*e (a selection, *picked out*), predi*lect*ion (a leaning toward, a *choosing* beforehand), *leg*ion (a body of soldiers *gathered* together), *leg*ume (a pod, a crop that may be *gathered* instead of cut), di*lig*ent (attentive to work, *choosing* between), e*lig*ible, e*leg*ant (fine, and therefore *chosen*). L. *leg*ere, *lect*us. G. *leg*ein, *lect*os.

Leg; lect—read;[2] *leg*ible, *leg*end (a story, something to be *read*), *lect*ure (an elaborate address, usually *read*), *lect*ion (a *reading*), *less*on. L. *leg*ere, *lect*us.

Leg—law; *leg*al, *leg*itimate (*lawful*), *leg*islate (make *laws*), alloy (a mixture allowed by *law*). L. *lex*, *leg*is.

Leger—light; *leger*-line (the *light* line above or below the musical staff), *leger*demain (*sleight of hand*). F. *leger*.

Lemm—take, seize; *lemm*a (an assumption, a *taking* for granted), di*lemm*a (the necessity of making a difficult decision, a *catching* both ways). G. *lamban*ein, ei*lemm*ai.

Lemur—ghost; *lemur* (a *nocturnal* animal). L. *lemur*.

Len—soft, mild; *len*ity, *len*ient. L. *len*is.

Lent—slack, loose; re*lent*. L. *lent*us.

Leo; leon—lion; *leo*pard (the spotted, or pard, *lion*), *leon*ine, chame*leon* (a kind of lizard, the *ground lion*), *Leon*ard (a very *lion*), dande*lion* (the *lion's tooth*). L. *leo, leon*is.

Lepid—scale; *lepid*odendron, *lepid*optera. G. *lepis, lepid*os.

Lepor—hare; *lepor*ine, *lever*et (a young *hare*). L. *lep*us, *lepor*is.

Leps—seize, catch, take; cata*leps*y (a sudden suppression of motion, a *seizing down*), epi*leps*y (a convulsive fit, a *seizing upon*). G. *lamban*ein, *leps*omai.

Les (*læs*)—hurt, injure; *les*ion (a rupture, an *injury*). L. *læ*dere, *læs*us.

Leth—oblivion; *leth*argy (a state of unconsciousness). G. *leth*e.

Lev—light; *lev*ity, al*lev*iate. L. *lev*is.

Lev—lift, raise, rise; *lev*er, *lev*y (to *raise* troops, or a *tax*), *leav*en (the substance which causes bread to *rise*), *lev*ee (a reception, formerly given in the morning, on *rising*), e*lev*ate, *Lev*ant (the eastern part of the Mediterranean, where the sun *rises*). L. *lev*are. L. *lev*is, light.

Lev—smooth; *lev*igate. L. *lev*is.

Lexi—a word, saying; *lexi*con (a dictionary, a book of *words*). G. *lex*is. G. *leg*ein, to speak.

Li—tie, bind, hold; *li*able, *li*en, al*l*y. F. *li*er. L. *li*gare.

Lib—taste, sip, pour out; *lib*ation (a *pouring out* of wine in honor of the gods). L. *lib*are.

Libell—little book; *libel* (a *published* defamation). L. *libell*us. L. *liber*.

Liber—free; *liber*ty, *liber*ate, *liber*al, de*liver*, *livery* (the uniform of a servant, *delivered* to him by his master). L. *liber*.

Liber; libr—balance, weigh; *libr*ate, de*liber*ate (*weigh thoroughly*). L. *libr*a.

Libidin—lust; *libidin*ous. L. *libid*o, *libidin*is.

Libr—book; *libr*ary. L. *liber*.

Lic—be permitted; *lic*ense (a *permission*), *lic*ense (*unrestrained* action), *lic*entiate (the holder of a *license* to practice a profession), *lic*entious (yielding to *license*, *loose* in conduct), *lei*sure, il*lic*it (*not allowed*). L. *lic*ere.

Lid (*læd*); **lis** (*læs*)—strike; col*lid*e, col*lis*ion, e*lid*e, e*lis*ion. L. *læd*ere, *læs*us.

Lieu—place; *lieu*, *lieu*tenant (a subaltern officer, ready to hold the *place* of the captain). F. *lieu*.

Lig—tie, bind; *lig*ament (a *band*), *lig*ature (a *bandage*), al*lig*ation (a rule for mixing, or *binding* together, ingredients), league (an alliance, or *binding* together), ob*lig*e (*bind* against). L. *lig*are.

Lign—wood; *lign*eous, *lign*iferous, *lign*ite (*wood*-coal), *lign*umvitæ (a very hard *wood*, the wood of life). L. *lign*um.

Limin—threshold, entrance; pre*limin*ary (before *entrance* upon the general subject, introductory), e*limin*ate (cast out, as if to *put out of doors*). L. *limen*, *limin*is.

Limit—boundary; *limit*. L. *limes*, *limit*is.

Limpid—clear. L. *limpid*us.

Lin—flax; *lin*en (made of *flax*), *lin*ing (made of *linen*), *lin*seed, *lin*net (the *flax bird*), crino*lin*e (hair cloth, as if made of *flax*), *lin*e (a mark compared to a thread of *flax*). L. *lin*um.

Lin—smear; *lin*iment (a substance *smeared* on). L. *lin*ere.

Line—line; *line*ar (composed of *lines*), *line*al (in the direct *line*), *line*ament (a feature, as if drawn in *lines*), de*line*ate (to sketch, as with *lines*). L. *line*a. L. *lin*um, flax.[3]

Lingu—tongue; *lingu*al, *lingu*ist (one versed in languages, or *tongues*), *langu*age, *ligu*le (a petal having the form of a strap, or *tongue*). L. *lingu*a.

Linqu; lict—leave; de*linqu*ent (remiss, *leaving* undone), re*linqu*ish, re*lict* (a widow, *left behind*), dere*lict*ion (complete *abandonment*), re*lic* (an object *left behind*). L. *linqu*ere, *lict*us.

Lip (*leip*)—leave; ec*lip*se (an observation, or *leaving out*), el*lip*se (an imperfect circle, a *leaving in*). G. *leip*ein.

Liqu—to be wet; *liqu*id, *liqu*or. L. *liqu*ere.

Liquid—clear; *liquid*ate (to pay off, and *clear*, an account). L. *liquid*us. L. *liqu*ere, to be wet.

Lit (*leit*)—public; *lit*urgy (a *public* service). G. *leit*os.

Lit (*lect*)—bed, couch; *lit*ter (a portable *couch*), *lit*ter (materials for a bed, as straw, etc., hence a confused mass of things scattered), cover*let*. L. *lect*us.

Litan—pray; *lit*any (a form of *prayer*). G. *litan*ein. G. *lite*, a prayer.

Lite (*lith*)—

Liter—letter; *liter*al (according to the *letter*), *liter*ary (relating to *literature*), *liter*ati (men of learning, or *letters*), *liter*ature (the writings of those skilled in *letters*, or learning), al*liter*ation (a succession of words beginning with the same *letter*), ob*liter*ate (to efface, as by painting over the *letters* of an inscription), *letter*. L. *liter*a. L. *lin*ere, *lit*us, to smear.

Lith—stone; *lith*ography (a process of drawing on *stone*), *lith*ology, *lith*otomy (the operation of cutting for *stone* in the bladder), *lith*arge (protoxide of lead, *silver-stone*), mono*lith* (a *single-stone* shaft), æro*lite* (a *stone* from the upper air). G. *lith*os.

Litig—dispute, contest; *litig*ate (*contest* at law). L. *litig*are. L. *lis*, *lit*es, strife; *ag*ere, to urge.

Littor—sea-shore; *littor*al. L. *littus*, *littor*is.

Liv—to be bluish; *liv*id. L. *liv*ere.

Liver—See *liber*.

Loc—place; *loc*al, *loc*ate, *loc*omotion (moving from *place*), *loc*omotive, dis*loc*ate (put *out of place*). L. *loc*us.

Locut (*loqu*)—

Loft—air, sky; a*loft* (on high, in the *air*), *loft*y (high up in the *air*), *loft* (an *upper* room), *lift* (to raise into the *air*). Scand. *loft*.

Log—speech, word, account, reason; apo*log*y (a defense, a *speaking* off the charge or fault), cata*log*ue (an enrollment, or list, a full *account*), deca*log*ue (the ten *commandments*), epi*log*ue (a concluding *speech*), eu*log*y (praise, a *speaking* well of some person or thing), mono*log*ue (a *speaking* alone), pro*log*ue (a *speaking* before), *log*ic (the science of *reasoning*), syl*log*ism (the three propositions involved in *reasoning* from premises to a conclusion[4]), ana*log*y (a comparison, a proportion, an equality of *ratios*). G. *log*os. G. *leg*ein, to speak.

Long—long; *long*itude (distance east and west on the earth, its supposed *length*), e*long*ate (*lengthen* out), ob*long* (a rectangle, *long* from side to side), *long*evity (*length* of life), pur*loin* (steal, originally to detain, or pro*long* the use). L. *long*us.

Lop (*loop*)—run; e*lop*e (*run* out or away), inter*lop*er (an intruder, one who *runs* in among). Du. *loop*en.

Loqu; locut—speak, talk; *loqu*acious (*talkative*), circum*locut*ion (*talking* around), col*loqu*y (a conversation, a *talking* together), e*locut*ion (a *speaking* out clearly), e*loqu*ent (*speaking* out with moving power), ob*loqu*y (calumny, a *speaking* against), inter*locut*or (a questioner, *speaking* between the several answers), soli*loqu*y (a *speaking* alone or to one's self), ventri*loqu*ist (one who *speaks*, as it were, from his *stomach*), al*locut*ion (an *address*). L. *loqu*i, *locut*us.

Lot—wash; *lot*ion (a *wash*). L. *lav*are, *lot*us.

Loy (*leg*)—law; *loy*al (faithful to the government, or *laws* of the land), al*loy* (a mixture of base metal provided by *law* for hardening coins). L. *lex*, *leg*is.

Lubric—slippery; *lubric*ate (make *slippery*). L. *lubric*us.

Luc—shine; *luc*id, trans*luc*ent (*shining* through), pel*luc*id (thoroughly *lucid*, or clear), e*luc*idate (clear up, make *lucid*, or clear). L. *luc*ere.

Luc—light; *luc*ubration (a production composed in seclusion, as by lamp-*light*), *Luc*ifer (the morning star, the bringing of *light*). L. *lux*, *luc*is.

Luct—a wrestling, struggling; re**luct**ant (unwilling, *struggling* back). L. *luct*a.

Lucr—gain; *lucr*e. L. *lucr*um.

Lud; lus—sport, play, laugh, mock; *lud*icrous (laughable, like something done in *sport*), al*lud*e (refer to lightly, as in *sport*), col*lud*e (act with, as in *play*), de*lud*e (mock at, as in *play*), e*lud*e (avoid, as in *play*), il*lud*e (deceive, *mock* at), il*lus*ion (deception, a *mocking* at), pre*lud*e (an introduction, a *play* beforehand), inter*lud*e (a pause, delay, like a break in the middle of a *play*). L. *lud*ere, *lus*us.

Lug—mourn; *lug*ubrious (*mournful*). L. *lug*ere.

Lumb—loin; *lumb*ar, *lumb*ago (rheumatism in the *loins* and back). L. *lumb*us.

Lumin—light; *lumin*ary, *lumin*ous, il*lumin*ate. L. *lumen*, *lumin*is.

Lun—the moon; *lun*ar, *lun*ate (shaped like a crescent *moon*), *lun*atic (a person having a disordered mind, supposed to be affected by the *moon*), *lun*ation (the revolution, or period, of the *moon*). L. *lun*a.

Lup—wolf; *lup*ine. L. *lup*us.

Lurid—pale yellow; *lurid* (gloomy, as of a *pale yellow* color). L. *lurid*us.

Lus—See *lud*.

Lustr—enlighten; *lustre*, il*lustr*ate. L. *lustr*um.

Lustr—expiatory sacrifice; *lustr*um, *lustr*al, *lustr*ation. L. *lustr*um.[5]

Lut—wash; ab*lut*ion, di*lut*e (thin out, *wash apart*), pol*lut*e (defile, as with an *over-washing* flood). L. *lu*ere, *lut*us.

Lut—a musical instrument. F. *lut*.

Lux—pomp, excess; *lux*ury. L. *lux*us.

Ly (*lu*)—loosen; ana*ly*ze (*loosen up*), para*ly*ze (render helpless, *loosen beside*). G. *lu*ein.

Lymph—water, liquid; *lymph*, lymphatic. G. *lymph*a.

Lyr (*lur*)—a lute[6]; *lyr*e, *lyr*ic (fitted for the *lyre*). G. *lyr*a.

NOTES

[1] The *Labyrinth* was an underground edifice on the island of Crete. It was composed of intricate passages, so that a person once at the center could scarcely find his way out. During the reign of the mythical King Minos, the labyrinth was made the abode of the minotaur, a monster half man and half bull. The Athenians had killed the son of Minos. In revenge, he threatened the destruction of their city; but he consented to spare them on condition of receiving every year seven youths and seven maidens to be devoured by the minotaur. The hero Theseus resolved to end the odious tribute by the destruction of the monster. He went as one of the youths and killed the minotaur in the labyrinth. Ariadne, the daughter of Minos, gave him a ball of thread, which he unrolled gradually as he passed through the labyrinth to the apartment of the minotaur. By means of this thread he was enabled to retrace his way out.

[2] Originally to *gather* the sense. See *Leg, lect*, to gather, choose.

³ A line is compared to a thread of *flax*.

⁴ The syllogism contains three propositions: a *major premise*, a *minor premise*, and the conclusion, as, for example: Man is mortal; William Jones is a man; Therefore William Jones is mortal.

The propositions are not always stated in this order; but they are involved in the argument. A fallacy, or false reasoning, is usually due to faulty premises. They are either not true, or else they do not correspond. The syllogism was first discovered and stated by Aristotle, the great scientist of antiquity. The science of logic, or the art of reasoning, received almost its full development at his hands. The specious reasoning of the *sophists* urged forward three great men in succession, Socrates, Plato, and Aristotle, to find the tests of truth and sound reasoning, with the result of creating the science of logic.

⁵ The *lustrum* occurred at Rome once in five years. Hence the period of five years came to be called a *lustrum*.

⁶ The lyre was the favorite instrument of Apollo, the god of music. According to ancient fable, the god was induced on two occasions to engage in musical contests designed to test the sweetness of the lyre and the skill of its master. In the first place, he competed with Pan, the good-natured but homely god of the shepherds, and who had invented the reed pipe. In this contest, Midas, King of Lydia, was made the judge. Apollo threw every grace of manner into his performance, and brought forth such heavenly strains of music that the neighboring mountains murmured ecstatic admiration. But the uncultivated sense of the king awarded the superiority to the squeaking pipes of Pan. He was punished for his bad taste by having his ears transformed into those of an ass. The renowned Phrygian cap was invented to conceal this deformity. But it was discovered by the barber, who, unable to retain so wonderful a secret, and not daring to divulge it to a mortal, dug a hole in the ground and laughed his secret into it. The following season large reeds grew up where the ground had been stirred; and their dry rattle made known to the world the convulsing secret of the barber. On another occasion a satyr, named Mansyas, dared to compete with the sun-god; but his performance was so abominable that Apollo, in disgust, had him flayed alive.

M

Macer—to steep; *macer*ate. L. *macer*are.

Machin—device, *machine*; *machin*e, *machin*ation (a wicked *device*). L. *machin*a. G. *mechan*e.

Maci—leanness; emaciate. L. *maci*es.

Macr—long, great; *macr*ocosm (the whole universe, the *great* world), *macr*on (the sign of the *long* sound). G. *macr*os.

Macul—spot, speck, hole, network; *macul*ate (to de-file, to *spot*), im*macul*ate (*unspotted*), *mack*erel (the *spotted* fish), *mail* (steel *net-work* for armor). L. *macul*a.

Madr (*mandr*)—herd, flock; *madr*igal (a *shepherd's* song). It. *mandr*a. L. *mandr*a, a stall, stable. G. *mandr*a, a fold.

Magister; magistr—master; *magister*ial (despotic, like a *master*), *magistr*ate. L. *magister*, *magistr*i.

Magn—great; *magn*itude, *magn*ificent, *magn*ani-mous, *magn*ify, *magn*ate. L. *magn*us.

Main—chief. O.F. *main*e, *magn*e. L. *magn*us, great.

Main (*man*)—hand; legerde*main* (sleight of *hand*), *main*tain (to hold as in the *hand*). L. *man*us.

Majest—dignity, honor; *majest*y (supreme *dignity*). L. *majest*us.

Major—greater; *major* (greater, also a military officer of *higher* rank than a captain), *major*ity (the greater number, also *full* age, the rank of *major*), *major*-domo (a steward, the *great* personage of the house), *may*or (the *chief* executive of a city). L. *major*.

Mal—bad, ill; *mal*ice (*ill*-will), *mal*ady (an *illness*), *mal*aria (*bad* air), *mal*ign (unfavorable, *ill*-disposed). L. *mal*us.

Malle—hammer; *malle*able (capable of being hammered out), mall (a kind of *hammer*), *malle*t (a small *mall*), *maul* (to strike or *hammer*). L. *malle*us.

Mamm—breast; *mamm*al (an animal that suckles its young at the *breast*), *mamm*illary (pertaining to the *breasts*). L. *mamm*a.

Mamm—the earth; *mamm*oth (a great extinct animal, supposed at one time to have burrowed in the *earth*). Tart. *mamm*a.

Man—hand; *man*ual (done by *hand*, also a brief treatise easily carried in the *hand*), a*man*uensis (one who writes with the *hand* from dictation), maintain (hold by the *hand*), *man*acle (a shackle for the *hand*), *man*age (to *handle*), *man*age (the control, or *handling*, of horses), *man*ifest (apparent, as is struck by the *hand*), *man*iple (a small company, or *handful*, of soldiers), *man*ipulate (to *handle*), *man*ner (way of doing or *handling*), *man*ufacture (a making by *hand*[1]), *man*umit (set free, send out of *hand*), *man*euver (a skillful piece of *handiwork*), *man*uscript (written by *hand*), e*man*cipate (set free, take out of *hand*). L. *man*us.

Man—flow; e*man*ate (*flow* forth). L. *man*are.

Man; mans—stay, dwell; *man*or (the *dwelling* of the lord, or owner), *man*sion (a fine *dwelling*), *man*se (a clergyman's *abode*), menial (employed about the *house*), per*man*ent (*staying* throughout), re*main* (*stay* back). L. *man*ere, *mans*us.

Manc (*mant*)—a seer; necro*man*cy (divining, or *foreseeing*, by means of dead bodies). G. *mant*is.

Mand—order; *mand*ate (an *order*), *mand*amus (an *order* of court), counter*mand* (to recall an *order*, *order* against it), de*mand* (require, *order* from), re*mand* (*order* back), com*mand* (*order* or entrust with). L. *mand*are.

Mand—chew; *mand*ible (the jaws). L. *mand*ere.

Mang—eat; *mang*er (an *eating* trough), *mang*e (a *scab* or itch in dogs). F. *mang*er.

Mani—frenzy, madness; *mani*a, *mani*ac. G. *mani*a.

Mans—See *man*.

Mar—the sea; *mar*ine (belonging to the *sea*), *mar*itime (pertaining to the *sea*), *mar*iner (a *sea*-man), rose*mary* (the *sea*-dew), cor*mor*ant (the *sea*-cow). L. *mar*e, *mar*is.

Maran (*marain*)—wither, fade; a*maran*th (the *unfading* flower). G. *maran*ein.

Margin—border. L. *marg*o, *margin*is.

Marit—husband; *marit*al (belonging to marriage, the relation of *husband* and wife). L. *marit*us. L. *ma*s, *mar*is, man, husband.

Marry (*marit*)—husband. L. *marit*us.

Marsupi—pouch; *marsupi*al (having a *pouch*, as the kangaroo). L. *marsupi*um. G. *marsup*os, a bag.

Marti—Mars; *marti*al (war-like, like *Mars*, the god of war). L. *Mar*s, *Marti*s.

Martyr—a witness. G. *martur*.

Mascul—male; *mascul*ine, e*mascul*ate (make weak, or *unmanly*). L. *mascul*us. L. *mas*, a male.

Mast—breast, nipple; *mast*oid (*nipple*-shaped). G. *mast*os.

Mastic—chew; *mastic*ate. L. *mastic*are. G. *mastax*, mouth. G. *mastiz*ein, to chew.

Mat—seek after, move; auto*mat*on (a self-*moving* figure or machine). G. *mat*eo.

Mater; matr—mother; *mater*nal (belonging to a *mother*), *matr*icide (the killing of a *mother*), *matr*imony (marriage, the state of *motherhood*), *matr*on (a *motherly* woman). L. *mater*, *matr*is.

Materi—stuff, substance; *materi*al. L. *materi*a.

Mathem—a lesson; *mathem*atics (*lessons* in quantity). G. *mathem*a, *mathem*atos.

Matin—morning; *matin*s (*morning* service), *matin*ee (an *early* performance). F. *matin*. L. *matutin*us, belonging to the morning. L. *Matut*a, the goddess of dawn.

Matur—ripe; *matur*e. L. *matur*us.

Matutin—belonging to the morning. L. *matutin*al. L. *Matut*a, the goddess of the dawn.

Maul (*mal*)—to paint; *maul*stick (a *painter's* stick). Ger. *mal*en.

Maxill—jaw-bone; *maxill*ary. L. *maxill*a. L. *macer*are, to chew.

Maxim—greatest; *maxim* (an opinion of the *greatest* importance), *maxim*um (the *greatest* limit). L. *maxim*us.

Me—go; per*me*ate (*go* through). L. *me*are.

Meagr (*maigr*)—thin, lean. F. *maigr*e. L. *macer*, *macr*i.

Mechan—device, machine; *mechan*ical (belonging to a *machine*). G. *mechan*e.

Med—heal; re*med*y (*heal* again). L. *med*eri.

Medi—middle, between; *medi*um (a *means*, in the *midst*), *medi*ate (go *between* and bring about settlement), *medi*eval (relating to the *middle* ages), *medi*ocre (of only *middling* talents), im*medi*ate (next, having nothing *between* or in the *middle*), *Medi*terranean (in the *middle* of the land), *me*an, *medi*an (in the *middle*), *meridi*an (the sun's *mid-day* line). L. *medi*us.

Medic—physician; *medic*ine. L. *medic*us. L. *med*eri, to heal.

Medit—ponder; *medit*ate. L. *medit*are.

Medl—to mix; *medl*ey (a *mixture*). O.F. *medl*er.

Medull—marrow. L. *medull*a.

Meer—the sea; *meer*schaum. Ger. *meer*.

Mega—great; *mega*therium. G. *megas*.

Mega—great; *mega*losaur (the *great* lizard), *mega*-lomyx (the *great* claw). G. *megas*, *megalos*.

Mel; mell—honey; *mell*ifluous (flowing sweet, like *honey*), *mol*asses (like *honey*), *mil*dew. L. *mel*, *mell*is.

Melan—black; *melan*choly (supposed to be due to *black* bile). G. *melas*, *melanos*.

Melior—better; a*melior*ate (to *better*). L. *melior*.

Melo—song; *melo*dy (the music of *song*), *melo*drama (acting with *songs*). G. *melos*.

Memento—be it remembered. L. *memento*. L. *memini*, to remember.

Memor—mindful; *memor*y, com*memor*ate, *memoir* (a short biographical sketch, a *recollection*). L. *memor*.

Menac (*minac*)—full of threatening; *menac*e. L. *minax*, *minac*is. L. *min*ere, to project.

Menager—keep house; *menager*ie (a place in which animals are kept, originally a place for *household* animals). F. *menager*. O.F. *mesnag*e, a household. L. *mans*is.

Mend—fault; e*mend* (to free from *fault*). L. *mend*um.

Mendaci—false; *mendaci*ous, *mendaci*ty. L. *mendax*, *mendac*is.

Mendic—beg; *mendic*ant. L. *mendic*are. L. *mendic*us, beggarly, poor.

Mens—measure; *mens*uration (the rules of *measuring*), com*mens*urate (great enough, *measuring* with), di*mens*ion (one of the *measurements* of a body), im*mens*e (great beyond *measure*), *mea*sure. L. *met*iri, *mens*us.

Ment—mind; *ment*al (belonging to the *mind*), de-

*ment*ed (out of one's *mind*), *ment*ion (call to *mind*). L. *mens, ment*is.

Mer—lake; *mere* (a *lake*), *mer*maid (the maid of the *lake*), *mar*sh. A.S. *mere*.

Merc—merchandise, trade, reward, pay; com*merc*e (*trade* with), *merc*antile (commercial, having to do with *trade*), *merc*enary (working for *pay*), *merc*er (a *trader*), *merc*handise (the goods of a *merchant*), *merc*hant (a person engaged in *trade*), *merc*y (pardon, a *reward*), *Merc*ury[2] (the god of *trade*), a*merc*e (to fine, fix a sum to be *paid*). L. *merx, merc*is.

Merg—dip, sink, mingle; im*merg*e (*dip* into), sub*merg*e (*dip* under), *merg*e (*sink* into), e*merg*e (come out, do the reverse of *dipping*). L. *merg*ere.

Merit—deserved; *merit*. L. *merere, merit*us.

Mes—middle; *mes*entery (a membrane in the *midst* of the entrails), *mes*ozoic. G. *mes*os.

Metall—metal; *metal, metall*urgy (working in *metals*). G. *metall*on.

Meter; metr—measure; anemo*meter* (an instrument for *measuring* the rate of the *wind*), baro*meter* (a *measure* of the *weight* of the atmosphere), chrono*meter* (a time-piece, a *measure* of *time*), dia*meter* (the *measure* directly *through* a circle), geo*metry* (the science of form, used in *measuring* the *earth*), hexa*meter* (having *six* feet or *measures*), peri*meter* (the entire boundary, or *measure around* of a polygon), sym*metry* (due proportion, in which the parts *measure*, or fit, exactly together), trigono*metry* (the science which investigates, or *measures*, triangles), thermo*meter* (a *measure* of heat). G. *metr*on.

Metr—mother; *metr*opolis (a great commercial center, like the *mother cities* of antiquity[3]). G. *meter*.

Miasm—stain, pollution; *miasm*a (*pollution* in the atmosphere). G. *miasm*a.

Micro—small; *micro*scope (the viewer of *small* objects), *micro*cosm (the *small* world or universe, the world of *small* life). G. *micro*s.

Migr—wander; *migr*ate, e*migr*ate (*wander* out of a country), *migr*atory (tending to *wander*), trans*migr*ate (*wander* across from one body to another). L. *migr*are.

Milit—soldier; *milit*ary, *milit*ia, *milit*ant, *milit*ate. L. *milit*es, *milit*is.

Mill—thousand; *mill* (the *thousandth* part of a dollar), *mill*ennium (the *thousand years* of the Savior's glorious reign on earth), *mill*foil (the *thousand-leafed* yarrow), *mill*e (formerly a *thousand* paces), *mill*ion (the great *thousand*).

Min—project; pro*min*ent (*projecting* forward), e*min*ent (*projecting* out above), im*min*ent (threatening, *projecting* upon). L. *min*ere.

Miniat—dye, paint; *miniat*ure (a small *painting*). It. *miniat*are, *miniat*o. L. *mini*um, cinnabar, red lead.

Minim—least. L. *minim*us.

Minister; ministr—a servant; ad*minister* (to direct, to *serve*), *minister* (a *servant*), *minstr*el (a band, a musical retainer, or old *servant*). L. *minister*, *ministr*i.

Minn; minut—diminish, lessen, make small; com*minut*ion (breaking into *small* pieces), di*minut*ion (a *lessening* apart), *minu*end (the number to be *diminished*), *minu*et (a dance with very *small* steps), *minut*e (made very *small*), *minut*e (one of the *small* divisions of time). L. *minu*ere.

Minor—less; *minor*, minority. L. *minor*.

Mio (*meio*)—less; *mio*cene (*less* recent). G. *meio*n.

Mir—wonder, behold, look; *mir*acle (a *wonder*), ad*mir*e (*wonder* at), marvel (a *wonderful* thing), *mir*age (an optical illusion due to certain conditions of the atmosphere, a *sight*), *mir*ror (a *looking-glass*). L. *mir*ari.

Mis—hate; *mis*anthrope (a *hater* of man), *mis*ogamist (a woman-*hater*). G. *mis*ein. G. *mis*os, hatred.

Misc—mix; *misc*ellaneous (of *mixed* kinds), pro*misc*uous (all *mixed* up). L. *misc*ere.

Miser—wretched. L. *miser*.

Miss—See *mitt*.

Mitt; miss—send, throw; *miss*ile (a weapon *thrown* forward), *miss*ion (the duty on which one is *sent*), *miss*ive (a letter *sent*), ad*mit* (*send* to), com*mis*sary (an officer to whom something is intrusted, or *sent* with), com*mit* (intrust to, *send* with), com*mit* (do, *send* out), demise (death, a *sending* away), di*miss*ory (giving leave to depart, a *sending* away), dis*miss* (*send* away), e*mit* (*send* forth), im*mit* (*send* into), inter*mit* (cease at times, interrupt, *send* apart), message (that which is *sent*), o*mit* (neglect, let go, *send* away), per*mit* (allow, *send* through), pre*miss* (a foundation, proposition *sent* forth, or stated before the other two propositions of the syllogism), promise (*send*, or set, forth what one will do), re*mit* (*send* back, hence to abate), compromise (settle by mutual yielding and *promising*), sub*mit* (yield, bow to, *send* under). L. *mitt*ere, *miss*us.

Mnemon—mindful; *mnemon*ics (the science calling to *mind*). G. *mnemon*. G. *mnao*mai, I remember.

Mobil—*mobile* (movable), *mob* (a disorderly, therefore *movable*, crowd). L. *mobil*is. L. *mov*ere, to move.

Mod—measure, manner, way; *mod*e, *mod*el (little *measure*), *mod*est (keeping within *measure*, or bounds), *mod*ify (make *measure*), *mod*ulate, *mood*. L. *mod*us.

Moder—measure, manner, mode; *moder*ate (reduced to *measure*), *moder*n (of the present *mode*). L. *moder*ari, *moder*atus.

Mol—mill; *mol*ar (used, like a *mill*, for grinding). L. *mol*a.

Mol—meal; im*mol*ate (to sacrifice, and begin, as the ancients did, by throwing *meal* upon the head of the victim). L. *mol*a.

Mol—heap, mass; *mol*ecule (a little *mass*), e*mol*ument, de*mol*ish (to take down the *heap*), *mol*e (a *mass* used as a break-water). L. *mol*es.

Mol—work, accomplish. L. *mol*iri.

Molest—troublesome. L. *molest*us. L. *moles*, a heap, mass.

Moll—soft; *moll*usc (a *soft*-bodied animal, as the snail and shell-fish), *moll*ify (to *soften*), e*moll*ient (a *softening* application). L. *moll*is.

Mon; mono—single, alone; *mon*arch, *mono*gram, *mono*logue, *mono*syllable. G. *mon*os.

Mon; monit—advise, remind, warn; *mon*ument (a memorial, or *reminder*), *mon*ster (a startling object, a *warning*), *mon*itor, *mon*ition, ad*mon*ish, pre*mon*ition, sum*mon* (*remind* privately). L. *mon*ere, *monit*us.

Monach—monk; *monach*ism, *monk*. G. *monach*os. G. *mon*os, alone.

Monast—monk; *monast*ery (an abode of *monks*). G. *monast*es. G. *mon*os, alone.

Monsoon (*mawsim*)—time, season; *monsoon* (a wind in the Indian Ocean which blows in one direction for a whole *season*[4]). Ar. *mawsim*.

Monstr—show, point out; de*monstr*ate (*show* to be *fully* reasonable), re*monstr*ate (expostulate, *show again* and *again* the folly of). L. *monstr*are. L. *monstr*um, a portent. L. *mon*ere, to advise, warn.

Mor—manner, custom; *mor*al (right, pure, in accordance of good *custom*), de*mure* (downcast, coy, of gentle *manner*). L. *mos*, *mor*is.

Mor—self-will; *mor*ose. L. *mos*, *mor*is.

Morb—disease; *morb*id, cholera *morb*us. L. *morb*us.

Mord; mors—bite; *mord*acity (*biting* sarcasm), *mor*sel (a little *bite*), re*morse* (a gnawing regret, a *biting again*). L. *mord*ere, *mors*us.

Morph—form, shape; a*morph*ous (*without form*), meta*morph*osis (a *change* of *form*), *Morph*eus (the god of dreams, or *shapes*), *morph*ine (the drug of *Morph*eus, that causes sleep). G. *morphe*.

Mors—See *mord*.

Mort—death; *mort*al (subject to *death*), *mort*ify (make *dead*), *mort*gage (the gage or pledge that became *dead*, or lost, on failure of the condition), *mort*uary (relating to *deaths*). L. *mors*, *mort*is.

Mot—moved, move; *mot*ion, *mot*ive (that which *moves*), *mot*or, pro*mote* (*move* forward), re*mote* (*moved* back). L. *mot*ere, *mot*us.

Mott—a saying; *mott*o. It. *mott*o. L. *mutt*um, a murmur, smothered sound.

Mov—move; *mov*e, *mo*mentum. L. *mov*ere.

Muc—slime; *muc*us, *muc*ilage. L. *muc*us.

Mulct—a fine. L. *mulct*a.

Muls—milked; e*muls*ion (a *milk*-like mixture). L. *mulg*ere, *muls*us.

Mult—many; *mult*itude, *mult*iply (make *manifold*), *mult*ifarious (of *many* kinds). L. *mult*us.

Mun; munit—fortify; *mun*iment (a *defense*), *muni*tion (a means of *defense*), am*mun*ition. L. *mun*ire, *munit*us.

Mund—the world; *mund*ane. L. *mund*us.

Municipi—a township, city; *municip*al (belonging to a

city). L. *municipi*um. L. *municeps*, *municipi*s, a free citizen. L. *mun*us, obligation, duty; *cup*ere, to take.

Mur—wall; *mur*al, im*mur*e (shut up within *walls*). L. *mur*us.

Muri—brine; *muri*atic (from, or resembling, *brine*). L. *muri*a.

Muric—prickly fish, spike; *muric*ated (covered with short *points*). L. *mure*x, *muric*is.

Murmur—murmur. L. *murmur*.

Mus—mouse; *mus*cle (that which creeps like a little *mouse*). L. *mus*.

Musc—moss; *musc*oid. L. *musc*us.

Mut—change; *mut*able, com*mut*e, *mut*ual, per*muta*tion, trans*mut*e. L. *mut*are.

Mutil—maimed; *mutil*ate. L. *mutil*us.

Mutin—tumultuous. O.F. *mutin*y. O.F. *mut*ente, a sedition.

Myriad—ten thousand. G. *muri*os, *muriad*os. G. *muri*os, numberless.

Myrm—ant; *Myrm*idones.[5] G. *murm*ex.

Myst—one who is initiated; *myst*ery (something unintelligible, or known only to the *initiated*), *myst*ic. G. *must*es. G. *mu*ein, to close the eyes.

Myth—fable; *myth* (a *fable*), *myth*ology (the stories of ancient *fable*). G. *muth*os.

NOTES

[1] Modern manufacture is carried on mostly by machinery. This allows an exactness not possible by hand. But is also gives a monotonous sameness of product, an endless repetition of the same identical thing. Human skill, on the contrary, cannot exactly duplicate its products, and it is, moreover, led into pleasing variety by the fancy or inspiration of the moment. This,

therefore, gives a special value to articles of ancient manufacture, and to those not fashioned by machinery.

[2] winged messenger of Jupiter. After him, therefore, was named the *swiftly*-moving *quicksilver*.

[3] The ancient Greek cities relieved their excess of population by colonization. Each city was the *metropolis*, or *mother city*, of its colony. A metropolis monopolized the trade of its colonies and amassed great wealth thereby. But as the ancient metropolitan cities shaped the thought of their dependencies, so a modern metropolis includes the idea of a great center of culture.

[4] The breeze flows to the point of greatest heat. The land becomes more highly heated in summer than the water. During half the year, or the northern summer, the breeze flows steadily toward the heated Peninsula or Hindostan. During the other half of the year, or the northern winter, the breeze flows with equal steadiness toward the highly heated regions of southern Africa. Voyages by sailing vessels on the Indian Ocean are so timed as to get the benefit of the monsoon, much the same as ships seek the trade-winds in sailing west, but avoid them and seek the region of the return trade-winds on returning east.

[5] The Myrmidones came originally from Ægina, and were fabled to have sprung from the *ants* of that island. During the reign of the good King Æacus, the island was depopulated by a plague. The gods, in pity to the stricken monarch, willed that the ants be transformed into men; and immediately the island was teeming with industrious people.

Nupti—a wedding; *nupti*al. L. *nuptiæ*. L. *nupt*a, a bride. L. *nub*ere, *nupt*us, to marry. L. *nub*es, a veil.

Nut—nod; *nut*ation (a *nodding* of the pole of a planet). L. *nut*are.

Nutr—nourish; *nutr*iment, *nutr*itive, *nutr*ition, *nur*se, *nurt*ure. L. *nutr*ire.

Nymph—bride; *nymph* (a beautiful maiden, fitted to be a *bride*). G. *numph*e.

N

Na—flow; *na*iad (a *water* nymph). G *na*ein.

Narc—numbness; *narc*otic (producing stupor, or *numbness*). G. *nark*e.

Narr—relate; *narr*ative. L. *narr*are.

Nas—nose; *nas*al, *nas*turtium (the flower whose odor twists the *nose*). L. *nas*us.

Nasc—be born; *nasc*ent. L. *nasc*i.

Nat—born; *nat*al (relating to birth), in*nat*e (in-*born*), *nat*ive, *nat*ure. L. *nat*us.

Nat—swim; *nat*atory. L. *nat*are.

Nau—ship; *nau*tical (relating to *ships*), *nau*sea. G. *nau*s.

Naus—ship; *naus*ea (the feeling produced by the motion of a *ship*). G. *nau*s.

Nautil—sea-man; *nautil*us (the little *navigator* of the deep). G. *nautil*os. G. naus, a ship.

Nav—ship; *nav*al, *nav*igate, *nav*y, *nav*e (the body of a church, the *ship* of Christ). L. *nav*is.

Nebul—little cloud; *nebul*a (one of the *cloudy* masses seen through the telescope). L. *nebul*a.

Nec—kill; inter*nec*ine (utterly *destructive*, as occurring among neighbors). L. *nec*are.

Necess—*necess*ary. L. *necess*e.

Necro—corpse; *necro*mancy (divination by means of a *corpse*), *necro*logy (an account of the recently *dead*). G. *necro*s.

Negat—deny; *negat*ive, *negat*ion, ab*negat*ion (self-*denial*). L. *neg*are, *negat*us.

Negoti—business; *negoti*ate. L. *negoti*um.

Neo—new; *neo*phyte (a *new* disciple, a *new* plant). G. *neo*s.

Ner—wet; *ner*eid (a *sea*-nymph, daughter of *Ner*eus), a*ner*oid (not having the *wet*, or liquid, mercury). G. *ner*os.

Neur—nerve; *neur*algia (*nerve* pain). G. *neur*on.

Neuter; neutr—neither; *neuter*, *neutr*al. L. *neuter*, *neutr*a. L. *ne*, not; *uter*, whether.

Nid—nest. L. *nid*us.

Nigr—black; *nigr*escent (becoming *black*). L. *niger*, *nigr*a.

Nihil—nothing; an*nihil*ate (reduce to *nothing*). L. *nihil*.

Nobil—well known; *nobl*e (distinguished, *well known*). L. *nobil*is.

Noc—hurt, harm; in*noc*uous (not *hurting*), in*noc*ent (not doing any *harm*). L. *noc*ere.

Noct—night; *noct*urnal, equi*noct*ial, *noct*urn (a *night* service). L. *nox*, *noct*is.

Nod—knot; *nod*e (one of the *knots*, or curves, in the moon's orbit). L. *nod*us.

Noi (*anoi*)—vexation; *noi*some (*vexing*). O.F. *anoi*. L. *in*, in; *odi*um, hatred.

Nom—pasture; *nom*ad (a member of a wandering tribe, wandering in quest of *pasture*). G. *nom*os. G. *nem*ein, to assign.

Nom—law; astro*nom*y (the *laws* of the stars), deutero*nom*y, eco*nom*y (the *law* of the household), auto*nom*y (the state of entire or virtual independence, the making of *laws* for self). G. *nom*os. G. *nem*ein, to distribute.

Nom (*nomen*)—name, term; bi*nom*ial (having two *terms*), bi*nom*ial, poly*nom*ial, mis*nom*er (a *misnaming*). L. *nomen*.

Nomen—name; *nomen*clature (terminology, the calling of *names*). L. *nomen*.

Nomin—name; nominal, *nomin*ate, de*nomin*ate. L *nomen*, *nomin*is.

Norm—rule; *norm*al, ab*norm*al (*irregular*), e*norm*o (beyond all *rule*). L. *norm*a.

Not—mark; de*not*e (*mark* down), *not*able, *not*ary writer, *mark*er), *not*e. L. *not*a.

Not—know; *not*ice (a making *known*), *not*ify (m *known*), *not*ion (a conception, what is *known*), n rious (too well *known*). L. *not*cere, *not*us.

Nounce; nunci (*nunti*)—bring tidings, tell; an*nou* de*nounce* (*tell* fully), e*nunci*ate, *nunci*o (a sp envoy or *messenger*), pro*nounce*, re*nounce* (giv *tell* back). L. *nunti*are. L. *nunti*us, a bring tidings.

Nov—new; *nov*el, *nov*ice (a *new* disciple), in*nov* introduce *new* things), re*nov*ate. L. *nov*us.

Novem—nine; *Novem*ber (the *ninth* month Roman year, which began with March). L.

Nox—night; equi*nox*. L. *nox*.

Nox—hurt; *nox*ious. L. *nox*a.

Nu—nod; in*nu*endo (an insinuation, as with the head). L. *nu*ere.

Nub—marry; con*nub*ial. L. *nub*ere.

Nuc—nut; *nuc*leus (a core or center, like the a *nut*). L. *nux*, *nuc*is.

Nud—naked. L. *nud*us.

Nugator—a trifler; *nugat*ory (worthless, as *nugator*. L. *nugar*i, to trifle. L. *nugæ*, tri

Null—none; an*nul*, *null*ify, *null*ity, *null*. none. L. *ne*, not; *ull*us, any.

Numer—number; *numer*ous, *numer*ate, in*numer*able, *numer*ical, super*numera* extra *number*). L. *numer*us.

Numism—current coin; *numism*atic (relat L. *numism*a. G. *nomism*a, *nomiz*ein, *nomos*, a law. G. *nom*ein, to distribute

O

Obed—obey; *obed*ient. L. *obed*ire. L. *ob*, against, near; *aud*ire; to hear, listen.

Obei—obey; *obei*sance (a bow, as if offering to *obey*). O.F. *obei*r. L. *obed*ire.

Obel—a spit; *obel*isk (a pointed shaft, resembling a little roasting *spit*). G. *obel*os.

Obes—fat; *obes*e. L. *obes*us. L. *obed*ere, *obes*us, to cut away. L. *ob*, against; *ed*ere, *es*us, to eat.

Obit—death; *obit*uary (a *death* notice). L. *obit*um. L. *obi*re, *obit*um, to go near, go down. L. *ob*, against, near; *i*re, to go.

Objurg—chide; *objurg*ation (reproof, censure). L. *objurg*are. L. *ob*, against; *jurg*are, to chide. L. *jus*, *jur*is, law; *ag*ere, to urge.

Obliqu—slanting, awry; *oblique*, *obliqu*ity. L. *obliqu*us.

Obliv—forget; *obliv*ion (*forgetfulness*). L. *obliv*isci.

Obscur—dark; *obscur*e (in the *dark*). L. *obscur*us. L. *ob*, against, over; *scur*us, covered.

Obsequi—compliance; *obsequi*ous (offering a groveling *compliance*). L. *obsequi*um. L. *ob*, near; *sequi*, to follow.

Obsol—decay; *obsol*ete, *obsol*escent. L. *obsol*ere.

Obstin—set about, be resolved on; *obstin*ate (determined). L. *obstin*are.

Obstreper—clamorous; *obstreper*ous. L. *obstreper*us. L. *ob*, against; *strepere*, to rattle.

Occiput—back of head. L. *occiput*. L. *ob*, against; *caput*, head.

Occult—concealed; *occult*ation (a *concealing*, observing). L. *occul*ere, *occult*us.

Occup—lay hold of; *occup*y, *occup*ation. L. *occup*are. L. *ob*, near; *cup*ere, to take.

Octav—eighth; *octav*e (an interval in music embracing *eight* notes), octavo (a book made from folding a sheet of paper into *eight* parts). L. *octav*us. L. *octo*, eight.

Ocul—eye; *ocul*ar (relating to the *eye*), *ocul*ist (one who treats the *eye*), bin*ocul*ar (two-*eyed*), mon*ocul*ar, in*ocul*ate (to insert a bud, or *eye*). L. *ocul*us.

Od—song; *od*e, ep*od*e (*sung* after), mel*od*y, mon*od*y (a single *song*), palin*od*e (a recantation, or *singing* back), par*od*y (a *song* beside another in imitation of the latter), pros*od*y (the laws accompanying *song*). G. *od*e. G. *aeid*ein, to sing.

Od—way, road, coming; *od*ometer (an instrument for measuring *roads*), meth*od* (a *way* after), peri*od* (a *way* round, or complete circuit), syn*od* (a *coming* together). G. *od*os.

Odi—hate; *odi*um, *odi*ous. L. *odi*, I hate.

Odyn—pain; an*odyn*e (a remedy that leaves one without *pain*). G. *odyn*e.

Oid (*eid*)—form; aster*oid*, etc. G. *eid*os.

Ol—emit odor; red*ol*ent. L. *ol*ere.

Ole—oil; *ole*aginous (*oily*), petr*ole*um (rock-*oil*). L. *ole*um. G. *elai*on.

Ole—olive-tree; *ole*aster. G. *elai*a.

Olfact—scented; *olfact*ory (relating to *smelling*). L. *olfac*ere, *olfact*us, to scent. L. *ol*ere, to smell; *fac*ere, to make.

Omal (*homal*)—even; an*omal*y (something irregular, and therefore *uneven*). G. *homal*os. G. *hom*os, one and the same.

Omin—omen; *omin*ous, ab*omin*ate (to shrink from as ill-*omened*). L. *omen*, *omin*is.

Omni—all; *omni*present (*all*, or everywhere present),

*omni*potent (*all*-powerful), *omni*scient (*all*-knowing), *omni*bus (designed for *all*). L. *omnis*.

Oner—burden; *oner*ous (*burdensome*), ex*oner*ate (to remove the *burden* of a charge). L. *onus, oner*is.

Onomato—name; *onomato*pœia (*name*-making). G. *onoma, onomatos*.

Onym (*onom*)—name; an*onym*ous (without *name*), hom*onym* (having same *name*), met*onym*y (change of *name*), patr*onym*ic (*father name*), syn*onym* (a *name*, or word, that goes with another). G. *onoma*.

Oo—egg; *oo*lite (a kind of limestone containing grains resembling the *eggs*, or roe, of fish). G. *oon*.

Op—riches; *op*ulent. L. *opes*.

Opac—dark, obscure. L. *opacus*.

Opaqu (*opac*)—dark, obscure; *opaqu*e. L. *opacus*.

Oper—work; *oper*ate, co-*oper*ate (*work* together), *oper*a (a musical *work* or production). L. *opus, oper*is.

Ophi—snake; *ophi*dian, *ophi*cleide (an instrument made by adding keys to an old instrument called, from its twisted form, a *serpent*). G. *ophis*.

Ophthalm—eye; *ophthalm*ia (disease of the *eye*), *ophthalm*oscope (an instrument for examining the *eye*). G. *ophthalmos*.

Opin—suppose; *opin*ion. L. *opin*ari.

Opl (*hopl*)—armor; pan*oply* (in complete *armor*). G. *hopl*a. G. *hopl*on, an implement. G. *hopo*, I am busy about.

Oppid—town; *oppid*an (relating to large *towns*). L. *oppid*um.

Opportun—convenient. L. *opportun*us. L. *ob*, near; *port*us, harbor, access.

Ops—sight, view; aut*ops*y (a post-mortem examination, a *seeing* for one's self), syn*ops*is (a connected *view*). G. *ops*is.

Opt—wish, choose; *opt*ion, *opt*ative (expression of a *wish*), ad*opt* (*choose* to). L. *opt*are.

Opt—see; *opt*ical (relating to *sight*), *opt*ician (a dealer in *optical* instruments). G. *opt*omai, I see.

Optim—best; *optim*ism (a belief that all is for the *best*). L. *optim*us.

Or—mouth; *or*al, *or*ifice (an opening, a *mouth*). L. os, *or*is.

Or; orat—pray, address; ad*ore*, inex*or*able (immovable by *prayer*), *or*ation, *or*ator, *or*ison, per*or*ation (the concluding *address*). L. *or*are, *or*atus. L. *os*, *or*is.

Or—gold. See *aur*.

Oracul—divine announcement; *oracul*ar, *oracle*. L. *oracul*um. L. *or*are, to pray. L. *os*, *or*is, the mouth.

Orama (*horama*)—a view; di*orama* (a *view* through a small opening), pan*orama* (a *view* of all). G. *horama*. G. *hora*o, I see.

Orb—circle, sphere. L. *orb*is.

Orbit—a track; *orbit* (the *path* of a planet), ex*orbit*ant (excessive, going out of the beaten *track*). L. *orbit*a. L. *orb*is, circle, sphere.

Orche—dance; *orche*stra (the place occupied by *dancers* in the ancient theater). G. *orche*omai.

Orcis (*orciz*)—adjure; ex*orcise* (to expel by solemn *adjuration*). G. *orciz*ein. G. *orc*os, an oath.

Ord—begin, weave; ex*ord*ium (the *beginning* of an oration), prim*ord*ial (at the first *beginning*). L. *ord*ire.

Ordin—order; *ordin*al (expressing the *order*), *ordin*ary (according to the customary *order*), *ordin*ation (the conferring of *orders*), sub*ordin*ate (of lower *order*, or rank). L. *ord*o, *ordin*is.

Ordin—order, command, arrange, regulate; co-*ordin*ate (*arranged* together), in*ordin*ate (*unregulated*),

ordinance (an *order* from authority). L. *ordin*are. L. *ord*o, *ordin*is, order.

Org (*erg*)—work; *org*an (a *working* part, an implement), *org*ies (excessive revelry, recalling the ancient rites, or *actions*, in honor of Bacchus), lit*urg*y (public *service*). G. *erg*ein.

Origin—beginning. L. *orig*o, *origin*is.

Orn—adorn, furnish; ad*orn*, *orn*ament, *orn*ate, sub*orn* (to supply, or *furnish*, with false testimony). L. *orn*are.

Ornith—bird; *ornith*ology (the science of *birds*), *ornith*orymcus (having a snout like a *duck*). G. *ornis*, *ornith*os.

Orphan—destitute; *orphan* (*destitute* of parents). G. *orphan*os.

Ortho—straight, correct; *ortho*dox (*correct* opinion), *ortho*epy (the *correct* pronunciation of *words*), *ortho*ceratite (a fossil in the form of a *straight horn*), *ortho*graphy (the *correct writing* of a word). G. *ortho*s.

Oscill—swing; *oscill*ate. L. *oscill*are. L. *oscill*um, a swing. L. *oscill*um, a little mask of Bacchus (*swinging* in the vineyard to propitiate the god of the vine). L. *os*, mouth, countenance.

Oscul—kiss; *oscul*ate. L. *oscul*are. L. *oscul*um, little mouth. L. *os*, mouth.

Oss—bone; *oss*eous (*bony*), *oss*ify (to convert into *bone*). L. *os*, *oss*is.

Oste—bone; *oste*ology (the science of *bones*), peri*oste*um (the covering of a *bone*). G. *oste*on.

Ostens—show, appear; *ostens*ible (in *appearance*). L. *ostend*ere, *ostens*us. L. *ob*, near; *tend*ere, stretch.

Ostrac—potsherd, tile; *ostrac*ize (to banish by voting on *tiles*, or shells). G. *ostrac*on. G. *ostre*on, oyster.

Outr—beyond; *outr*age (*excessive* violence). F. *outr*e. L. *ultr*a.

Ov—egg; *ov*al (*egg*-shaped), *ov*iform, *ov*iparous (*egg*-producing), syn*ov*ium (the membrane encasing the *egg*-shaped bone at a joint). L. *ov*um.

Ov—shout; *ov*ation (a *loud-voiced* welcome). L. *ov*are.

Overt—opened, open; *ov*ert (public, *open* to view), *ov*erture (a piece of music rendered at the beginning, or *opening*, also a proposal, an *opening* of a question), *ov*erture (a *beginning*, a proposal). O.F. *ov*eir, *ov*ert.

Oxy—sharp, acid; *oxy*gen (the *acid*-producer), *oxy*mal (a mixture of the *acid* vinegar with *honey*), par*ox*ysm (the fit of a disease, a *sharpening* beside). G. *ox*us.

Oz—smell; *oz*one (a peculiar principle in the atmosphere, noticed by its *smell* after an electric discharge). G. *oz*ein.

P

Pabul—food. L. *pabul*um. L. *pasc*ere, to feed.

Pac—peace; *pac*ify (to quiet, make *peace*). L. *pax*, *pac*is.

Pac (*pass*)—step; *pac*e. L. *pass*us. L. *pand*ere, *pass*us.

Pachy—thick; *pachy*derm (having *thick* skin), *pachy*-cephalous (having *thick* head). G. *pach*us.

Pact—fastened; com*pact* (*fastened* together), im*pact* (a *fastening*, or sticking, against). L. *pang*ere, *pact*us.

Pact—agreed; *pact* (an *agreement*), com*pact* (an *agreement* or bargain with). L. *pacisc*i, *pact*us. L. *pac*ere, to agree.

Pæd—child; *pæd*obaptism, *ped*agogue (a *child*-instructor). G. *pais*, *paid*os.

Palæ (*palai*)—old, ancient; *palæ*ography (the study of *ancient* writings), *palæ*ology (the study of *ancient* remains), *palæ*ontology (the study of life in *ancient* geological ages). G. *palai*os. G. *palai*, long ago.

Pale (*palai*)—wrestle; *pale*stra (a *wrestling*-school). G. *palai*ein. G. *pale*, a wrestling.

Palin—again; *palin*drome (a word or sentence which is the same whether read forward of back; it therefore runs back *again*; as, *madam*), *palin*ode (an *ode* in which a recantation, or recalling *again*, is made), *palim*psest (a manuscript on which a second writing has been made, and to receive which the surface was *rubbed*, or prepared, *again*[1]). G. *palin*.

Palis—pale, stake; *palis*ade (a defense of heavy *stakes*). F. *palis*. F. *pal*.

Pall—man- L. *pall*a.

Pall (*paill*)—straw; *pall*et (a *straw* bed or mattress). F. *paill*e.

Pall—become pale; *pall*id, *pall*or, *pale*. L. *pall*ere.

Palli—cloak; *palli*ate (to excuse, as if covering with a *cloak*). L. *palli*um.

Palp—feel; *palp*able. L. *palp*are. L. *palp*ari, to handle.

Palpit—throb; *palpit*ate. L. *palpit*are. L. *palp*are, to feel, quiver.

Pamp—cram, glut; *pamp*er. Low Ger. *pamp*en. Low Ger. *pamp*e, broth.

Pan—bread; *pan*try (the *bread* room), *pan*nier (a *bread*-basket), ap*pan*age (a dependency granted to a relative for his *bread*, or maintenance), com*pan*y (those eating *bread* together). L. *pan*is.

Pand; pans—spread out; ex*pand*, ex*panse*, ex*pans*ive. L. *pand*ere, *pass*us.

Papaver—paper. L. *papaver*.

Papilion—butterfly; *papilion*aceous. L. *papilio*, *papilion*is.

Par—equal; dis*par*ity (*inequality*), dis*par*age (make light of, render *unequal*), *par* (an amount *equal* to the face value), *par*ity (a putting of like, or equal, things together), *pair* (two equal things), *peer* (an *equal*), com*peer* (an associate, a familiar *equal*). L. *par*.

Par—get ready, set; com*pare* (*set* together), *par*ade (a display *gotten up* specially), pre*pare* (*get ready* beforehand), re*pair* (*get ready* again), se*par*ate (*set* apart), se*ver* (*set* apart), se*ver*al (more than two, separated, or *set* apart), *pare* (to trim, *get ready*). L. *par*are.

Par—ward off, guard; *par*asol (a shade to *ward off* the sun), *par*apet (a rampart for *guarding* the breast), *par*achute (an apparatus for breaking, or *warding* *off*, the fall from a balloon). F. *par*er. It. *par*are. L. *par*are, to get ready.

Par—produce, bring forth, come into sight; *par*ent (one who *brings forth* offspring), ap*pear* (to *come into view*). L. *par*ere.

Pariet—wall; *pariet*al (forming the *wall* of the skull). L. *paries*, *pariet*is.

Parl—speak; *parl*ance (a form of *speech*), *parl*ey (to *speak* with an enemy about conditions), *parl*iament (a deliberative, or *speaking*, body), *parl*or (a room for *conversation*), *parol*e (a *verbal* promise). F. *parl*er.

Parochi—neighborhood, parish; *parochi*al (belonging to a *parish*), *parish*. L. *parochi*a. G. *paroiki*a. G. *paroic*os, neighboring. G. *para*, near; *oic*os, house.

Parr (*patr*)—father; *parr*icide (the killing of a *father*). L. *pater*, *patr*is.

Pars; part—part; a*part* (to one side, or *part*), a*part*ment (a room a*part* from others), *parc*el (a little bundle, or *part*), *pars*e (to give the *parts* of speech and their properties), *part*ial (leaning to one side, or *part*), *part*icle (a little *part*), *por*tion. L. *pars*, *part*is.

Pars (*parc*)—sparing; *pars*imony (stinginess, excessive *sparing*). L. *parc*us.

Part; partit—divide, share, separate; com*part*ment (one of *similar divisions* of an inclosed space), de*part*, im*part* (give a *share to*), *part*isan (one who adheres strongly to a side, as a *sharer* in its fortunes), *part*ition, *part*y (a *division*), re*part*ee (a witty reply, a *sharing again*), tri*part*ite (of *three parts*). L. *part*ire.

Particip—sharing in; *particip*ate, *particip*al. L. *particep*s, *particip*is. L. *pars*, *part*is, part; *cap*ere, to take.

Pass—step; com*pass* (a circuit, a *step* around, hence to embrace), *pace* (a *step*), *pass* (to *step* by), *pass*age (a means of *passing*), *pass*port (a permission to *pass* through the *port*), sur*pass* (*pass* beyond), tres*pass* (*pass* beyond the limit of another's right). L. *pass*us.

Pass—See *pat.*

Past—feed; *past*ure (a *feeding* place for animals), *past*oral (relating to shepherds, the *feeders* of flocks), *past*or (the *feeder* of a flock), *past*ern (the joint by which a horse is tethered at *pasture*), *past*el (a colored crayon resembling a little roll of *bread* or *food*), *past*ille (a small cone of aromatic substance, resembling a little roll of *bread*), re*past* (a meal, a *feeding* again), *pest*er (to bother, hamper, like hobbling a horse, in the *pasture*). L. *pass*ere, *past*us.

Pat—lie open; *pat*ent (quite apparent, *open* to view). L. *pat*ere.

Pat; pass—suffer, feel, endure; *pat*ient (a *sufferer*), *pat*ient (*enduring*), com*pat*ible (harmonizing with, *enduring together*), *pass*ive (*suffering*, submitting, *enduring*), *pass*ion (strong *feeling*), com*pass*ion (*suffering* or *feeling* with). L. *pat*i, *pass*us.

Pat—walk; peri*pat*etic (*walking* around). G. *pat*eo. G. *pat*os, path.

Pater; patr—father; *pater*nal, *patr*ician (of noble rank, like the Roman senators, or *fathers*[2]), *patr*iarch, *patr*imony (inheritance from a *father*), *patr*on (a protector, as of a *father*), *patr*onymic (a *father's* name modified[3]). L. *pater*, *patr*is.

Path—feel, suffer; *path*etic (stirring the *feelings*), *path*os (that which causes *feeling*), anti*path*y (intense dislike, a *feeling against*), homœo*path*y (see *homœ*), hydro*path*y (see *hydr*), allo*path*y (see *all*), sympa*th*y (a *feeling with* another in his troubles). G. *path*ein.

Patr—See *pater*.

Patri—country, race; *patri*ot (a lover of his *country*), ex*patri*ate (to send into exile, *out* of one's *country*). L. *patri*a. G. *patri*a. L. G. *pater*,[4] father.[5]

Pau—cease; *pau*se, re*pos*e (*pause*, or rest, *again*). G. *pau*ein.

Pauper—poor; *pauper*, *pover*ty, *poor*. L. *pauper*.

Pecc—sin; *pecc*able, *pecc*ant, *pecc*adillo. L. *pecc*are.

Pectin—comb; *pectin*al. L. *pecten*, *pectin*is.

Pector—breast, chest; *pector*al, ex*pector*ate (to spit, to expel as from the *chest*). L. *pect*us, *pector*is.

Pecul—appropriate to one's own use; *pecul*ate (to *appropriate* trust funds). L. *pecul*ari.

Peculi—private property, uncommon; *peculi*ar. L. *peculi*um.

Pecuni—property, money; *pecuni*ary (relating to *money*). L. *pecuni*a. L. *pecus*, cattle, property.

Ped (*pæd*)—boy, child; *ped*obaptism (the baptism of a *child*), *ped*agogue (the leader of a *child*[6]). G. *pai*s, *paid*os.

Ped—foot; *ped*al (pertaining to the *foot*), bi*ped* (a two-*footed* animal), ex*ped*ite (to make *foot*-loose), im*ped*e (to entangle the *foot*), *ped*estal (the *foot*-stall), *ped*icel (the *foot*-stalk of a leaf), quadru*ped* (a four-*footed* animal). L. *pes*, *ped*is.

Pelag—sea; archi*pelag*o (a sea interspersed with many islands, like the Ægean, the *chief sea* of the ancient Greeks). G. *pelag*os.

Pell; puls—drive, urge; com*pel* (*drive with*), dis*pel* (*drive apart*), ex*pel* (*drive out*), im*pel* (*urge against*), pro*pel* (*drive forward*), re*pel* (*drive back*), re*puls*e (an overthrow, a *drive back*), *puls*e (the throb, or *drive*, of blood through the arteries), appeal (call, or *urge, upon*). L. *pell*ere, *puls*us.

Pell—skin, fur; *pell*icle (a thin film, a *small skin*), *pel*t (a *skin*), *pel*isse (a silk habit, formerly a *furred* robe), peel (strip off the *skin*), sur*pl*ice (an outer garment, formerly made of *skins*). L. *pell*is.

Pelv—a base; *pelv*is (the bony cavity at the *base* of the abdomen). L. *pelv*is.

Pen (*pœn*)—pain, punishment, penalty; *pen*al (related to *punishment*), *pen*itent (deeply sorry, suffering the *punishment* of regret), *pun*ish (to inflict a *penalty*), im*pun*ity (*freedom from punishment*), sub*pœn*a (an order to appear at court *under* a *penalty* for disobedience), *pain*, re*pent* (suffer *pain*). L. *pœn*a.

Pend; pens—hang, weigh (as in a hanging scale), pay (as if by weight); *pend*ant (a *hanging* ornament), *pend*ent (*hanging*), *pend*ulous (*hanging*), *pend*ulum (the *hanging* wire of a clock), *pens*ile (*suspended*), *pens*ion (a sum *paid* at intervals as a gratuity), *pens*ive (sad, thoughtful, tending to ponder or *weigh* matters), ap*pend* (add to, *hang* to), com*pend*ium (an abridgment, a saving of *expense*), com*pens*ate (*pay* an equivalent, or what will *weigh with* the article or favor received), de*pend* (*hang from, hang* on), ex*pend* (*pay out, weigh out*), im*pend* (*hang over*), pansy (the flower of thought, a pondering or *weighing*), per*pend*icular (forming a right angle, as does the *hanging* plummet with the horizon), pre*pense* (*weighed*, or pondered, *beforehand*, premeditated), pro*pens*ity (a leaning toward, a *hanging forward*), sus*pend* (*hang under*). L. *pend*ere, *pens*us.

Penetr—pierce into; *penetr*ate. L. *penetr*are.

Penn—feather, wing; *pen* (a writing implement, formerly made of a quill or *feather*), *penn*on (a streamer, beating the air like a *wing* or *feather*). L. *penn*a.

Pens—See *pend*.

Penuri—want, need; *penury* (extreme *destitution*),

*penuri*ous (extremely sparing, as if in great *need*). L. *penuri*a.

Peps; pept—cook, digest; *peps*ine (a substance that aids *digestion*), dys*peps*ia (*bad digestion*). G. *pept*ein.

Per—try; experience (*thorough trial*), expert (*thoroughly tried*, hence skilled), *per*il (great danger, or *trial*). L. *per*iri.

Per—come to naught; *per*ish (to be lost, to decay, *come to naught*). L. *per*ire.

Peregrin—travel; *peregrin*ation (*traveling* about), *pilgrim*[7] (a *traveler*). L. *peregrin*ari. L. *peregrin*us, foreign. L. *per*eger, a traveler. L. *per*, through; *eger, ager*, a field, land.

Perfid—treacherous; *perfid*y (*treachey*). L. *perfid*us (literally "putting *away faith*"). L. *per*, away; *fides*, faith.

Pernici—destruction; *pernici*ous (extremely injurious, or *destructive*). L. *pernici*es (literally "*thorough slaughter*"). L. *per*, thorough; *nex, nec*is, slaughter.

Perpendicul—plummet; *perpendicul*ar (forming a right angle, as does the plummet with the horizon). M. *perpendicul*um (literally "the *careful measurer*"). L. *per*, thoroughly; *pend*ere, to weigh.

Perpetr—perform thoroughly; *perpetr*ate. L. *perpetr*are.

Perpetu—continuous; *perpetu*al (*continuing* forever). L. *perpetu*us. L. *perpes, perpet*is.

Pervicac—willful; *pervicac*ious. L. *pervicax, pervicac*is.

Pessim—worst; *pessim*ist (one who sees in society a tendency to the *worst*). L. *pessim*us.

Pest—plague; *pest*, *pest*iferous (*plague*-bringing, detestable), *pest*ilent (hurtful as a *plague*), *pest*ilence (the *plague*). L. *pest*us.

Pest (*paist*)—struck; ana*pest* (a foot in prosody, the exact reverse, or *strike back*, of a dactyl). G. *paist*os. G. *pai*ein, to strike.

Pet (*pett*)—breast; para*pet* (a defense for the *breast*). It. *pett*o. L. *pect*us.

Pet; petit—attack, seek, ask; *petit*ion(a request, an *asking*), ap*petit*e (the desire for food, the inclination to make an *attack upon* food), com*pet*ent (being sufficient for, *seeking with*), com*petit*or (a rival, one who *seeks* an object *with* another), im*pet*us (an *attack upon*), im*pet*uous (rushing forward, as to an *attack*), *pet*ulant (fretful, ready to *attack*), repeat (*attack again*). L. *pet*ere, *petit*us.

Petal—leaf; *petal* (one of the *leaves* of a flower). G. *petal*on.

Petiol—little stalk; *petiol*e (the *footstalk* of a leaf). L. *petiol*us.

Petr—stone, rock; *petr*ify (turn into *stone*), *petr*oleum (*rock-oil*), salt*peter* (the *salt* of the *rock*), *Peter* (a *rock*), *Petr*æa (the *Rocky* Arabia), *pier* (a mass of *stone*-work). G. *petr*os, *petr*a.

Phag—devour, eat; anthropo*phag*i (cannibals, *man-eaters*), eso*phag*us (the gullet which *carries* to the stomach what is *eaten*), sarco*phag*us (a stone receptacle for a body, formerly supposed to consume, or *devour*, the *flesh*). G. *phag*ein.

Phalanx; phalang—a battalion. G. *phalanx*,[8] *phalang*os.

Phan—show, bring to light, appear; *phan*tom (an *appearance*, a specter), dia*phan*ous (transparent, *showing through*), Epi*phan*y (the feast of the *showing forth* of the Savior to the wise men of the East), *fan*cy (the power of mind which causes images to *appear*), *fan*tastic (odd, in the nature of a *phan*tom of the imagination). G. *phan*ein.

Pharmac—drug; *pharmac*y (a place where *drugs* are

compounded), *pharmaco*poeia (a treatise on the *making* of *medicines*). G. *pharmaco*n.

Phas—appearance, declaration; *phase* (an *appearance* presented), em*phasis* (special *stress upon* a word). G. *phasis*.

Phem—speech; blas*pheme* (to *speak hurtful* things of sacred personages or subjects) eu*phemism* (a figure by which a harsh expression is softened, a *well speaking*). G. *pheme*. G. *phemi*, I say.

Phen (*phain*)—show, appear; *phen*omenon (an *appearance*), *phen*ogam (see *gam*). G. *phain*ein.

Pher—carry, bear, bring; peri*phery* (the circumference, or line *bearing around*, of a polygon), para*pher*nalia (apparel and ornaments, like the outfit of a bride *brought* to the *side* of her husband's possessions), Christo*pher* (the *Christ bearer*[9]). G. *pher*ein, to bear.

Phet—spoken; pro*phet* (one who *foretells*). G. *phet*es. G. *phemi*, I say.

Phil—fond, loving; *phil*anthropy (see *anthrop*), *phil*osophy (*love* of *wisdom*), *phil*ology (the history of language, *love* of *words*), *phil*ter (a *love* potion), *Phil*ander (a *lover* of *man*), *Phil*ip (a *lover* of *horse*), Theo*phil*us (a *lover* of *God*). G. *phil*os.

Phleb—vein; *phleb*otomy (blood-letting, and therefore *vein-cutting*). G. *phlebs*, *phleb*os.

Phleg—burn; *phleg*m (a viscous humour supposed to be due to inflammation, a *burning*). G. *phleg*ein.

Phoc—seal; *phoc*ine (relating to *seals*). L. *phoc*a. G. *phoc*e.

Phon—sound; *phon*ic (belonging to *sounds*), *phon*etic (representing *sounds*), eu*phony* (*sounding well*), sym*phony* (harmony, *sounding together*). G. *phon*e.

Phor—bringing; phos*phor*us (see *phos*; *bringing* light), meta*phor* (a transferring, or *carrying over*, of a word from one use to another). G. *phoro*s. G. *phere*in, to bear.

Phos; phot—light; *phos*phorus (the *light-bearing* substance), *phot*ograph (*written*, or produced, by *light*). G. *phos*, *phot*os.

Phrag—fence; dia*phrag*m (the great *fence* between the thorax and abdomen). G. *phrag*numi, I fence.

Phras—a speaking; *phras*e. G. *phras*is. G. *phras*ein, to speak.

Phren—brain, mind; *phren*ology (the science of the special parts of the *brain*). G. *phren*.

Phtheg (*phtheng*)—cry out, utter; apo*phtheg*m (a terse saying, or *utterance*). G. *phtheng*omai.

Phthis—consumption; *phthis*is (*consumption* of the lungs), *phthis*ic. G. *phthis*is. G. *phthin*ein, to decay.

Phthong—sound; di*phthong* (*double sound*), a*phthong* (*without sound*). G. *phthong*os. G. *phtheng*omai, I cry out.

Phylacter—guardian; *phylacter*y (an amulet used as a *protection*). G. *phulacter*. G. *phulass*ein, to guard.

Phyll—leaf; *phyll*ophagous (*leaf-devouring*, living on leaves), chloro*phyl* (the *green* pulpy substance in a *leaf*). G. *phull*on.

Physi—nature; *physi*ognomy (*knowledge* of one's *nature* obtained from the features), *physi*ology (the *science* of the *nature*, or functions, of the organs of a body), *physi*c (a remedy adapted to the *nature* of the body), *physi*cs (the science of the *nature* of material things). G. *phusis*. G. *phue*in, to produce.

Phyt—plant, grown; *phyt*ology (the *science* of *plants*), *phyt*ionous (living on *plants*, or *plant-devouring*), neo*phyte* (a new convert, one *newly planted*). G. *neos*, *phyt*on. G. *phue*in, to grow.

Pi—propitiate; ex*pi*ate (to atone for, to suffer for,

hence to satisfy or *propitiate*), *pi*acular (having power to atone, or *propitiate*). L. *pi*are (literally "to appease with pious rites"). L. *pi*us.

Pi—devout; *pi*ous, *pi*ety, *pi*ty (sympathy, a characteristic of *piety*). L. *pi*us.

Piano—even, smooth, soft; *piano*forte (see *fort*). It. *piano*. L. *plan*us, even, level (see *plane*).

Pict—paint; *pict*ure (a *painting*), de*pict* (to describe vividly, as if to *paint down*). L. *ping*ere, *pict*us.

Pig (*ping*)—paint; *pig*ment (a *paint*). L. *ping*ere.

Pil—rob; com*pil*e (gather together from various sources, as *robbers* do theirs spoils). L. *pil*are.

Pil—hair; de*pil*atory (removing *hair*), *pl*ush (a *hairy* fabric). L. *pil*us.

Pil—pillar; *pil*lar, *pil*e. L. *pil*a.

Ping (*pang*)—fasten; im*ping*e (*fasten against*). L. *pang*ere.

Pinn—feather, wing; *pinn*ate (having leaflets like *feathers*), *pin*ion. L. *pinn*a, *penn*a.

Pinn—peak; *pinn*acle. Low L. *pinn*a. L. *pinn*a, a feather.

Pir (*peir*)—a trial, attempt; em*pir*ic (settling by *trial* or experience), *pir*ate (a *daring* rover). G. *peir*a.

Pisc—fish; *pisc*atorial, *pisc*iculture. L. *pisc*is.

Pist—pound; *pist*on (the *pounding* cylinder in a pump barrel, or in the cylinder of a stem-engine), *pest*le (an implement for *pounding* substances in a mortar), *pist*il (a *pestle*-like part of a flower). L. *pins*ere, *pist*us.

Plac—please; *plac*able (capable of being mollified, or rendered *pleased*), *plac*id (composed, as if thoroughly *pleased*), com*plac*ent (being thoroughly *pleased with* one's self). L. *plac*ere.

Plag—stroke, blow; *plag*ue (a heavy *blow*, a destructive disease). L. *plag*a.

Plagi—kidnapping; *plagi*ary (the stealer of another's writing, as if a *kidnapper* of the child of his brain). L. *plagi*um.

Plain (*plan*)—level, flat; *plain* (a *level* surface), ex*plain* (to make *thoroughly* clear, or *level*). L. *plan*us.

Plain (*plang*)—lament, bewail. L. *plang*ere.

Plaint (*planct*)—bewail, complain; *plaint*, *plaint*ive, *plaint*iff, com*plaint*. L. *plang*ere, *planct*us.

Plais—please; com*plais*ant (endeavoring to *please*). F. *plais*ic.

Plan—flat, level, smooth; es*plan*ade (a *leveled* place in a park), *plan* (a representation on a *flat* surface), *plan*e, *plan*k. L. *plan*us.

Plan—wandering; *plan*et (one of the *wandering*, as contrasted with the fixed, stars). G. *plan*e.

Plant—plant. L. *plant*a.

Plant—sole of the foot; *plant*igrade (walking on the *sole of the foot*). L. *plant*a.

Plas(s)—mold, form; *plas*ter (a substance easily *molded* on), *plas*tic (soft, easily *molded*), proto-*plas*m (the vital vegetable substance, the *first form* of life in matter). G. *plas*sein.

Plat—flat; *plat*itude (a *flat* expression), *plat*form, *plat*eau, *plat*e. F. *plat*. G. *plat*us, broad.

Plat—silver; *plat*ina (a *silver*-like metal). Sp. *plat*a. O.F. *plat*e, hammered plate. F. *plat*, flat.

Plaud; plaus—clap hands; ap*plaud*, *plaud*it, *plau*sible, ex*plode*. L. *plaud*ere.

Ple; plet—fill; com*ple*ment (that which *completes*, or *fills out*), com*ple*te (*filled out*), de*ple*tion (emptying, or *un-filling*), ex*ple*tive (a word that *fills out* an expression without adding to the sense), im*ple*ment (a tool used in executing, or *filling in*, a work), re*ple*te (thoroughly *filled, filled back*), sup*ple*ment (an addition, a *fill up*), supply (to provide, to *fill under*). L. *ple*re, *plet*us.

Ple—to sail; *Ple*iades[10] (a constellation of seven stars, whose rising indicated a safe time to *sail*). G. *ple*ein.

Pleb—the people; *pleb*eian (of the common *people*). L. *pleb*s, *pleb*is.

Plen—full; *plen*ty, re*plen*ish (*fill again*), *plen*itude, *plen*ary (complete, very *full*), *plen*ipotentiary (having *full powers*). L. *plen*us.

Pleon—more; *pleon*asm (a *redundancy* of speech). G. *pleon*, *pleion*. G. *pleo*s, full.

Pleth—crowd, throng; *pleth*ora (fullness, as of a *thronging* quantity). G. *pleth*os.

Pleur—rib, side; *pleur*a (the covering of the lungs, secluded near the *ribs*), *pleur*isy (inflammation of the *pleura*). G. *pleur*a.

Plev—be in surety; re*plev*y (to reclaim goods on a *pledge* to try the right in a suit). Low L. *pleb*ere.

Pli—fold, bend; *pli*able, *pli*ant (easily *bent*), ap*ply* (*bend* to a task), ap*ply* (*fold* to), de*ploy* (*unfold*), dis*play* (un-*fold*), em*ploy* (*fold* in), im*ply* (*fold* in), re*ply* (*fold* back), sup*pli*ant (*bending* under). F. *pli*er. L. *plic*are.

Plic—fold, bend, embrace, twine; com*plic*ate (make complex, or *twined* together), ex*plic*ate (explain, un-*fold*), ex*plic*it (distinct, unmistakable, thoroughly un-*folded*), im*plic*ate (to involve, *embrace*, or include in some questionable transaction), im*plic*it (complete, unreserved, *embracing* fully), sim*plic*ity (of a single, or the *same*, *fold*), sup*plic*ate (to entreat on *bended* knee), du*plic*ate (a copy, making the original *twofold*). L. *plic*are.

Plinth—brick, tile; *plinth* (the lower, or *brick*-shaped, part of the base of a column). G. *plinth*os.

Plio (*pleion*)—more; *plio*cene (pertaining to the *more recent* tertiary deposits). G. *pleion*, more; *cain*os, recent.

Plo—folded; di*plo*ma (a document conferring some

power or honor, formerly double, or *twofold*). G. *plo*os.

Plor—to cry out, wail; de*plore* (to *wail thoroughly*, to lament), ex*plore* (to search *out*, like the *crying* hounds on the chase). L. *plor*are.

Plum—feather; *plum*age (the *feathers* of a bird), *plume* (a waving *feather*), *plume* (to take pride in, as a *feather* in the cap), nom de *plume* (the "*name of the pen*," which was formerly a quill, or feather, an assumed name of a writer). L. *plum*a.

Plumb—lead; *plumb* (a piece of *lead* on a string), *plumb*ago (like *lead*), *plumb*er (a worker in *lead*), *plummet* (a *lead*-line), *plump* (straight downward, like the *lead*). L. *plumb*um.

Plur—more; *plur*al (expressing *more* that one). L. *plus*, *plur*is.

Pluvi—rain; *pluvi*al (*rainy*), *plov*er (the bird of the *rainy* season). L. *pluvi*a.

Pneumat—wind, air; *pneum*atic (relating to *wind* or *air*). G. *pneuma*, *pneumat*os. G. *pne*ein, to blow.

Pneumon—lung; *pneumon*ia. G. *pneumon*. G. *pne*ein, to blow.

Po (*poi*)—make; *po*em (a production, or thing *made*), *po*esy, *po*et (the *maker*), onomatopæa (*word-making*). G. *poi*ein.

Poach (*poch*)—pouch, bag; *poach* (to steal game and carry it off in a *bag*), *poach* (to cook an egg so as to preserve it in the form of a *pouch*). F. *poch*e.

Pod—foot; anti*pod*es (those with *feet* directly *opposite*), chiro*pod*ist (one who attends to the *hands* and *feet*), tri*pod* (a *three-footed* frame). G. *pous*, *pod*os.

Poign (*pung*)—prick; *poign*ant. L. *pung*ere.

Pois—weigh, balance; *pois*e, equi*pois*e. O.F. *pois*er, *peis*er.

Pol—make smooth; *pol*ish, inter*pol*ate (insert, *polish*, in between), *pol*ite (*polished*). L. *pol*ire.

Pol—sell; mono*poly* (*selling alone*). G. *pol*ein.

Polem—war; *polem*ical (*war*-like). G. *polem*os.

Polis—city; acro*polis* (an upper *city*), metro*polis* (a great commercial center, like an ancient *mother city*, or founder of colonies), necro*polis* (the *city* of the *dead*). G. *polis*, city.

Polit—citizen, subject of government; *polit*y (form of *government*), cosmo*polit*e (a *citizen* of the *world*). G. *polit*es. G. *polis*, city.

Poll—fine flour; *poll*en (the *flour*-dust of flowers). L. *poll*is.

Pom—apple; *pom*egranate (the *apple* with *grains* or seeds in it), *pom*mel (the *apple*, or knob of a saddle), *pom*ade (formerly made of *apples*). L. *pom*um.

Pomp—a sending, procession; *pomp* (display, like a *procession*). G. *pomp*ein, to send.

Pon—to place, put; com*pon*ent (composing, or *placing together*), de*pon*ent (*putting down, putting aside*), ex*pon*ent (*placing out*), op*pon*ent (one opposing, or *placing against*), post*pon*e (*place after*). L. *pon*ere.

Ponder—weigh; *ponder*, *ponder*able, *ponder*ous, im*ponder*able, pre*ponder*ate (*out-weigh*). L. *ponder*are. L. *pond*us, *ponder*is, a weight.

Pont—bridge; *pont*oon (a float used in the construction of a temporary *bridge*), *pont*iff (the chief priest at Rome; the pope; originally an officer having charge of the construction of roadways and *bridges*). L. *pons*, *pont*is.

Popul—people; *popul*ar, *popul*ate, *popul*ace, de*popul*ate. L. *popul*us.

Por—passage; *por*e. G. *por*os.

Porc—pig; *porc*ine (*pig*-like), *pork*, *porc*upine (the *pig* with the *spines*), *por*poise (the *pig*-fish). L. *porc*us.

Port—carry, bear, bring; *port*able (capable of being

moved about, or *carried*), *port*er (a *carrier* of burdens), *port*age (a *carrying* place between two lakes or streams[11]), *port*folio (a case for *carrying* papers), *port*manteau (a bag for *carrying clothes*), *port*ly (of large size and dignified *bearing*), com*port* (suit, *carry with*), de*port* (*bear*), dis*port* (amuse, *carry away*), ex*port* (*carry out*), im*port* (*carry into*), im*port* (to signify, *bring in*), im*port* (*signification*), im*port*ant (of serious *import*), pur*port* (to imply, *carry* through), re*port* (*bring back*), s*port* (for *disport*), su*pport* (uphold, *bear under*), trans*port* (*carry across*, beyond). L. *port*are.

Port—harbor, entrance, door, gate, access; *port* (an *entrance* for vessels), *port*al (a *gate*), *port*cullis (a *sliding gate.* See *col*), *port*er (a *gate-keeper*), *port*ico (a porch at an *entrance*), op*port*une (timely, having ready *access*), im*port*une (to urge, when there is not ready *access*). L. *port*us.

Pos—place, put, lay; com*pose* (*put together*), de*pose* (*put aside*), dis*pose* (*place apart*), ex*pose* (*place out*), im*pose* (*lay upon*), inter*pose* (*put between*), op*pose* (*place against*), *pose* (to *oppose* with troublesome questions), pro*pose* (*place before*), pur*pose* (intend, *place before* the mind), *puz*zle (a difficult question presented, or *opposed*, for solution), re*pose* (*place back*), sup*pose* (imagine, *place under*), trans*pose* (*put across*), *pose* (an attitude, a *placing*). F. *pos*er. G. *paus*is, a pause. G. *pau*ein, to cease. G. *pau*esthai, to cease.

Pos—a drink; sym*pos*ium (a merry feast, a *drinking together*). G. *pos*is.

Posit—place, put, settle; *posit*ion (a *placing*), *posit*ive (decided, *settled*), ap*posit*e (suitable, *put near*), com*posit*ion (a *placing together*), de*posit* (*place* *down*), dis*posit*ion (a *placing apart*), ex*posit*ion (an exposing, or *placing out*), im*posit*ion (an imposing, or *putting upon*), im*post* (a tax *put upon* goods), im*post*or (a deceiver, one who *imposes* or *puts upon*), inter*posit*ion (an interposing or *putting between*), juxta*posit*ion (a *placing near*), op*posit*e (*placed against*), *post*ure (a *placing*), pre*posit*ion (a word *placed before* a noun or pronoun to show its relation to some other word), pro*posit*ion (a statement *put forward*), re*posit*ory (a store-house where things are *laid away*), sup*posit*ion (a supposing or *putting under*), trans*posit*ion (a transposing or *putting across*). L. *pon*ere, *posit*us.

Poss—be able, have power; *poss*ible (within the scope of *ability*), *poss*e (a sheriff's party, the *power* of the county). L. *posse*.

Poster—coming after; *poster*ity (the generations *coming after*), *poster*ior (later, *coming after*, also hinder), *poster*n (a *back* door or gate), pre*poster*ous (thoroughly absurd, reversing all the suggestions of reason, placing the *after before*). L. *poster*us.

Posthum (*postum*)—latest born; *posthum*ous (*born after* the death of the father, hence, appearing after the death of the author). L. *posthum*us.

Postul—ask, demand; *postul*ate (an assumed, or *demanded*, supposition), ex*postul*ate (to reason earnestly with, to *ask from*). L. *postul*are.

Pot—drink; *pot*ion (a *draught*), *pot*ation (a drinking bout), *pot*able (fit to *drink*). L. *pot*are. L. *pot*us, drunken.

Potent—powerful; *potent*ate (one having great political *power*), omni*potent* (*all-powerful*), *potent* (*powerful*), *potent*ial (having latent *power*), pleni*potent*iary (a person invested with *full power*, such as power to negotiate a treaty). L. potens, *potent*is.

Poul—a hen; *poultry* (domestic *fowls*), *pullet* (a *young hen*). F. *poule*.

Pract (*pracs*)—do; *practice* (to *do*), *practical* (capable of being *done*). G. *prass*ein.

Practic—fit for business. G. *practic*os. G. *prass*ein, to do, accomplish.

Pragm—a deed, thing done; *pragm*atic (pertaining to *business*). G. *pragm*a.

Prais—See *preci*.

Pras—leek; chryso*pras*e (a stone of a yellow-green color, resembling a combination of *gold* and the green *leek*). G. *pras*on.

Prav—crooked; de*prav*e (make *utterly crooked*). L. *prav*us.

Precari—to pray; *precari*ous (doubtful, calling for *prayer*). L. *precari*.

Precat—pray; de*precat*e (*pray* to remove), im*precat*e (call down *upon* in *prayer*). L. *precari*, *precatus*.

Preci (*preti*)—price, value; *preci*ous (of *value*), ap*preci*ate (to *value*, to increase the *value* of), de*preci*ate (to put *down* the *value*), *prais*e (to *value*). L. *preti*um.

Precipic (*precipit*)—headlong; *precipic*e (a *headlong* descent). L. *præceps*, *præcipit*is. L. *præ*, before; *caput*, *capit*is, the head.

Precipit—headlong; *precipit*ate (to cast *headlong*). See *precipic*.

Precoci—prematurely ripe; *precoci*ous. L. *præcox*. L. *præ*, before; *coqu*ere, to cook, ripen.

Pred (*præd*)—booty; *pred*atory (in quest of *booty*). L. *præd*a.

Predic—proclaim, declare; *predic*ate (to *assert* as belonging to something), *predic*ate (that which is *predic*ated, or asserted, of a thing), *preach* (to *declare* the word). L. *prædic*are, literally "to *say before*." L. *præ*, before; *dic*ere, to say.

Pregn—See *prehend*.

Prehend; prehens—take, seize, grasp; ap*prehend* (to *seize upon*), com*prehend* (to *grasp together*, to include), re*prehend* (to reprove, to *hold back*), *prehens*ile (capable of *grasping*), im*pregn*able (not to be *taken*). L. *prehend*ere, *prehens*us.

Prem—See *prim*.

Premi—See *em*.

Presbyter—elder; *presbyter*y (an assembly of the *elders* of a church[12]), *priest* (the *elder*). G. *presbuteros*.

Prestigi—weight or influence; *prestige*. L. *præstigi*um.

Prim—first; *prim*e (in the *first* stage or condition), *prim*ary (in the *first* stage), *prim*er (a *first* book), *prim*eval (of the *first age*), *prim*itive (in the *first* stage), *prim*ogenitive (the system of favoring the *first-born*), *prim*rose (the *first* rose of spring), *prim* (neat, delicate, like a *first* crop of hair), *prem*ier (the *first* officer of a cabinet). L. *prim*us.

Princip—chief; *princip*al, *princip*le (a truth of *chief* importance), *princip*ality (the domain of a prince or *chief*), *princ*e (one of the *chief* men). L. *princ*eps, *princip*is.

Prior—before. L. *prior*.

Pris (*prehens*)—seize, grasp, hold; *pris*on, *pris*e (a *seizing* lever), com*pris*e, enter*pris*e (an undertaking, a *seizing* among), re*pris*al (a *seizing* in return), sur*pris*e (a *seizing* upon). L. *prehend*ere, *prehens*us.

Pris (*priz*)—saw; *pris*m (having the form of a piece *sawn* off). G. *priz*ein.

Pristin—ancient; *pristine*. L. *pristin*us.

Priv—single; *priv*ate, *priv*acy, *priv*ilege (a favoring opportunity, like a *law* for the benefit of a *single* person), de*priv*e (to take from, and thus leave the possessor *single*, or destitute). L. *priv*us.

Prob—test; *prob*ation (a *testing*), *prob*e, *prob*able (likely to stand the *test*), ap*prob*ation, re*prob*ate (rejected on *test*), *prov*e, re*prov*e. L. *prob*are. L. *prob*us, good, excellent.

Prob—honest, excellent; *prob*ity. L. *prob*us.

Prodigi—token, portent; *prodig*y. L. *prodigi*um.

Prol—offspring, increase; *prol*ific (rapidly *increasing*). L. *prol*es.

Prolix—extended. L. *prolix*us. L. *pro*, forth; *liqu*ere, to flow.

Promen—walk; *promen*ade (a *walk*). O.F. *promen*er. Low L. *promin*are, to drive forward. Low L. *pro*, forward; *min*are, to drive, lead.

Prompt—brought, forward. L. *prom*ere, *prompt*us.

Promulg—publish; *promulg*ate (to *publish* abroad). L. *promulg*are.

Pron—inclined forward; *pron*e. L. *pron*us.

Propag—peg down; *propag*ate (to extend, like a series of layers *pegged down*). L. *propag*are.

Propinqu—near; *propinqu*ity (*nearness*). L. *propinqu*us. L. *prope*, near.

Propiti—favorable; *propiti*ous, *propiti*ate. L. *propiti*us.

Propri—one's own, peculiar, select; ap*propri*ate, *propr*ty, *propri*ety (*select* or approved behavior). L. *propri*us.

Proselyt—an arrival; *proselyt*e (a convert, a new *arrival* to a cause). G. *proselut*os. G. *pros*, toward; *erch*omai, to come.

Proto—first; *proto*martyr (the *first* martyr), *proto*-

plasm (see *plass*), *proto*type (an original or model, the *first* type), *proto*xide (the *first* oxide), *proto*zoan (an animal of the lowest, or *first*, division). G. *protos*.

Prov—See *prob*.

Province (*provinci*)—a territory, conquest; *province*. L. *provincia*.

Provis—provide; *provis*ion (that which is *provided*), *proviso* (a *provision*). L. *provid*ere, *provis*us. See *vid*.

Proxim—nearest, very near; *proxim*ity, ap*proxim*ate (to approach *very near*), *proximo* (the next, or *nearest*, month). L. *proxim*us.

Prud (*provid*)—foresee, provide; *prud*ent (careful, *providing* against trouble), *prude* (an over-nice, or *prudent*, woman), juris*prud*ence (the science of law, as made and *provided*). L. *provid*ere. L. *pro*, before; *vid*ere, to see.

Prun—plum. L. *prun*um.

Prur—itch; *prur*ient. L. *prur*ire.

Psall—touch, twang a harp; *psal*m, *psalt*ery. G. *psall*ein.

Psest—scraped; palim*psest*. (See *palin*.) G. *psest*os.

Pseud—false; *pseud*onym (*false* or assumed *name*). G. *pseud*os.

Psych—soul, mind; *psych*ology (the science of *mind*), *psych*ical (pertaining to the *soul*), metem*psych*osis (a *change* or passage of the *soul* from one body *into* another). G. *psuch*e. G. *psuch*ein, to blow.

Pubert—age of manhood; *pubert*y. L. *pubert*us.

Pud—feel shame, blush; im*pud*ent (*unblushing*). L. *prud*ere.

Puer—boy; *puer*ile (*boyish*). L. *puer*.

Pugil—boxer; *pugil*ist. L. *pugil*.

Pugn—fight; *pugn*acious, re*pugn*ant (thoroughly

distasteful, *fighting back*), im*pugn* (attack, *fight against*), op*pugn* (discredit, *fight against*). L. *pugn*are. L. *pugn*us, a fist.

Pulmon—lung; *pulmon*ary. L. *pulmo, pulmon*is.

Puls—drive; *puls*e (the *drive* of the blood through the arteries), re*puls*e (*drive back*). L. *pell*ere, *puls*us.

Pulver—dust, powder; *pulver*ize (reduce to *powder*). L. *pulv*is, *pulver*is, dust.

Pun—punish; im*pun*ity (escaping *without punishment*). L. *pun*ire. L. *pœn*a, pain.

Punct—prick, point; *punct*ure, *punct*ual (on the *point*), *punct*uate (to attach the limiting *points*), *punct*illio (a nice little *point* of honor), com*punct*ion (a *pricking* of conscience). L. *pung*ere, *punct*us.

Pung—prick; *pung*ent, ex*pung*e (remove, *prick out*). L. *pung*ere.

Pup—boy, girl, doll; *pup*il (the *boy* or *girl* learner, also the central spot in the eye in which the *little image* may be seen), *pup*pet (a *little doll*), *pup*a (a chrysalis, the little *child*). L. *pup*us, *pup*a.

Pur—pure. L. *pur*us.

Pur—pus; *pur*ulent. L. *pus, pur*is.

Purg—purify; *purg*e, ex*purg*ate. L. *purg*are. L. *pur*us, pure; *ag*ere, to compel, make.

Pusill—mean; *pusill*animous (*mean-spirited*). L. *pusill*us. L. *pus*us, small.

Pustul—blister, pimple. L. *pustul*a. L. *pusul*a.

Put—think, reckon, suppose; com*put*e (*reckon together*), dis*put*e (*think apart*), im*put*e (*reckon against*), *put*ative (accounted, *reckoned*), re*put*e (*think again*). L. *put*are. L. *put*us, clean, clear.

Put—cleanse, lop off (as in cleansing trees of worthless branches); am*put*ate (*lop off* around), de*put*e (*cut off* from). L. *put*are. L. *put*us, clean, clear.

Putr—rotten; *putr*id. L. *puter, putr*is. L. *putr*ere, to be rotten. L. *put*ere, to stink.

Pygm—fist; *pygm*y (a very small person about as large as from the elbow to the *fist*). G. *pugm*e.

Pyl—gate, passage; *pyl*orus (the *passage* to the entrails), Thermo*pyl*æ (the *Passage* of the *Hot* Springs). G. *pule*.

Pyr—fire; *pyr*e (a funeral *fire*), *pyr*otechnics (*fireworks*), em*pyr*ean (the lofty region exposed to the *fire* of the sun). G. *pur*.

NOTES

[1] By the application of heat, a palimpsest is often caused to reveal the original composition. In this way some very valuable records have been recovered.

[2] The Roman senate was restricted to wealthy and noble families, the common people (or *plebs*, plebeians) being excluded for centuries from participation in the government. Hence the real nobility or aristocracy came to mean those families of senatorial rank and dignity; that is, those families which had supplied at some time a member to the senate (*patres*). On account of the exclusiveness of the patricians, and their undisguised disdain for the plebeians, or common people, the term *patrician* came to include, somewhat, the idea of haughtiness or disdain. But its principal sense includes the better qualities of a true nobility.

[3] Patronymics were very common in early Greece. The heroes of the Iliad all (or nearly all) had *patronymics*. Achilles, the son of *Peleus*, was called *Pelides*; Agamemnon, the son of *Atreus*, was called *Atrides*; Diomed, the son of *Tydeus*, was called *Tydides*, etc. Such names as *Johnson*, *Williamson*, *Jameson*, *Robertson*, *Stephenson*, etc., were all originally patronymics. The system of surnames, or family names, has superseded, in most countries, the system of patronymics.

[4] The number of identical words and formative elements in the Greek and Latin languages indicates a close relationship between the men speaking them, and a common ancestry at a date comparatively recent. The separation occurred in prehistoric times. But the evidence is conclusive that they left the Aryan hive as one migration or tribe, and that they divided on reaching the Bosporus, a portion moving southward to occupy the coasts, islands, and peninsulas of the Ægean Sea, while another portion bore to the right, beyond the mountains and the Adriatic, entering Italy as its final population. The material remains of the prehistoric races have nearly all disappeared from the face of the earth; but their history is, nevertheless, written with great exactness and considerable fullness from the evidence fixed in speech, a material that defies the corroding effects of time and the track of vandalism. See *Aryan*.

[5] One's native *country* is spoken of as the *fatherland*, while one's speech is one's *mother* tongue.

[6] Originally a slave, who *led* the *child* to school.

[7] For many centuries Christians have been making pilgrimages to Jerusalem, the Holy City which contains the tomb of the Savior, and which was the scene of His ministration and His sufferings. The violence done to Christian pilgrims led to the great uprising of the Middle Ages called the Crusades (the wars under the banner of the *cross*). Those wars called into service the knighthood and chivalry of the period. Conspicuous among the Christian knights were the kings of England and France, Richard Cœur de Lion and St. Louis, while the crescent had among its champions the renowned Saladin. After the varying fortunes of a most romantic and world-stirring struggle, Jerusalem became a Christian city, and remained so for two hundred years, when it again sank under the domination of the infidel. But the Crusades were not in vain; the stir and movement of a universal war disseminated ideas of geography and history, shook off the torpor of the Dark Ages, started the human mind anew on the lines of scientific inquiry, precipitated the revival of learning, and with it the mental illumination that has transformed the modern world. The Mahommedans likewise have ever made

their pilgrimages to their own holy city, Mecca, the burial-place of their prophet, Mohammed.

8 The famous *Macedonian phalanx* enabled King Philip and his son Alexander the Great to conquer the world. This phalanx was an invention of Philip's, and consisted of a close array of men several ranks deep trained to lock their shields together, and, with their long spears projecting outward, to rush forward as a single mighty machine of war. Before this irresistible machine the armies of brave singles warriors were unable to make a stand, and the nations of the world fell in succession under the domination of Macedon.

9 A term first applied in medieval legend to St. Christopher, who was said to have *carried Christ* across a stream, in the form of a little child.

10 The Pleiades were fabled to be the seven daughters of Atlas transferred by Jupiter to be a constellation in the sky. But six of the stars are visible to the naked eye, and the ancients supposed that the seventh concealed herself out of shame for having given her love to a mortal, Sisyphus, while her sisters were sought by the gods themselves. This is the famous myth of the *lost Pleiad.*

The group, Pleiades, is supposed to be the central group in the Milky Way, and one of its stars, Alcyone, is considered to occupy the apparent central point of the universe, around which it revolves.

11 Previous to the introduction of railroads, goods were moved almost exclusively by inland navigation. Not only were the larger bodies of water and rivers utilized by sailing vessels (and later by steam-boats), but even the smaller streams were traversed by flat-boats pushed along with poles. By thus pushing up to the headwaters of one stream and carrying across (portage) to the headwaters of another basin, navigation was managed over vast distances. The most noted portages of history were those between the heads of Persian Gulf and Red Sea respectively and the Mediterranean. The vast trade of India flowing up during all ages to the markets of the Western world was carried in caravans over these great portages. Famous cities, such as Persepolis,

Baalbek, Palmyra, and Bagdad, sprang up on the route of this overland trade, this general *portage*, and grew wealthy and populous, in the midst of deserts, by simply supplying the passing needs of those engaged in the mighty stream of trade. To avoid the expense and delay of that portage, Columbus faced his vessel to the west and discovered a new world.

[12] The expedition of Ponce de Leon into Florida in quest of the fountain of youth is familiar to all. Of the same visionary nature were the numerous expeditions into Central Asia in quest of the mythical *Prester* John. A rumor had reached Europe that some missionaries had penetrated to the capital of a powerful and wealthy Tartar chief, and had made of him such an exemplary convert that he consented to become a *presbyter (prester)* in the Christian Church and to adopt the Christian name John. It was further reported that toward Europeans, those who hailed from Christendom, his liberality was lavish, even unbounded. There was, therefore, a wide-spread desire to visit this Eastern wonder. Parties, great and small, were for ages wandering over the steppes of Asia. They found not the wonderful *prester*; but they found Asia, and, like Ponce de Leon, they contributed to the growing science of Geography.

Q

Quadr—square, fourfold; *quadr*ate (make *square*), *quadr*angle (a court having *four* angles), *quadr*ant (one of the *four* equal parts of a circle), *quadr*ennial (recurring once in *four* years), *quadr*ilateral (a *four*-sided plane figure), *quadr*ille (a *square* dance), *quadr*illion (a million raised to the *fourth* power), *quadr*uped (a *four-footed* animal), *quadr*uple (*fourfold*), s*quadr*on (a troop of horse forming a *square*). L. *quadr*us.

Qual—what sort; *qual*ity, *qual*ify (to limit, to *make* of a particular *kind*). L. *qual*is.

Quant—how much; *quant*ity (the *how much*). L. *quant*us.

Quarant—forty; *quarant*ine (a *forty* days' detention to prevent the spread of disease). F. *quarant*e. L. *quadragint*a. L. *quadr*us, fourfold.

Quart—fourth; *quart* (the *fourth* of a gallon), *quart*an (recurring on the *fourth* day, as a *quartan* ague), *quart*er, *quart*et (music in *four* parts), *quart*o (having the sheet of paper folded into *four* parts). L. *quart*us, fourth. L. *quattu*or, four.

Quass—shatter, shake, strike; *quas*h (to annul, to *crush*), con*cuss*ion (a violent *shaking together*), dis*cuss* (to debate, to *shake asunder*), per*cuss*ion (*striking through*), res*cue* (to save, to *drive away* danger *again*). L. *quat*ere, *quass*us.

Quater (*quattuor*)—four; *quater*nary (consisting of *fours*), *quater*nian (a set of *four*), *quat*rain (a stanza of *four* lines). L. *quattuor*.

Quer—complain; *quer*ulous (given to *complaining*), *quer*imonious, *quar*rel (a dispute, as over some *complaint*). L. *quer*i.

Quer (*quær*); **quisit** (*quaisit*)—seek, ask; *quer*y (an *asking*), ac*quire* (to obtain *to* one's self, as after *seeking*), con*quer* (to overpower, as if after going in *quest* of, to *seek with*), dis*quisit*ion (an *inquiry*, a *seeking apart*), en*quire* (to *seek into*), ex*quisit*e (very fine, and therefore *sought out*), in*quest* (an *inquiry into*), in*quire* (to *search into*), in*quisit*ion (an *inquiring into*), per*quisit*e (an incidental profit, *thoroughly sought*), *quest* (a *search*), *quest*ion, re*quest* (a *seeking back*), re*quire* (to *seek back*). L. *quær*ere, *quæsit*us.

Quiesc—rest, become quiet; *quiesc*ent (remaining *quiet*), ac*quiesc*e (to yield, to *rest in* a conclusion requested). L. *quiesc*ere.

Quiet—quiet; *quiet*, ac*quit* (to discharge, to *quiet* the charge), *quit* (free, put *at rest*), *quit*e (free, therefore *at rest*), re*quiem* (a mass for the dead, a service for the *repose* of a soul), re*quit*e (to pay back, to *quit* again), *coy* (*quiet, still*), de*coy* (to allure, to *quiet down*). L. *quiet*us.

Quin—five at a time; *quin*ary. L. *quini*.

Quinc (*quinque*)—five; *quinc*unx (an arrangement by *fives*). L. *quinque*.

Quint—fifth; *quint*uple (*five-fold*), *quint*essence (the pure essence of a thing, the *fifth essence* as distinct from the four elements). L. *quint*us. L. *quinque*, five.

Quir—See *quer*.

Quisit—See *quer*.

Quorum—of whom; *quorum* (the number, *of whom*, who may transact business). L. *quorum*. L. *qui*.

Quot—how many; *quot*a (a share, a *how many*), *quo*-

tient (the result in division, the *how many* times), ali*quot* (contained an exact *number of times* in *another* number). L. *quot*.

R

Rab—rage, rave; *rab*id, *rab*ies. L. *rab*ere.

Rabbel—chatter; *rabbel* (a crowd of noisy *chatterers*). O.Du. *rabbel*n.

Racem—cluster; *receme* (a *clustering* inflorescence). L. *racem*us.

Ract (*rhact*)—break; catar*act* (a fall, *break* down, of water). G. *rhegn*umi.

Rad—scrape; abr*ade* (*scrape* away). L. *rad*ere.

Radi—ray, shine; *radi*ant, irr*adi*ate (to send out *rays*). L. *radi*are. L. *radi*us, a ray.

Radi—ray; *radi*us (a *ray* from the center of the circle). L. *radi*us.

Radic—root; *radic*al (going to the *root*), er*adic*ate (pull out by the *root*), *radi*sh (a *root* vegetable). L. *radix, radic*is.

Ram—branch; *ram*ify (*branch* off). L. *ram*us.

Ran—frog; *ran*unculus (little *frog*). L. *ran*a.

Ranc—smell ill, strong, harsh; *ranc*id, *ranc*or. L. *ranc*us.

Rant—be enraged. O.Du. *rant*en.

Rap; rapt—seize, grasp; *rap*acious (*grasping*), *rap*ine (the *seizing* of plunder), *rap*id (*snatching* away), *rapt*ure (a seizing), *rapt*ores (birds that *seize* their prey). L. *rap*ere, *rapt*us.

Rar—thin, rare. L. *rar*us.

Ras—scrape; er*ase* (*scrape* out), abr*as*ion (a scraping away), *ras*e (to demolish, as of *scraping* away), *raz*or, *ras*orial (a term applied to *scraping* birds). L. *rad*ere, *ras*us.

Rat—think, calculate, determine, settle; *rat*io (a *calculation*), *rat*ify (to confirm, make *settled*), *rat*e (a *settled* price or value), *rat*ion (a *fixed* allowance of provision), *rat*ional (having reason, or the *thinking* faculty). L. *re*or, *rat*us.

Rav—bear away; *rav*age, *rav*ine. F. *rav*ir. L. *rap*ere.

Re—thing; *re*al (belonging to *things*), *re*bus (a word represented by *things* or objects), *re*public (the public *matter*). L. *re*s.

Reav (*reafi*)—pluder; ber*eav*e (*deprive* of). A.S. *reafi*an. A.S. *reaf*, clothing, robe. A.S. *reof*an, *reaf*, deprive.

Rebuk (*rebouqu*)—blunt, a weapon, put aside a request. O.F. *rebouqu*er. F. *rebouqu*er, to obstruct, stop the mouth. F. *bouque* (*bouche*), mouth. L. *bucca*, the puffed cheek, mouth.

Rebut (*rebout*)—repulse, overcome; *rebut*. O.F. *rebout*er.

Recent—fresh. L. *recen*s, *recent*is.

Recip—receive, take; *recip*ient (the *receiver*), *recip*e (a prescription, a *take thou*). L. *recip*ere. L. *re*, back; *cap*ere, to take.

Reciproc—returning, alternating; *reciproc*al, *reciproc*ity, *reciproc*ate. L. *reciproc*us.

Rect—ruled, right, straight; *rect*angle (having only *right* angles), *rect*ify (make *right*), *rect*ilinear (made up of *straight* lines), *rect*itude (*uprightness*), cor*rect*, di*rect* (*rule* apart), e*rect* (*upright*). L. *regere*, *rect*us.

Recuper—recover; *recuper*ative. L. *recuper*are.

Recus—reject, escape, dodge; *recus*ant (*rejecting* a *cause* or opinion), *ruse* (a trick, a *dodge*). L. *recus*are. L. *re*, back; *caus*a, cause.

Redol—emit odor; redolent. L. *red*, again; *ol*ere, *od*ere, to be odorous.

Redout—fear; *redout*able (inspiring *fear*). O.F. *redout*er.

Refrag—oppose, thwart; re*frag*able, ir*refrag*able. L. *refrag*are. L. *re*, back; *frang*ere, to break.

Reg—rule, govern; *reg*ent (one *ruling* in the stead of another[1]), *reg*imen (a course of life conforming to *rule*), *reg*iment (an organization of soldiers under *government*), *reg*ion (an extent of country *governed* by some authority). L. *reg*ere.

Reg—king; *reg*al (*kingly*), *reg*icide (the slaying of a *king*). L. *rex, reg*is.

Regn—reign; *regn*ant (*reigning*), inter*regn*um (a period *between* two regular *reigns*), *reign*. L. *regn*are. L. *regn*um, kingdom. L. *reg*ere, to rule.

Regul—a rule; *regul*ar, *regul*ate. L. *regul*a. L. *reg*ere, to rule.

Relev—assist, help; *relev*ant (bearing upon, so as to *help*). F. *relev*er. L. *re*, again; *lev*are, to lift, raise. L. *lev*is, light.

Religion—piety. L. *religio, religion*is.

Reminisc—remember; *reminisc*ence (a *remembrance*). L. *reminisci*.

Remn (*reman*)—remain; *remn*ant (a *remaining* part). L. *reman*ere. L. *re*, back; *man*ere, to remain.

Ren—kidney; *ren*al, *rein*s. L. *ren*is.

Rend—give up; *rend*er, surren*der*, *rend*ezvous (a place to report, *give yourselves up*). F. *rend*re. L. *redd*ere, to give back. L. *red*, back; *da*re, to give.

Reneg—forsake the faith; *reneg*ade. Sp. *reneg*ar. L. *re*, again; *neg*are, to deny.

Repart—re-divide, answer thrust with thrust, reply; *repart*ee (a witty reply). F. *repart*ir. F. *re*, again; *part*ir, part, dart off.

Repriev (*reprev*)—reject, disallow; *repriev*e (the arrest of an execution, therefore a *rejecting* of the

sentence). M.E. *reprev*en. L. *re*, back; probare, to
test.

Reprim—repress, reprove; *reprim*and (a *reproof*
from one in authority). L. *reprim*ere. L. *re*, back;
primere, to press.

Reprob—reject, cast away; *reprob*ate. L. *prob*are. L.
re, back; *prob*are, to prove.

Reprov—condemn; *reprov*e. O.F. *reprov*er. L. *re*,
back; *prob*are, to test.

Rept—creep; *rept*ile (a *creeping* thing), sur*rept*itious
(secret, sly, *creeping under*). L. *rep*ere, *ript*us.

Repudi—reject; *repudi*ate. L. *repudi*are. L. *repudi*um, a casting off. L. *re*, back; *pud*ere, to feel
shame.

Requi—repose; *requi*em (a service for the *repose* of a
soul). L. *requi*es. L. *qui*es, rest.

Respit (*respect*)—respect; *respit*e (a delay in the execution of a sentence, through a *respect* for the suit
on the part of some judge). L. *respic*ere, *respect*us.

Rest—stay, stop, remain; ar*rest* (cause to stop), *rest*ive
(stubborn, wishing to *stop*). L. *rest*are. L. *re*, back;
*st*are, to stand.

Restaur—restore; *restaur*ant (a place of refreshment
or *restoration*). L. *restaur*are.

Resuscit—revive; *resuscit*ate. L. *resuscit*are. L. *re*,
again; *sub*, under; *cit*are, to arouse.

Ret—net; *ret*icule (a little *net* for the hair), *ret*ina (the
net-like innermost coating of the eye). L. *rete*.

Retali—requite; *retali*ate (*requite* in kind). L. *retali*are.

Retic—be very silent; *retic*ent (observing *silence*). L.
*tac*ere, to be silent.

Retin (*reten*)—hold back, retain; *retin*ue (a band of
retainers). O.F. retenir. L. *retin*ere. L. *re*, back;
*ten*ere, to hold.

Reveal (*revel*)—draw back a veil. L. *revel*are. L. *re*, back; *vel*um, veil.

Rever—stand in awe of; *rever*e, *rever*end. L. *rever*eri. L. *re*, again; *ver*eri, to fear, feel awe.

Rh—See *rhe*.

Rhaps (*rhapt*)—stitch together; *rhaps*ody (an outburst of sentiment, recalling the old fragmentary and, as it were, *stitched together*, songs of the early Greek period[2]). G. *rhapt*ein.

Rhe—flow; diar*rhe*a (a *flow through* the bowels), *rhe*um (a thin *fluid* secreted by the glands), *rhe*umatism (a disorder attributed to *rheum*), catar*rh* (a *downward flow* from the head), *rhy*thm (the measured motion, the regular *flow*, in verse). G. *rhe*ein.

Rhetor—orator; *rhetor*ic (the art of composition, the *orator's* art[3]). G. *rhetor*.

Rhin—nose; *rhin*oceros (the beast with the *horn* on the *nose*), platy*rhin*e (having a *flat nose*). G. *rhis*, *rhin*os.

Rhiz—root; *rhiz*ophagous (living on *roots*), *rhiz*opod (*root foot*), licorice (see *glyc*). G. rhiza.

Rhod—rose; *rhod*odendron (the *rose tree*, an evergreen shrub having rose-like flowers), *Rhod*e Island (the *Island of Roses*[4]). G. *rhod*on.

Rhomb—a spindle; *rhomb*us (a figure in the form of a *spindle*), *rhomb*oid (resembling a *rhombus*), *rhumb*, *rumb* (a line for directing a ship's course on a chart, so called because consisting of spiral lines on a globe, and suggestive of the magician's circle, or rhombus). G. *rhomb*os. G. *rhemb*ein, to revolve.

Rid; ris—laugh; *rid*iculous (causing *laughter*), de*rid*e (to *laugh down*), *ris*ible. L. *rid*ere, *ris*us.

Rid (*ræd*)—discern, explain; *rid*dle[5] (an enigma to be *explained*). A.S. *ræd*an.

Rig—moisten; ir*rig*ate (to *moisten* land by letting in a flood of water). L. *rig*are.

Rig—be stiff; *rig*id. L. *rig*ere.

Rip—bank, shore; *rip*arian (relating to the *bank* of a stream), *riv*er (a stream within *banks*), ar*riv*e (to come to *shore*). L. *rip*a.

Ris—See *rid*.

Riv—stream; *riv*ulet (a little *stream*), de*riv*e (to deduce from a source, as by draining, or *streaming off*, water), *riv*al (a contestant, originally one who disputed about the use of a *brook*). L. *riv*us.

Robor—strength; cor*robor*ate (to *strengthen* fully). L. *robor*.

Robus—strength; *robus*t (having great *strength*). O.L. *robus*.

Rod; ros—gnaw, eat; *rod*ent (a *gnawing* animal), cor*rod*e (to *eat up*), e*rod*e (to *eat away*). L. *rod*ere, *ros*us.

Rog; rogat—ask, demand; ab*rogat*e (repeal, *ask* to have done away with), ar*rog*ate (assume, *ask to* one's self), de*rogat*e (detract *from*, as in *asking* the repeal of a law), inter*rog*ate (*ask thoroughly*), pre*rog*ative (a special privilege or right,[6] originally precedence in voting, being *asked* first), pro*rog*ue (adjourn, defer, as in publicly *asking* an extension of office), super*e*rogat*ion (a doing *beyond* what is necessary, as in paying out, or *asking*, an excessive sum of money), sur*rog*ate (an officer having jurisdiction of wills, and the settlement of the estates of deceased persons, originally an assistant judge elected, or *asked* for, as a substitute). L. *rog*are, *rogat*us.

Ros—dew; *ros*emary (the *seadew* flower). L. *ros*.

Rostr—beak; *rostr*um (a speaker's platform, like that in the Roman forum, which was adorned with the *beaks* of captured galleys). L. *rostr*um.

Rot—wheel; *rot*ary (*wheel*-like). L. *rot*a.

Rot—route, path; *rot*e (the beaten *track*). O.F. *rot*e. L. *rump*ere, *rupt*us, break.

Rotund—round; *rotund*ity. L. *rotund*us. L. *rot*a, wheel.

Roug—red; *roug*e (*red* paint), Baton *Roug*e (the City of the *Red Staff*). F. *roug*e. L. *rub*eus.

Rout—a way, path; *rout*e, *rout*ine, *rut*, *rot*e. F. *rout*e. L. *rupt*us, broken.[7]

Roy (*roi, reg*)—king; *roy*al (*kingly*), vice*roy* (the governor of a province, who takes the place of the *king*), cordu*roy* (the *cord* of the *king*), pome*roy* (the apple *king*). F. *roi*. L. *rex, reg*is.

Rub—red; *rub*y (a *red*-colored gem), *rub*icund (very *red*), *rub*ric (a direction printed in *red*[8]), e*rub*escent (becoming *red*). L. *rub*er. L. *rub*ere, to be red.

Ruct—belch; e*ruct*ate. L. *ruct*are.

Rud—raw, crude; *rud*e (raw, uncultured), e*rud*ite (scholarly, freed from *rudeness*), *rud*iment (the thing in its first or *crude* stages). L. *rud*is.

Rug—wrinkle; cor*rug*ate (*wrinkle together*), *rug*ose (full of *wrinkles*). L. *rug*a.

Ruin—overthrow. L. *ruin*a. L. *ru*ere, to rush, fall down.

Rumin—chew the cud; *rumin*ant (having the trait of chewing the cud), *rumin*ate (to *chew the cud* of reflection). L. *rumin*are.

Rumor—noise, murmur. L. *rumor*.

Rupt—break; *rupt*ure (a *break*), ab*rupt* (*breaking off*), cor*rupt* (*break up*), dis*rupt* (*break apart*), e*rupt*ion (a *breaking out*), inter*rupt*ion (a *breaking in among*), ir*rupt*ion (a *breaking into*), bank*rupt* (one whose *bank*, or credit, is *broken*). L. *rump*ere, *rupt*us.

Rur—the country; *rur*al. L. *rus*, *rur*is.

Rus—the country; *rus*tic, *rois*tering. L. *rus*.

Russ—reddish; *russ*et. L. *russ*us.

NOTES

[1] During the infancy or disability of a king, it is customary to appoint a *regent*, who shall exercise all the powers of a king until the period of infancy is past or the disability removed. In his later life, the mind of King George III, of England, became affected. In consequence, his son, afterward George IV, was appointed *regent*. The unfortunate monarch rallied for a time and resumed the reins of government. But he again relapsed hopeless, and the same regency, reappointed, continued until his death, ten years later.

[2] In ancient Greece there were a class of persons who made a business of reciting poetry. They became, as it were, the publishers of poetry in bringing it before the public. Oftentimes they would be a manuscrit or library: for a book would be carried for generations in the memories of the rhapsodists. In this manner the works of Homer were transmitted down from his dim eleventh century before Christ to the time of Pisistratus in the sixth century B.C. That accomplished tyrant had the works of the great bard compiled and edited, and they have since been a part, as well as the foundation, of the written literature of Greece. The rhapsodists would recite a book at a time, and it seemed like sewing or *stitching* them *together*. Hence the name applied to them.

[3] Rhetoric was cultivated by the ancient Greeks as the art of persuasion; and, as such, it became endowed with the most fascinating charms. The artful speaker presented such an appearance of wisdom that he received the name of the *sophist* or *wise one*. Socrates attacked the rhetoricians or sophists as trying to confuse the human mind instead of leading it up to a perception of truth.

[4] Meaning the Island of Rhodes, in the Mediterranean. The American Rhode Island was so called from its resemblance to the island made famous by the ancient Colossus.

[5] The most famous riddle was that of the sphinx, a female monster said to have once infested Bocotia, in ancient Greece. She busied herself in capturing straggling people and propounding to them the following riddle: "What animal is it that starts into life on four legs, passes to the use of two, and ends on three?" If the captive failed to solve the riddle, he was strangled. (The term *sphinx* means the "strangler.") The hero Œdipus, on his travels, fell into the toils of the sphinx. He solved the riddle and slew the monster, and was made king of the country by the grateful people. He said that the animal alluded to is man, who starts into life crawling on hands and knees (*four feet*), passes to the upright posture or use of his two feet proper, and who, in old age, is compelled to resort to a staff (his *third* leg).

[6] The *prerogative* of the House of Commons (from which that of the House of Representatives was taken as a *precedent*) had its origin in an early custom of the Anglo-Saxon kings of calling into council some representative men of the realm on the subject of royal revenue, or ways and means of carrying on the government. In fact, this custom gave rise to the House of Commons itself. The prerogative was confirmed in *Magna Carta* (the *Great Charter*) or the great bill of rights wrested by force from the tyrannical King John. It was deemed essential to freedom that the people who paid the money should have the privilege of granting or withholding it, and of stating the exact purposes for which it could be used. A king having power to take money at will from his subjects could call into his service an unlimited number of mercenary soldiers and reduce his people to slavery. The great war of the seventeenth century between king and parliament was fought on the question of prerogative, and resulted in victory for the people and for the cause of freedom.

[7] A path is *broken*, or beaten, by travel.

[8] The middle ages were called the *dark ages* because learning and cultivation had disappeared from the home of men, and

were succeeded by the darkness of ignorance and the reign of violence. The monasteries were held sacred, and thus escaped the vandalism of the period. In those secluded asylums the monks patiently cultivated letters. The ancient books that had escaped the torch of barbarism were collected in and put under safe-keeping; and many copies of them were made by the slow process of writing, for the mighty art of printing had not been invented yet. The work was done with loving care by those nameless benefactors of mankind. Many of the manuscripts are models of taste, and even of art; for the red coloring was caused to have an ornamental effect, as well as to distinguish important parts of the work. These manuscript treasures of the monasteries came forth at the revival of learning to be the educators of the modern world.

S

Sac (*sacc*)—sack. L. *sacc*us.

Sacchar—sugar; *sacchar*ine. G. *sacchar*on.

Sacerdot—priest; *sacerdot*al (belonging to a *priest*). L. *sacerdos, sacerdot*is. L. *sacer*, sacred; *d*are, to give.[1]

Sacr—holy; *sacr*ed, *sacr*ament (a *sacred* vow or engagement), *sacr*ifice (to *make* a *holy* offering), *sacr*ilege (the stealing or desecration of *holy* things), *sacr*istan (a keeper of the *holy* vestments), conse*cr*ate (make *entirely holy*), dese*cr*ate (to profane or render *unholy*), exe*cr*ate (to declare accursed by the use of a *holy* name). L. *sacer, sacr*i.

Sag—perceive by the senses; *sag*acious (*perceiving* quickly), pre*sag*e (a *perceiving beforehand*). L. *sag*ire.

Sagitt—arrow. L. *sagitt*a.

Sal—salt; *sal*ine, *sal*ad (a *salted* or seasoned dish), *sal*t, *sal*ary (a stated compensation, originally an allowance for the purchase of *salt*). L. *sal*.

Sal—leap, spring forward; *sal*ient (prominent, *springing* forth), as*sail* (*spring at*), re*sil*ient (*leaping back*), *sal*ly (a *springing* forth), *sal*mon (the *leaping* fish). L. *sal*ire.

Sal (*sall*)—hall, room; *sal*oon (a *large room*). F. *sall*e.

Saliv—saliva. L. *saliv*a.

Salt—dance; *salt*ation, *salt*atory. L. *salt*are. L. *sal*ire, *salt*us, to leap.

Salt—leap, spring forward; as*sault* (*spring at*), de*sult*ory (*leaping from*), ex*ult* (*leap out* as with joy), in*sult* (*spring upon*), re*sult* (*spring back*). L. *sal*ire, *salt*us.

Salubr—healthful; *salubr*ious. L. *salubr*is. L. *salus*, health.

Salut—health; *salut*ary (*healthful*), *salut*e (wish *health* to). L. *salus*, *salut*is.

Salv—save; *salv*ation, *salv*age (allowance for *saving* vessels), *salv*er (a platter from which the victuals were tasted by a menial to *save* his lord from poison), *salv*e (an ointment for healing or *saving*). L. *salv*are. L. *salv*us, safe.

San—sound; *san*e. L. *san*us.

San—heal; *san*atory, *san*itarium. L. *san*are. L. *san*us, sound.

Sanct—holy; *sanct*ify (*make holy*), *sanct*imony (*holiness*), *sanct*ion (an authorization making a transaction *sacred*), *sanct*ity, *sanct*uary (the *holy* place), *saint*. L. *sanct*us.

Sanguin—blood; *sanguin*ary (bloody), *sanguin*e (hopeful from having a free circulation of *blood*), con*sanguin*ity (relationship by *blood*). L. *sanguis*, *sanguin*is.

Sanit—health; *sanit*ary, *sanit*arium. L. *sanit*as. L. *san*us, sound.

Sap—to taste, be wise; *sap*id (having pleasant *taste*), *sap*ient (being *wise*), in*sip*id (*tasteless*). L. *sap*ere.

Sapon—soap; *sapon*aceous. L. *sapo*, *sapon*is.

Sarc—flesh; *sarc*asm (a remark that tears the *flesh*), *sarc*ophagus (see *phag*). G. *sarx*, *sarc*os.

Sat; satis—enough, sufficient; *sat*e (surfeit, give *enough*), *sat*iate (surfeit, give *enough*), *satis*fy (*make enough*), as*set*s (effects deemed *sufficient* to meet liabilities). L. *sat*, *satis*.

Satell—an attendant; *satell*ite. L. *satell*es.

Satur—full; *satur*ate (make *full*), *satir*e (originally a medley, or *full* dish). L. *satur*.

Saur—lizzard; *saur*ian (one of the *lizzard* tribe). G. *saur*os.

Sav (*silv*)—forest; *sav*age (belonging to the *forest*). L. *silv*a.

Sax—stone; *sax*ifrage. L. *sax*um.

Scal—ladder; *scal*e (having steps like a *ladder*). L. *scal*a.

Scalen—uneven; *scalen*e (having *unequal* sides). G. *scalen*os.

Scalp—cut; *scalp*el (a *dissecting* knife). L. *scalp*ere.

Scand; scans—climb; *scan* (to trace out the measure of poetry, or *climb* along its several feet), a*scend* (*climb up*), de*scend* (*climb down*), tran*scend* (*climb beyond*). L. *scand*ere.

Scapul—shoulder-blades; *scapul*ar. L. *scapul*æ.

Scen—tent, sheltered place; *scen*e (a view such as is given on the *sheltered* stage[2]), pro*scen*ium (the place before the stage or *scen*e). G. *scen*e.

Scend—See *scand*.

Scept—consider, inquire; *scept*ic (one who does not accept a belief, but *inquires* into its soundness; in other words, a doubter). G. *scept*omai, I consider.

Scept—prop, support; *scept*er (a monarch's wand, originally his supporting *staff*). G. *scept*ein.

Sched—a strip of papyrus bark; *sched*ule (a scheme written out on a small *strip* of paper). L. *sched*a.

Schis (*schiz*)—cleave, rend; *schis*m (a *rending* apart of the members of a society), *schis*t (slate-rock easily cleft). G. *schiz*ein.

Schol—leisure; *schol*o (a place of instruction that employs *leisure* time[3]). G. *schol*e.

Sci (*ischi*)—the socket in which the thigh-bone turns; *sci*atic (pertaining to the hip-joint). G. *ischi*on.

Sci—know; *sci*ence (classified *knowledge*), con*sci*ence (*knowledge* within us), con*sci*ous (aware of, or having *knowledge*), omni*sci*ent (*knowing* all things), pre*sci*ence (*knowing* before). L. *sci*re.

Sci—cut; *sci*on (a small branch *cut* off for grafting. Hence a younger *branch*). F. *sci*er. L. *sec*are.

Scind—cut; re*scind* (undo, *cut* back). L. *scind*ere.

Scintill—spark; *scintill*ate (*sparkle*), *scintill*a (the merest *spark*). L. *scintill*a.

Scler—hard; *scler*otic (*firm, hard*). G. *scler*os.

Scop—a watcher, viewer; *scop*e (a reach or *view*), epi*scop*al (relating to a bishop, or *overseer*), horo*scop*e (see *hor*), kaleido*scop*e (an instrument for *viewing beautiful forms*), micro*scop*e (an instrument for *viewing small* objects), stetho*scop*e (an instrument for *viewing*, or examining, the *chest* or lungs), tele*scop*e (an instrument for *viewing* objects *afar off*). G. *scop*os.

Scor—ordure, dung; *scor*ia (dross, *waste*). G. *scor*.

Scorbut—scurvy; *scorbut*ic. L. *scorbut*us.

Scrib; script—write; *scrib*e (a *writer*), a*scrib*e (allow, as if in *writing*), de*scrib*e (to give an account of, as if in *writing*), circum*scrib*e (mark, or *write*, a boundary *around*), in*scrib*e (*write upon*), pre*scrib*e (*write* out *beforehand*), pro*scrib*e (to outlaw, as by a *written* document posted in a public place), *scrib*ble (*write* carelessly), sub*scrib*e (*write under*), con*script* (enrolled in a *written* list), post*script* (*written after*), re*script* (a *written reply*), *script* (*written* characters), *script*ure (that which is *written*), super*script*ion (the *writing* on the *outside*), tran*scrib*e (to *write across*, or over again). L. *scrib*ere, *script*us.

Scrupul—a sharp stone; *scrupl*e (a little perplexity, like a *sharp stone* in the shoe). L. *scrupul*um. L. *scrup*um.

Scrut—search into carefully; *scrut*iny, in*scrut*able (*unsearchable*). L. *scrut*ari.

Sculpt—cut, carve; *sculpt*ure. L. *sculp*ere.

Scurr—buffoon; *scurr*ilous (extremely abusive, worthy of a *buffoon*). L. *scurr*a.

Scut—shield; *scut*iform, e*scut*cheon (a painted *shield*). L. *scut*um.

Seb—fat, tallow; *seb*aceous. L. *seb*um.

Sec; sect—cut; *sec*ant (a radius that *cuts* the circumference of a circle), *sick*le (a *cutting* instrument), bi*sect* (*cut* into *two* equal parts), dis*sect* (*cut apart*), in*sect* (an animal whose body is *cut into* three *sect*ions), inter*sect* (*cut between*), *sect*ion (a *cutting*), *seg*ment (a portion *cut* off), tri*sect* (*cut* into *three* equal parts). L. *sec*are, *sect*us.

Secul (*sæcul*)—a generation, age, the world; *secul*ar (belonging to the *world*). L. *sæcul*um.

Sed—sit, settle; *sed*entary (involving much *sitting*), *sed*ate (calm, *settled*), *sed*iment (a *settling*), super*sede* (*set over*), dissi*dent* (*sitting apart*), pre*side* (*sit before*), re*side* (*sit* or remain *back*), re*sid*ue (a remainder, *sitting* or staying *back*), sub*side* (*settle down*), sub*sid*y (a reserve, *sitting under* or near). L. *sed*ere.

Sedul—diligent; *sedul*ous. L. *sedul*us.

Seg (*sec*)—cut; *seg*ment (a piece *cut* off). L. *sec*are.

Selen—the moon; *selen*ography. G. *selen*e.

Sembl—seem, appear, be like; *sembl*ance, re*sembl*e, dis*sembl*e (to pretend, to *seem otherwise* than one is). O.F. *sembl*er. L. *simul*are, to pretend.

Sembl—See *simul*.

Semin—seed; dis*semin*ate (scatter the *seed apart*), *semin*ary (a place where the *seeds* of knowledge are sown). L. *semen*, *semin*is.

Sen—old; *sen*ior (*older*), *sen*ate (a council of *elderly* men[4]), *sen*eschal (an *old* servant), *sen*ile (showing *old* age), *sir*e (a parent, a venerable one). L. *sen*ex.

Sent; sens—perceive, feel, think; *sent*iment (something strongly *felt*), pre*sent*iment (a *feeling* *beforehand*), sent*ence* (the expression of a *thought*), *sense*, as*sent* (agree to, and *think* in the direction required), con*sent* (*feel with*), dis*sent* (*think apart*), re*sent* (*feel* deeply), *sense* (the power of *perceiving*), *sens*ible (having *keen senses*, or *feelings*), *sens*ual (beastly, yielding to the grosser *impulses*). L. *sent*ire, *sens*us.

Sept—hedge, inclosure; tran*sept* (the cross-inclosure). L. *sept*um. L. *sep*ire, *sept*us. L. *sæp*es, a hedge.

Sept—rotten; anti*sept*ic (a substance that *arrests decay*). G. *sept*os. G. *sep*ein, to rot.

Septem—seven; *Septem*ber (the *seventh* month of the Roman year, which began with March), *sept*ennial (belonging to *seven* years). L. *septem*.

Septuagint—seventy; *Septuagint* (the Greek version of the Old Testament translated from the Hebrew by *seventy* scholars at Alexandria during the reign of Ptolemy Philadelphus, King of Egypt[5]). L. *septuagint*a.

Sepul (*sepult*)—bury; *sepul*cher (a tomb, or *burial* place), *sepul*ture (*burial*). L. *sepel*ire, *sepul*tus.

Sequ; secut—follow; *sequ*el (that which *follows*), *sequ*ence (a regular succession or *following*), con*sequ*ent (*following with*), exe*qu*ies (funeral ceremonies or *followings*), ob*sequ*ies (funeral rites, *following near*), ob*sequ*ious (*following* each beck and nod), sub*sequ*ent (*following after*), con*secut*ive (*following together*), exe*cut*e (*follow out*), per*secut*e (*follow* with intense determination to punish or annoy), pro*secut*e (*follow forward*). L. *sequi*, *secut*us.

Sequester—to surrender, set aside; *sequester*, *seques*trate. L. *sequest*rare.

Ser; sert—join bind, put; *ser*ies (a *connected* row), *ser*ried (*joined* closely together), as*sert* (make claim, *join* issue), con*cert* (*joined together*), de*sert* (leave, *unjoin*), dis*sert*ation (a treatise, discussion, a *joining apart*), exert (*put forth*), insert (*join into*). L. se*re*re, se*rt*us.

Ser—whey; se*r*um. L. se*r*um.

Seren—bright, clear; *seren*e, *seren*ade (designed to cheer or make *bright*). L. *seren*us.

Seri—grave, serious; *seri*ous. L. *seri*us.

Sermon—a speech, discourse. L. *sermo, sermon*is.

Serp—creep; *serp*ent (a *creeping* thing). L. *serp*ere.

Serr—saw; *serr*ated (notched like a *saw*). L. *serr*a.

Serv—serve, keep; con*serv*e (*keep* fully), de*serv*e (*serve* fully), ob*serv*e (*keep* near), pre*serv*e (*keep* beforehand), re*serv*e (*keep* back), sub*serv*e (*serve* under). L. *serv*are.

Sess—sit; *sess*ion (a *sitting*), *sess*ile. L. *sed*ere, *sess*us.

Set—bristle. L. *set*a.

Sever—serious, earnest; *sever*e, as*sever*ate (make an *earnest* assertion), per*sever*e (be *earnest* throughout). L. *sever*us.

Sever (*separ*)—separate; *sever* (*separate*), *sever*al (a number of *separate* things). L. *separ*are. L. *se*, aside; *par*are, arrange, set.

Sexagen—sixty; *sexagen*ary. L. *sexagen*i. L. *sex*, six.

Sext—sixth; *sext*uple (*six*-fold), *sext*ant (the *sixth* part of a circle), bis*sext*ile (a name for leap-year in which formerly the 24th of February, being the *sixth* before the calends of March, occurred twice). L. *sext*us. L. *sex*, six.

Shal (*scalh*)—servant; mar*shal* (a commanding officer; a commander of horse; originally a groom or horse-*servant*), sene*schal* (high steward, an old *retainer*). O.H.Ger. *scalh*. Goth. *skalks*.

Shevel (*chevel*)—hair; di*shevel*ed (with disordered *hair* streaming apart). O.F. *chevel*. L. *capill*us.

Sibil—hiss; *sibil*ant. L. *sibil*are.

Sicc—dry; de*sicc*ate (*dry* out). L. *sicc*us.

Sid—See *sed*.

Sider—star; *sider*eal (belonging to the *stars*), con*sider* (reflect, as if with eyes upraised contemplating the *stars*). L. *sid*us, *sider*is.

Sign—mark. L. *sign*um.

Sil—be silent; *sil*ence. L. *sil*ere.

Sil (*sal*)—leap, spring; re*sil*ient. L. *sal*ire.

Silex; silic—flint; *silic*on, *silex*, *silic*ate. L. *silex*, *silic*is.

Silv—forest; *silv*an[6]. L. *silv*a.

Sim—same; *sim*ple (of the *same*, or one, fold). L. *sim* (from a base *sam*a).

Simi—an ape. L. *simi*a. L. *sim*us, flat-nosed.

Simil—like; *simil*ar, *simil*e (a *like* thing), *simil*itude (a *likeness*), as*simil*ate (make *like*). L. *simil*is.

Simul—make like; *simul*ate. L. *simul*are. L. *simul*, together.

Simult—at the same time; *simult*aneous. L. *simult*im. L. *simul*, together.

Sincer—pure, sincere. L. *sincer*us.

Sinciput—half the head. L. *sinciput*. L. *semi*, half; *caput*, head.

Singul—single. L. *singul*us.

Sinister—on the left hand, hence evil. L. *sinister*.

Sinu—fold, bend; *sinu*ous, insinuate (introduce by winding or *bending*). L. *sinu*s.

Siphon—a small pipe or reed; *siphon* (a bent pipe for drawing of liquids[7]). G. *siphon*.

Sist—to place, stand; as*sist* (step, or *stand* to), con*sist* (*stand together*), de*sist* (*put away*), ex*ist* (*stand out*), in*sist* (*stand against*), per*sist* (*stand through*), re*sist* (cause to *stand back*), sub*sist* (to stay, *stand under*). L. *sist*ere. L. *st*are, to stand.

Sit—wheat, food; para*site* (one who *feeds* upon another, *sit*ting *beside* the latter at his table). G. *sit*os.

Sit—site. L. *sit*us.

Situ—to place; *situ*ate (put in *place*). L. *situ*are. L. *situ*s, a site.

Skelet—dried; *skelet*on (the *dry* bones). G. *skelet*os. G. *skell*ein, to dry.

Sobri—sober; *sobri*ety. L. *sobri*us. L. *se*, aside (hence not); *ebri*us, drunk.

Soci—companion; *soci*able, *soci*ety, asso*ci*ate. L. *soci*us.

Sol—the sun; *sol*ar (belonging to the *sun*), *sol*stice (the place in the ecliptic where the *sun* seems to stand), para*sol* (an article that *wards off* the *sun*). L. *sol*, *sol*is.

Sol—alone; *sol*e, *sol*o, *sol*itude, *sol*itary, de*sol*ate, *sol*iloquy (*speaking alone* to one's self). L. *sol*us.

Sol—console; *sol*ace, con*sol*e, discon*sol*ate. L. *sol*ari.

Sol—be accustomed; in*sol*ent (offensive, and therefore *not* in accordance with the kindly *customs* of society). L. *sol*ere.

Solemn—religious; *solemn* (serious, like a *religious* rite). L. *soll*us, entire; *ann*us, year.[8]

Solicit—agitate, urge. L. *solicit*are. L. *sollicit*us, wholly agitated. L. *soll*us, whole; *ci*ere, *cit*us, to shake, arouse.

Solid—firm; *solid*, *sold*ier (he who receives the *solid* pay), *sold*er (to make *solid*), con*solid*ate. L. *solid*us.

Solv; solut—loosen; dis*solv*e (*loosen apart*), re*solv*e (separate into parts, *loosen*), *solv*e (*loosen* up, explain), ab*solut*e (*loosened from* limit or restraint), dis*solut*e (altogether *loose*), *solut*ion. L. *solv*ere, *solut*us.

Somn—sleep; *somn*ambulist (a *sleepwalker*), *somn*olence (*sleepiness*), *somn*iferous (*sleep-bringing*), in*somn*ia (inability to *sleep*). L. *somn*us.

Son—sound; con*son*ant (*sounding with*), dis*son*ant (*sounding apart*, hence not harmonious), per*son* (a character in a play whose voice formerly *sounded through* a mask), reson*ant* (*sounding back*), *son*orous (*sounding*), unis*on*(having *one* harmonious *sound*). L. *son*are.

Soph—wise; philo*soph*y (the general doctrine on a subject,[9] the *love* of *wisdom*). G. *soph*os.

Sophis—instruct; *sophis*try (fallacious reasoning, like that of the old Greek *instructors* in oratory). G. *sophiz*ein. G. *soph*os, wise.

Sopor—sleep; *sopor*iferous (*sleep-bringing*). L. *sopor*.

Sopran—supreme; *sopran*o (the highest, or *supreme*, voice in music). It. *sopran*o. L. *superan*us, chief. L. *super*, above.

Sorb—sup up; ab*sorb*. L. *sorb*ere.

Sord—dirt; *sord*id. L. *sord*es.

Sort—lot,[10] kind; as*sort* (put like *kinds* together), con*sort* (have *lot with*), *sort*, *sorc*ery (magic, a casting of *lots*). L. *sors*, *sort*is.

Sort—obtain; re*sort* (*obtain again*). L. *sort*iri. L. *sors*, *sort*is, lot.

Sort—sally forth; *sort*ie (a *sally* from a place besieged). F. *sort*ir. L. *surg*ere, *surrect*us, to rise.

Sound (*sund*)—a swimming; *sound* (a channel or strait so narrow that a strong man can *swim* across it.[11] Hence to measure the depth of water, as in a *sound*). A.S. *sund*.

Sover—See *super*.

Spa—draw, pluck; *spa*sm (a convulsion, a *drawing* together). G. *spa*ein.

Spars—scattered; *spars*e, a*spers*e (calumniate, as if *sprinkling* with dirty water), di*spers*e, inter*spers*e. L. *sparg*ere, *spars*us.

Spati—roam; ex*pati*ate (*roam* at large in a subject). L. *spati*ari. L. *spati*um, space.

Spec; spect—look, see, appear; *spec*ies (a kind or

appearance), *spec*ie (hard money *visible* to the eye), *spec*imen (something *seen*), *spec*ious (fair to *see*), con*spic*uous (thoroughly *seen*), de*spic*able (fit to be despised, or *looked down* upon), per*spic*acity (keenness of *sight*), per*spic*uous (clear, easily *seen through*), a*spect* (*outlook*), circum*spect* (careful, as if *looking around*), ex*pect* (*look out* for), in*spect* (*look into*), intro*spect*ion (a *looking within*), per*spect*ive (a *look through* distance), pro*spect* (a *look ahead*), re*spect* (*look* upon with approbation), retro*spect* (*look back*), *spect*acle (a show to be *looked* at), *spect*acles (glasses for *looking* through), *spect*ator (an *on-looker*), *spect*er (an *apparition*), *spect*rum (the *appearance* of analyzed light[12]), su*spect* (*look under*). L. *spec*ere, *spect*us.

Speci—kind; *spec*ies, e*spec*ial (of a particular *kind*), *spec*ial (of a particular *kind*), *spec*ify (to particularize, make of a particular *kind*), *spic*e (a *kind* of fruit). L. *spec*ies. L. *spec*ere, to see, appear.

Specul—watchtower; *specul*ate (to contemplate, as from a lofty *watchtower*). L. *specul*um. L. *spec*ere, to look.

Specul—a mirror; *specul*ar. L. *specul*um. L. *spec*ere, to see.

Spell—a saying, story; *spell* (to *tell* the names of the letters[13]), *spell* (an incantation), go*spel* (the *story* of *God* or the *good*). A.S. *spell*.

Sper (*spe*)—hope; de*spair* (to be *without hope*), pro*sper* (to have one's *hopes advanced*). L. *spes*.

Sper (*speir*)—sow, scatter; *sper*m (spawn, *seed*), *spo*radic (*scattered* here and there), *spore* (a *seed*). G. *speir*ein.

Sperm—seed. G. *sperm*a. G. *speir*ein, to sow, scatter.
Spher (*sphair*)—ball. G. *sphair*a.

Sphing—throttle; *sphinx* (a fabulous female, said to have *strangled* travelers who could not solve her riddle[14]). G. *sphing*ein.

Sphyx (*sphuz*)—pulsate; a*sphyx*ia (suffocation, a stoppage of the *pulse*). G. *sphus*ein.

Spic—See *spec*.

Spin—thorn; *spin*e (a *thorn*), *spin*e (the *thorny* backbone), porcu*pin*e (the *pig* with the loose *spines* or *thorns*[15]). L. *spin*a.

Spir—breathe; *spir*acle (a *breathing*-hole), *spir*it (formerly supposed to be the *breath*), a*spir*e (*breathe toward*), a*spir*ate (a *breath* sound), con*spir*e (*breathe together*), ex*pir*e (*breathe out*), in*spir*e (*breathe into*), per*spir*e (*breathe through*), su*spir*ation (*under breath* expression), re*spir*e (*breathe again*), tran*spir*e (*breathe*, or ooze, out). L. *spir*are.

Spiss—thick; in*spiss*ate (make *thick*). L. *spiss*us.

Splend—shine; *splend*id, *splend*or, re*splend*ent. L. *splend*ere.

Spoli—spoil, booty; *spoli*ation (the taking of *booty*), *spoli* (plunder, take *booty*), de*spoil* (take *booty* from[16]). L. *spoli*um.

Spond; spons—promise, answer; de*spond* (give up and *promise* nothing), re*spond* (*promise back*), *spons*or (a *promise* in baptism), re*spons*ible (liable to answer or *promise* back). L. *spond*ere, *spons*us.

Spont—of one's own record; *spont*aneous. L. *spont*e.

Spor—See *sper*.

Spum—foam; *spum*e, *pum*ice (a volcanic mineral, the *foam*-stone). L. *spum*a.

Spuri—false; *spuri*ous. L. *spuri*us.

Squal—be rough, dirty; *squal*id, *squal*or. L. *squal*ere.

St—stand; contra*st* (*stand against*), co*st* (*stand together*), ob*st*acle (something *standing against*), re*st* (*stand back*), *st*able (*standing* firm, also a *stand* for horses). L. *st*are.

Stagn—a still pool; *stagn*ate. L. *stagn*um.

Stala—drip; *stala*ctite (a hanging crystal in a cave, caused by the *drip* from the limestone), *stala*gmite (a cone on the floor on a cave, caused by the limestone *drip*). G. *stala*ein.

Stamen; stamin—a thread (especially the standing up warp in an upright loom); *stamen* (the *thread*-like part of a flower), *stamin*a (the principal strength of any thing, compared to the woven *threads* in cloth). L. *stamen*, *stamin*is. L. *st*are, to stand.

Stann—tin; *stann*iferous. L. *stann*um.

Stant—standing; con*stant* (*standing together*), di*stant* (*standing apart*), ex*tant* (*standing forth*), in*stant* (*standing against*), *stanz*a (a division of poetry ending with a pause or *standing* still), circum*stance* (a thing *standing around*), sub*stance* (*standing under* or near). L. *stans*, *stant*is. L. *st*are, to stand.

Stas—a standing; apo*stasy* (a desertion or *standing* away), ec*stasy* (a *standing* out). G. *stasis*. G. *histe*mi, I stand.

Stat—stand; *state* (condition, *standing*), *stat*ion (*standing* still), *stat*ue (a *standing* figure), *stat*ure (one's *standing* height), *stat*us (state, *standing*). L. *st*are, *stat*us.

Stat—standing; *stat*ics (the science of bodies at rest, *standing* still), apo*state* (a deserter *standing apart* from his party), hydro*statics* (the doctrine of *standing water* and other liquids at rest.). G. *stat*os. G. *histe*mi, I stand.

Statut—place, put, set, establish; *statut*e (a law duly *established*), con*stitut*e (*place together*), de*stitut*e (*put away*), in*stitut*e (*establish in*), re*stitut*e (a *placing back*), sub*stitut*e (*put under* or instead of). L. *statu*ere. L. *st*are, to stand.

Stell—star; *stell*ar, con*stell*ation. L. *stell*a.

Steno—narrow, close; *steno*graphy (writing close). G. *steno*s.

Stereo—solid, stiff; *stereo*type (a *solid* plate of type), *stereo*scope (an instrument that gives the appearance of *solidity* to objects presented in a picture). G. *stereo*s.

Steril—barren. L. *steril*is.

Stern—strew; con*stern*ation (a *throwing down*). L. *stern*ere.

Sternut—sneeze; *sternut*ation. L. *sternut*are.

Stert—snore; *stert*orous. L. *stert*ere.

Stetho—the chest; *stetho*scope (see *scop*). G. *stetho*s.

Sthen—strength; cali*sthen*ics (exercises designed to promote beauty and *strength*). G. *sthen*os.

Stich—row, line; acro*stic* (a word or sentence formed by a *row* of beginning letters). G. *stich*os.

Stigm—a prick, mark, brand; *stigm*a, *stigm*atize. G. *stigm*a. G. *stig*ein, to prick.

Stil—an iron pin; *stil*etto. L. *stil*us.

Still—drop; di*still* (*drop* down), in*still* (*drop* into). L. *still*are. L. *still*a, a drop.

Stimul—goad; *stimul*ate (*goad* on). L. *stimul*us.

Stipendi—tax, tribute; *stipend* (a salary). L. *stipend*ium. L. *stip*s, *stip*is, small coin.

Stipul—settle by agreement; *stipul*ate. L. *stipul*ari.

Stirp—trunk, stem of a tree; e*xtirp*ate (root out, as if pulling up by the *stem*). L. *stirp*s, *stirp*is.

Stitut—See *stat*.

Stol (*stell*)—place, put, send; *stol*e (a robe to be *put* on), dia*stol*e (the dilation, or *putting* aside, of the heart), apo*stle* (one *sent* abroad), epi*stle* (a missive *sent to*), sy*stol*e (contraction, or *putting together*, of the heart). G. *stell*ein.

Stolid—firm, stupid. L. *stolid*us.

Stom—mouth. G. *stom*a.

Strangl (*strangal*)—halter; *strangle* (to choke, as with a *halter*). G. *strangale*. G. *strangos*, twisted.

Strat—spread; *stratum*, pro*strate*, *street* (a *broad* passage). L. *stern*ere, *strat*us.

Strateg—a general; *strategy* (the planning of a *general*), *stratagem* (a scheme worthy of a *general*). G. *strategos*. G. *stratos*, an army; *agein*, to lead.

Strenu—vigorous; *strenuous*. L. *strenuus*.

Strep—rattle; ob*strep*erous (noisy, *rattling* against). L. *strep*ere.

String; strict—draw tight, bind, compass, urge; *stringent*, *strict*, a*striction*, a*string*ent, boa-con*strictor*, ob*striction* (obligation, a *binding against*), re*strict* (*bind back*), con*strain* (compel, *bind together*), di*strain* (seize goods for debt, *pull asunder*), di*strict* (a region, such as that in which a lord could *distrain*), di*stress* (a calamity, a *pulling* asunder), re*strain* (*bind back*), *strain* (*draw tight*), *strait* (*compressed*, narrow). L. *string*ere, *strict*us.

Stroph (*streph*)—turn; *strophe* (a part of a poem sung during a *turn* of dancing shows), apo*strophe* (a *turning* away *from* the audience to address one person or object only). G. *streph*ein.

Stru; struct—build; con*strue* (*build together*), con*struct* (*build together*), de*stroy* (*unbuild*), in*stru*ment (an implement, as if for *building* in), *struct*ure (a *building*), in*struct* (*build* into the mind), ob*struct* (*build* against). L. *stru*ere, *struct*us.

Strychn—nighshade, poison; *strychn*ine. G. *struchnos*.

Stucc—hardened, incrusted; *stucco* (a kind of *plaster*). It. *stucco*.

Stud—be busy about, *study*; *stud*ent. L. *stud*ere.

Stult—foolish; *stult*ify (*make foolish*). L. *stult*us.

Stup—be amazed; *stup*id, *stup*efy, *stup*endous. L. *stup*ere.

Styl (*stil*)—an iron point used in writing; *styl*ographic (writing with an *iron point*), *styl*e (one's mode of *writing*). L. *stil*us.

Styp (*styph*)—contract, draw together; *styp*tic. G. *stuph*ein.

Su—follow; purs*ue* (to *follow forward*), s*ue* (to petition, to *follow*), s*uite* (a *following*), s*uit* (a case at law, that which is *followed* up, also a set, or *succession*, of clothes). O.F. s*ui*r. L. s*equi*.

Suad; suas—persuade; diss*uade* (*persuade* apart), pers*uade* (*persuade thoroughly*). L. s*uad*ere.

Suav—sweet; s*uav*e. L. s*uav*is.

Sublim—raised on high. L. *sublim*is.

Subtil—fine, thin; *subt*le. L. *subtil*is. L. *sub*, under (or closely); *tel*a, a web. L. *tex*ere, to weave.

Succ—juice; *succ*ulent (full of *juice*). L. *succ*us.

Sud—to sweat; *sud*atory, *sud*orific, ex*ud*e. L. *sud*are.

Suffoc—choke; *suffoc*ate. L. *suffoc*are. L. *sub*, under; *fauc*es, the throat, gullet.

Suffragi—a vote; *suffrag*e (the privilege of *voting*). L. *suffragi*um.

Sui—one's self; *sui*cide (the *killing* of one's *self*). L. *sui*.

Sulc—furrow; *sulc*ated. L. *sulc*us.

Sult—See *salt*.

Sultan—victorious; *sultan* (a ruler, the winner of *victories*[17]). Arab. *sultan*.

Sum; sumpt—take; as*sum*e (*take into*), con*sum*e (*take wholly*), pre*sum*e (imagine, *take beforehand*), re*sum*e (*take again*). L. *sum*ere, *sumpt*us.

Summ—highest; *summ*it (the *highest* point), *sum* (the amount, the *highest* result), con*summ*ate (to perfect, bring into one *sum*). L. *summ*us.

Sumptu—expense; *sumptu*ous (*expensive*), *sumptu*ary

(relating to one's *expenses*). L. *sumptus*. L. *sum*ere, *sumptus*, to take.

Super—over, above; *super*ior, *super*nal, *super*b, *su*preme, *sover*eign (chief, *over* all), *sopr*ano (the *highest* voice in music), *suzer*ain (an *over* lord, a *sover*eign). L. *super*.

Supercili—eyebrow; *supercili*ous (haughtly, having a tendency to lift the *eyebrows*). L. *supercili*um. L. *super*, over; *cili*um, eyelid.

Superfici—surface; *superfici*al (on the *surface*). L. *superfici*es. L. *super*, above; *faci*es, face.

Superstiti—witness; *superstiti*on (the awe of one who *witnesses* something supposed to be supernatural). L. *superst*es, *superstitis*. L. *super*, over; *stare*, to stand.

Supin—lying on one's back; *supin*e. L. *supin*us.

Suprem—highest; *suprem*e. L. *suprem*us.

Surd—deaf (hence irrational, or deaf to reason); ab*surd*, *surd* (having no *rational* root). L. *surd*us.

Surg; surrect—rise; *surg*e (the *rise* or swell of the waves), in*surg*ent (a rebel, *rising upon* authority), in*surrect*ion (an *uprising*), re*surrect*ion (a *rising again*), *sourc*e (the *rise* or start, origin). L. *surg*ere, *surrect*us.

Surveill—superintend, watch; *surveill*ance. F. *surveill*er. L. *super*, over; *vigil*are, to watch.

Suscept—receive; *suscept*ible (ready to *receive*). L. *suscip*ere, *suscept*us. L. *sub*, under; *cap*ere, *capt*us, to take.

Sut—sewed; *sut*ure (a *seam*). L. *su*ere, *sut*us.

Swart—dark; *swart*hy.[18] A.S. *sweart*.

Swer—speak, swear; an*swer* (to *speak in reply*), *swear*. A.S. *swer*ian.

Syc—fig; *syc*amore (the *fig-mulberry*), *syc*ophant (a fulsome parasite, like one of those in ancient Athens, who *showed* were the stolen *figs* were kept). G. *suc*on.

Syl—right of seizure; a*syl*um (a place in which a person may not be *seized*,[19] a place of refuge in distress). G. *sul*e.

Sylv—See *silv*.

Symposi—drinking party, banquet; *symposi*um. G. *sumposi*on. G. *sun*, together; *posis*, a drink.

Symptom—an accident, a happening to one. G. *sumptom*a. G. *sun*, together; *pipt*ein, to fall.

Syncop—a cutting short; *syncop*ate (to contract, or *cut short*, a word), *syncop*e (a swoon, a *cutting short* of strength). G. *sun*, together; *copt*ein, to cut.

Syndic—censor, regulator, controller; *syndic*ate (a combination to *regulate* or *control* a line of business). G. *sundic*os, helping in a court of justice.[20] G. *sun*, together; *dice*, justice.

Syring—reed, pipe, tube; *syring*e. G. *surinx, suring*os.

NOTES

[1] The priest was the offerer (or *giver*) of sacrifice (*sacred* gifts).

[2] In the ancient Greek theater the stage alone was covered. The auditorium was without a roof or shelter.

[3] People whose time and thoughts are crowded with practical duties nevertheless should reserve a certain portion of time for special study. All have the leisure for study if they have the will.

[4] "Old men for council; young men for war," has become a proverb. Wisdom and judgment come only with age and experience. The old are best fitted to decide what should be done; while the young are best fitted to do it. Hence, the Constitution fixes a qualification of age for membership in the United States Senate. The Roman Senate was distinguished by its wise and far-seeing enactments. It laid deep the foundations on which were

built the greatness of the Roman Empire. But it also rose on many occasions to the sublimity of patriotism and sacrifice where the safety or honor of the commonwealth was concerned. On one occasion it even sacrificed itself. When Rome was sacked by the Gauls, the Senate deemed it proper to die at their posts instead of withdrawing into the citadel with the rest of the people. The venerable men sat in their chairs and awaited the stroke of death. The plundering barbarians were amazed at the scene. They stroked the white beards to satisfy themselves that those placid forms were real; they felt the flesh to ascertain if life were still active within; but, at a signal, they drove the murderous axes into their victims and passed on.

5 The first Ptolemy (Soter) was a Greek, one of the generals of Alexander the Great. At the death of Alexander, Ptolemy seized upon Egypt, and became the founder of a remarkable line of monarchs, terminating with the famous Cleopatra. Ptolemy was thoroughly imbued with Greek culture. He gathered around him the scholars and artists of Greece, making Alexandria a typical Greek city. He laid the foundation of that immortal mass of erudition called the Alexandrian Library. His sons inherited his tastes and aspirations. Such enlightened collectors could not overlook such an important book as the Jewish Scriptures; so the translation was made. It was made with such care and was so accurate in all respects as to become a standard of nearly equal authority with the original Hebrew text.

6 Pennsylvania meant the *Forest* Land bought by *Penn*.

7 The principle of the siphon is the pressure of the atmosphere which causes water to rise in a vacuum. The same principle operates in the working of water-pumps, the pump being simply a contrivance for forcing the air out of a tube, and thereby creating a vacuum into which the water may flow. There is no such force as suction: the force is pressure, or gravity, the suction being merely a process of creating a vacuum. The vacuum in the siphon is created by filling the tube with water (or other liquid), and then reversing its position, place the small arm in a vessel of liquid whose depth is less than the longer arm of the siphon. The downward flow through the long arm creates a vacuum at the curve, into which the liquid is forced up through the short arm.

The movement thus caused will continue until the vessel is empty. The siphon is useful in transferring a liquid from one vessel into another.

8 The solemnity of a Roman religious rite was proportioned to the infrequency of its recurrence. It took high rank as a *solemn* ceremonial when it did not recur within the space of an *entire* year.

9 Science is an orderly arrangement of what is known on a subject; philosophy is the ultimate doctrine or highest reasoning on the subject. So far as the philosophy is proven, it has all the authority of science or demonstrated truth. But the term philosophy is extended to any body of doctrine, though it may be only tentative or purely hypothetical. For example, we have at present a *science* of astronomy embodying much knowledge in regard to the visible universe. Thales, the ancient philosopher, taught a *philosophy* of the universe which coincided wonderfully with the present *science* of the universe. His teachings, however, had no authority further than a strong probability of truth. *Science* teaches what is true; *philosophy*, in the narrower sense of theory, teaches what *seems* to be true.

10 The hope of gain has always been a powerful stimulus. It is the mainspring to most voluntary individual enterprise. In ancient times troops were deliberately stimulated by this motive. They were authorized to seize all kinds of property, private as well as public, in an enemy's country. But each man could not plunder for himself. The spoils were first collected into one mass and then distributed according to rank among the soldiers of the expedition. Separate piles were made as nearly equal as possible, and the privilege of choosing a pile was determined by *lot*. The plunder included not only the material property, but even the wretched people themselves, who were taken as the prizes of conquest and sold into slavery. Homer's great poem, the "Iliad," opens with the convulsions produced in the Greek army before Troy by the final disposition of two young and beautiful captives. Achilles was driven almost into open rebellion, and the cause of the Greeks was jeopardized while he nursed his wrath and "sulked in his tent."

11 The channel of the Hellespont, so celebrated on account of the famous bridge of boats built by Xerxes for the passage of his mighty army, has been made doubly celebrated by the exploits of two famous swimmers. Leander, of ancient story, swam across it nightly from Abydos to visit his mistress, Hero, the beautiful priestess of Venus, at Sestos. One tempestuous night he was drowned, and in the morning the billows cast his body forth upon the shore. At the sight of her drowned lover, Hero plunged into the flood and drowned herself. The second swimmer was Lord Byron, a passionate lover of Greek history and story. At the beginning of the nineteenth century he swam across the Hellespont to prove the correctness of the legend.

12 Light is analyzed or separated into its elementary rays, or colors, by being passed through a triangular prism. Such passage subjects it to the greatest possible amount of refraction, inasmuch as the ray enters one oblique surface and emerges from another. The elementary rays composing white light possess different degrees of refrangibility. So the one ray of white light entering the prism emerges as seven rays of color seen distinctly on the screen in the following order: *red*, *orange*, *yellow*, *green*, *blue*, *indigo*, and *violet*. These are the colors seen in the rainbow, which is but a *spectrum* resulting from the refraction of sunlight through falling drops of water. The red color of sunset is the result of refraction delivering the red ray to the eye when the others have been refracted out of range. The spectrum cast by the light of a solid substance fused to a white heat contains breaks or dark vertical lines. Each substance has its own peculiar form of breaks. Hence, scientists have been enabled to determine the substances composing the sun and other luminous heavenly bodies by an examination of their light on the spectroscope.

13 To be more exact in definition, the art of spelling is the art of making up the written word, or putting in the needed letters in their proper order. This view is expressed by the more critical word *orthography*.

14 This being was said to capture wayfarers and propound to them a riddle, on the failure to solve which she strangled them. Hence the name *sphinx* or *strangler*. (See *Riddle*.) A famous piece of ancient sculpture is the colossal Sphinx of the Nile

Valley, situated near the Great Pyramid. This Sphinx was carved out of a great granite rock, forming in itself a mound. The total length of the reclining body of the lion is one hundred and forty-six feet. The head measures twenty-eight feet six inches from the top to the chin. Across the shoulders it measures thirty-six feet, and the paws are extended about fifty feet. The features have been mutilated, in accordance with a tenet of the Mohammedan religion, which prohibits the use in art of the figure of any living being.

[15] When attacked, the porcupine gathers himself into a ball, presenting in every direction his terrible quills. He can even discharge his quills, like arrows, striking his enemy at a distance.

[16] See *Trophy*.

[17] The Mahommedan rulers were, for a time, the conquerors of the earth, and were properly called the *"Victorious Ones."* Claiming authority from Heaven to propagate their religion by the sword, and promising an immediate entrance into Paradise with an eternity of voluptuous enjoyments to those of their followers who fell in battle, they were enabled to sweep the east and the south with their fanatical hordes. They also overran Spain and poured in upon the plains of south France preparatory to overrunning all Europe. But they met a final repulse in that quarter of Tours from the troops of Charles, the great general of France, who thus saved Christianity from destruction, gaining also for himself the surname of *Martel*, or the *"Hammerer."* The grandson of Charles was the scarcely less renowned Charlemagne. Eight hundred years after Tours, the Sultan, still trying to vindicate his name, effected a foothold in Europe, and made Constantinople his capital. Another Martel, in the person of John Sobieski, of Poland, met and overthrew the conquering Sultan on the Danube. Since then, the Sultan's name has become a misnomer; the victories went against him, his empire gradually crumbling. The world-conqueror (the Victorious One) became the "Sick Man of Constantinople."

[18] Literally *blackened by heat*. It was long supposed that a dark skin is due to exposure to the heat of the sun. It is noticed, for example, that the people in the south of Europe have dark complexions, while those in the north are fair. It is noticeable,

moreover, that there is a shading off from the blue-eyed, flaxen-haired, fair-skinned Scandinavian through the brunette French, the dark-eyed equatorial tribes. In fact, a superstition once prevailed in Europe that a black skin was due to the intense heat of the equator, and that a white man would become black the instant he reached the *"line."* This superstition caused the greatest trepidation among the Portuguese mariners who explored the African coast prior to the discovery of America by Columbus. Only after a brave crew had passed the dreaded line was the superstition exploded.

[19] Judæa had cities of refuge, three on each side of the Jordan, into which persons who had committed unintentional homicide could flee and be safe from the vengeance of the friends of the slain. The ancient temples were sanctuaries in which it was not lawful to lay violent hands upon any one. The case of Pausanias, the Spartan, is a noted example of the ancient right of asylum. The hero of Platæa stained his laurels by treasonable correspondence with the Persian king whom he had so brilliantly defeated. Being detected, and finding himself pursued by the whole populace, he fled into a temple for protection. The people stood foiled at the entrance, recognizing the right of *asylum.* In the dilemma, the aged mother of the culprit took a stone and laid it on the threshold. The hint was taken, the entrance walled up, and the traitor starved to death. In the Middle Ages, the Christian churches and monasteries retained the right of sanctuary.

[20] The *assistant judge* was a *censor* or *regulator* of manners.

T

Tab—waste away; *tab*id. L. *tab*ere.

Tabern—booth, hut; *tabern*acle (a tent, a little *booth* or *hut*), *tavern* (a wayside inn, originally a *hut*). L. *tabern*a.

Tabul—plank, table; *tabul*ar (in the form of a *table*), *tabul*ate (make *tables* or synopses of), en*tabl*ature (the part of a building surmounting the columns, though originally the pedestal or *planked* flooring), *table*.[1] L. *tabul*a.

Tac—be silent; *tac*it, *tac*iturn (having a tendency to *silence*), reti*c*ent (remaining *silent*). L. *tac*ere.

Tach—fasten; at*tach* (*fasten* to), de*tach* (un*fasten*). Bret. *tach*a.

Tact—touch; con*tact* (*touch* together), in*tact* (*untouched*), *tact* (delicacy of *touch*), *tact*ile (*touchable*). L. *tang*ere, *tact*us.

Tact (*tass*)—arrange, order; *tact*ics (the art of maneuvering, or *arranging*, troops). G. *tass*ein.

Tag—See *tang*.

Tagli—cut; in*tagli*o (a kind of carved, or *cut into*, work). It. *tagli*are.

Taill—cut; *tail*or (a *cutter* of cloth), de*tail* (*cut* into pieces), en*tail* (to bestow as a heritage, like the abridged, or *cut* into, title to real estate[2]), re*tail* (*cut* small), *tall*y (a *notched* stick). F. *taill*er. F. *taill*e, a slitting, an incision. L. *tal*ea, a wand rod.

Tain—See *ten*.

Tal—heel; *tal*on (a *claw*). L. *tal*us.

Talent—a sum of money, a gift. L. *talent*um. G. *talent*on.

Talism (*telesm*)—mystery; *talism*an (a *charm*). G. *telesm*a.

Tandem—at length; *tandem*[3] (one after the other, making great *length*). L. *tandem*.

Tang—touch; *tang*ent (a straight line just *touching* the circumference of a circle), con*tag*ion (*touching together*), con*tig*uous (*touching together*), con*ting*ent (dependent, *touching upon*), *tang*ible (capable of being *touched*). L. *tang*ere.

Tant—so great; *tant*amount. L. *tant*us.

Tapes—carpet, woolen rug, cloth; *tapes*try (*cloth* hangings), *tape*, *tipp*et. L. *tapes*, *tapet*is.

Taph—tomb; epi*taph* (an inscription *on* a *tomb*), ceno*taph* (a monument without a grave, hence an *empty tomb*). G. *taph*os.

Tard—slow; *tard*y, re*tard*. L. *tard*us.

Tart (*tirit*)—shiver; *tart*an (the woolen material of the Scotch plaid.[4] Originally a flimsy woolen cloth of Spain that caused its wearer to *shiver* with cold). Sp. *tirit*ar.

Taur—bull. L. *taur*us.

Tauto—the same thing; *tauto*logy (speaking *the same thing* over and over). G. *tauto*. G. *to auto*.

Tax—order, arrangement; *tax*idermy (the *arrangement* of skins to resemble the living animals), syn*tax* (the treatment of the *arrangement* of words in a sentence). G. *tax*is. G. *tass*ein, to arrange.

Techn—art; *techn*ical (relating to an *art*), pyro*techn*ics (the art of *fireworks*), poly*techn*ic (devoted to *many arts*). G. *techn*e.

Tect—carpenter, builder; archi*tect* (the *chief builder*). G. *tect*on.

Tect—See *teg*.

Tedi (*tædi*)—irksomeness; *tedi*ous. L. *tædi*um. L. *tæd*et, it irks.

Teg; tect—cover; *teg*ument (a *covering*), in*teg*ument, de*tect* (*uncover*), pro*tect* (*cover* in front), *tog*a (a mantle, for covering). L. *teg*ere.

Tegul—tile; *tegul*ar, *til*e. L. *teg*ula. L. *teg*ere, to cover.

Tele—afar off; *tele*graph, *tele*scope, *tele*phone. G. *tele*.

Telluri—the earth; *tellur*ian (an instrument illustrating the motions of the *earth*). L. *tellus, tellur*is.

Tem—strong drink; abs*tem*ious (refraining *from strong drink*). L. *tem*um.

Temer—rash; *temer*ity (rashness). L. *temer*us.

Temn—despise; con*temn*. L. *temn*ere.

Temper—regulate, qualify. L. *temper*are.

Tempest—season, weather. L. *tempest*as.

Templ—temple; *templ*e, con*templ*ate (consider, as did the augurs in the *temple*). L. *templ*um.

Tempor—time; *tempor*ary (enduring for a short *time*), *tempor*al (belonging to *time*), *tempor*ize (to serve the present *time*), con*tempor*aneous (at the same *time*), ex*tempor*ary (*out* of the *moment* or *time*). L. *tempus, tempor*is.

Tempt—prove, try; *tempt*, at*tempt*. L. *tempt*are, *tent*are.

Ten; tent—hold; *ten*able, *ten*ant, *ten*acious, *ten*ement, *ten*et, *ten*on, *ten*or, *ten*ure, abs*tain*, con*tain*, con*tent* (contained, *held* together), con*tin*ent, con*tin*ue, con*tin*uous, coun*ten*ance (visage, *holding* together), de*tain*, enter*tain* (*hold* among), ob*tain* (*hold* near), per*tain* (*hold*, or extend, through to), re*tain*, sus*tain* (uphold, *hold* under). L. *ten*ere.

Tend; tent—stretch, reach; *tend* (*reach* toward), at*tend* (*stretch*, or give heed, to), con*tend* (*stretch* out thoroughly), dis*tend* (*stretch* apart), ex*tend* (*stretch* out), in*tend* (*stretch* into), por*tend* (point out, *stretch* forth), pre*tend* (*stretch* or spread before, as a veil), sub*tend* (*stretch* under), *tend*er (to offer, *stretch* out toward), *tend*er (to *reach* to), *tend*on (the *stretcher* at the end of a muscle). L. *tend*ere, *tent*us.

Tender (*tener*)—thin, *tender*. L. *tener*.

Tens (*temps*)—time. F. *temps*. L. *tempus*.

Tens—stretched; *tens*e (tightly *stretched*), *tens*ion (*stretching*), in*tens*e (*stretched* into). L. *tend*ere, *tens*us.

Tent—stretched; *tent* (a pavilion *stretched*, or spread, out), *tent*er (a frame for *stretching* cloth), in*tent* (purpose, *stretching* into), os*tent*ation (display, *stretching* before the eyes). L. *tend*ere, *tent*us.

Tent—feel, try; *tent*acle (a *feeler*), *tent*ative (on *trial*). L. *tent*are. L. *ten*ere, to hold.

Tenu—thin; *tenu*ity, at*tenu*ate (make *thin*), ex*tenu*ate (excuse, *thin out*). L. *tenu*is.

Tep—be warm; *tep*id. L. *tep*ere.

Terg—the back; *terg*iversation (a subterfuge, as if shuffling around and around and showing one's *back*). L. *terg*um.

Terg; ters—wipe; de*terg*e (*wipe* off), *ters*e (condensed, clean). L. *terg*ere, *ters*us.

Termin—boundary, end; *termin*ate (to end), *terminu*s (the end), de*termine* (to settle or end the matter), ex*termin*ate (destroy utterly, as if driving beyond the *boundaries*). L. *termin*us.

Tern—by threes; *tern*ary. L. *tern*i. L. *ter*, three times.

Terr—earth, land, ground; in*ter* (bury, put *into the earth*), par*terre* (an even piece of garden extending *along* the *ground*), *terr*ier (a dog that burrows in the *ground*), *terr*itory (an extent of *land*), *terr*a firma (the *solid ground*), *terr*a incognita (the *unknown land*), *terr*a cotta (*baked earth*), *terr*a alba (*white earth*), *terr*ene, *terr*estrial, *terr*ace (a platform of *earth*), *terr*aqueous (consisting of *land* and *water*),

subterr**an**ean, Medi**terr**anean (the Sea in the *Midst* of the *Lands*). L. *terr*a.

Terr—to frighten; *terr*ible, *terr*or, *terr*ific, de*ter* (*frighten* from). L. *terr*ere.

Terti—third; *terti*ary. L. *terti*us.

Tessell—little cube, small square piece of stone; *tessell*ated. L. *tessell*a.

Test—shell; *test*aceous (having a hard *shell*). L. *test*a.

Test—witness; at*test* (bear *witness* to), con*test* (call to *witness*), de*test* (execrate, call upon the gods to *witness*), in*test*ate (without a will duly *witnessed*), pro*test* (bear *witness* publicly), *test* (cause to *witness*), *test*ify (bear *witness*), *test*imony (the evidence of a *witness*). L. *test*is.

Test—head; *test*y (hot-*headed*). O.F. *test*e. L. *test*a, shell, skull.

Testat—male a will; *testat*or (the *maker* of a *will*), in*test*ate (without a *will*), *test*ament (a *will*). L. *test*are, *testat*us.

Tetra—four; *tetra*syllable, *tetra*rch, *tra*pezium (a small table, a *four-footed* bench). G. *tetra*.

Text—woven; *text*ile, *text*ure, *text* (the subject *woven* out in the discourse), con*text* (*woven*, or joined, *together*), pre*text* (*woven in front*, as a veil). L. *text*ere, *text*us.

The—a god; *the*ology (the *doctrine* relating to *God*), a*the*ism (denial of the existence of *God*), *the*ism (belief in *God*), *the*ocracy (*government* directly by *God*), apo*the*osis (a deification, or causing to be a *god* on departing *from* this life), Pan*the*on (a temple at Rome dedicated to *all* the *gods*[5]), en*thu*siasm (inspiration, having a *god within*). G. *the*os.

The—place, put; *the*me (a subject *put* down for argument), anti*the*sis (a contrast, a *placing opposite*), epi*the*t (a term or expression *put upon* one), hypo*the*sis (a supposition, a *placing under*), meta*the*-sis (a transposition, a *placing over*), paren*the*sis (a pair of brackets inclosing something added or *put in beside*), syn*the*sis (a *putting together*), *the*sis (an argument or treatment *laid* down). G. ti*the*mi.

Thea—see; *thea*ter (a place for *seeing* shows), am-phi*thea*ter (a place for *seeing* all *around*). G. *thea*omai, I see.

Theor—behold, contemplate; *theor*y (a line of *con-templation* or *reasoning*), *theor*em (something to be *contemplated* or reasoned out). G. *theor*ein. G. *theor*os, a spectator. G. *thea*omai, I see.

Therapeut—attendant; *therapeut*ic (relating to the physician's, or *attendant's*, art). G. *therapeu*ein. G. *therap*, an assistant.

Theri—wild beast; mega*theri*um (the *great beast*), dino*theri*um (the *terrible beast*). G. *theri*on. G. *ther*.

Therm—warm, heat; *therm*al, *therm*ometer, iso*therm* (lines showing equal annual *heat*), *Therm*opylæ (the Pass of the *Hot* Springs). G. *therm*os.

Thorax—breast-plate, chest. G. *thorax*.

Thur—frankincense; *thur*ible (the censer for the burning of *incense*). L. *thus*, *thur*is.

Tic—See *tac*.

Tid—time, hour, season; *tid*e (the *seasonable* rise of the water[6]), *tid*ings (news of the happenings of the *time*), *tid*y (neat, *seasonable*). A.S. *tid*.

Tim—to fear; *tim*id, *tim*orous, in*tim*idate. L. *tim*ere.

Tin—See *ten*.

Ting; tinct—dyed; *ting*e, *tinct*ure, *tint* (a tinge, or *dye*, of color), *taint* (to stain, or *dye*). L. *ting*ere, *tinct*us.

Tir—pull, draw; re*tir*e (*draw back*), *tir*ade (a long-*drawn*-out reproof). F. *tir*er. It. *tir*are.

Tir—a novice; *tir*o. L. *tir*o.

Tiss—weave; *tiss*ue (a *web*). F. *tiss*er.

Titill—tickle; *titill*ation. L. *titill*are.

Titul—inscription, *title*. L. *titul*us.

Toc (*toqu*)—strike; *toc*sin (the striking of the *alarm* bell). O.F. *toqu*er.

Tog—See *teg*.

Toil—cloth; *toil*et (apparel, *clothes*). F. *toil*e. L. *tela*, a web, thing woven.

Toler—put up with; *toler*ate. L. *toler*are.

Tom (*temn*)—cut; ana*tom*y (the structure of a body as revealed in dissection or *cutting up*), a*tom* (an ultimate part that admits no division or *cutting up*[7]), phlebo*tom*y (blood-letting, a *cutting* of the veins), epi*tom*e (an abridgment, a *cutting* on the surface), *tom*e (a volume, formerly a *section* of papyrus). G. *temn*ein.

Tomb (*tumb*)—tomb. G. *tumb*os.

Ton—tone (as if obtained by the *stretching* of a string); *ton*e, *ton*ic (giving *tone*), dia*ton*ic (proceeding by *tones*), in*ton*e, tune. G. *ton*os. G. *tein*ein, to stretch.

Tons—clipped; *tons*ure (the *clipping* of the hair or beard). L. *tond*ere, *tons*us.

Tons—an oar; *tons*il (the little *oar*). L. *tons*a.

Top—a place; *top*ography (*description* of a *place*), *top*ic (a common *place*). G. *top*os.

Torn—turn; *torn*ado (a violent wind suddenly *returned*), at*torn*ey (see *attorn*). L. *torn*are. L. *torn*us, a lathe.

Torp—benumb; *torp*id, *torp*edo (a fish that electrifies or causes numbness). L. *torp*ere.

Torr—be dry; *torr*id (*dry*, scorched, hot). L. *torr*ere.

Torrent—hot, boiling, raging. L. *torrens*, *torrent*is. L. *torr*ere, to heat.

Tors—stump, trunk; *tors*o (the *trunk* of a statue). It. *tors*o. L. *thyrs*us, a stalk, stem. G. *thurs*os, a stalk, rod, thyrsus.

Tors—twist; *tors*ion (a *twisting*). L. *torqu*ere, *tors*us.

Tort—twist, wring; con*tort* (*twist together*), dis*tort* (*twist apart*), ex*tort* (*twist out*), re*tort* (*twist back*), *tort*ure (a *wringing* pain), *tort*oise (the reptile with the *twisted* feet), *tort*uous (crooked, *twisted*), *tart* (the *twisted* cake or pie), *torch* (made of a *twisted* piece of tow), *tort*ment (to *wring* with pain). L. *torqu*ere, *tort*us.

Tot—entire, all; *tot*al, sur*tout* (over *all*). L. *tot*us.

Tour (*tourn*)—turn; *tour* (a circuit or *turn*), con*tour* (an outline, a *turn* together), de*tour* (a *turn* aside). F. *tour*ner. L. *torn*are.

Tourn—turn; *tourn*quet (a *turning* instrument for tightening a bandage, and stanching the flow of blood), *tourn*ey (a joust, a *turning* round about), *tourn*ament (a jousting or *turning* about). F. *tourn*er. L. *torn*are. L. *torn*us, a lathe.

Tout—See *tot*.

Toxic—poison for arrows; *toxic*ology (the science of *poisons*), in*toxic*ate (to put *poison* into the blood). G. *toxic*on. G. *tox*on, a bow.

Trach—rough; *trach*ea (the *rough*-surfaced windpipe). G. *trach*us.

Tract—draw; at*tract* (*draw to*), con*tract* (*draw together*), dis*tract* (*draw apart*), ex*tract* (*draw out*), pro*tract* (*draw forward*), re*tract* (*draw back*), *tract* (a short treatise *drawn* up), *tract* (a region *drawn* or spread out). L. *trah*ere, *tract*us.

Tradit—deliver, betray; *tradit*ion (the story of the past *delivered* by one generation to another), *trait*or (one who *betrays* or delivers up), be*tray* (to *deliver up*). L. *trad*ere, *tradit*us.

Trag—goat; *trag*edy (a drama presenting a fatal issue, originally a play or *song* at which a *goat* was sacrificed to Dionysios). G. *trag*os.

Trah—draw; sub*trah*end (the part to be *subtracted*

or *drawn down*), por*tray* (to represent with *lines drawn* forth), *tra*il. L. *tra*here.

Trait—draw, drawn; *trait* (a feature, as if a *line* or *stroke*), por*trait* (a likeness *drawn* out). F. *tra*ire, *trait*. L. *tra*here, *tract*us.

Trait—See *tradit*.

Tranquill—at rest. L. *tranquill*us.

Trans—across; *trans*om (a *cross*-beam over a door). L. *trans*.

Trap (*trapp*)—stair; *trap* (an igneous rock of columnar structure, and seeming to rise in *steps*[8]). M.E. *træpp*e.

Trapez—a table; *trapez*ium (having the form of a small *table*), *trapez*e (having the form of a *trapezium*). G. *trapez*a. G. *tetra*, four; *pez*a, foot.

Trav (*traf*)—beam; archi*trav*e (the lower portion of the entablature, being the *chief beam* resting immediately on the columns). F. *traf*. L. *trabs*.

Travail—toil, labor. F. *travail*.

Treacher (*tricher*)—to trick; *treacher*y. O.F. *trichier*.

Treasur (*thesaur*)—store, hoard; *treasur*e, *treasur*y.[9] G. *thesaur*os. G. ti*the*mi, *thes*o, I place.

Treat (*tract*)—handle; *treat*, *treat*ise, *treat*y, en*treat*. L. *tract*are. L. *tra*here, *tract*us, to draw.

Trebl (*tripl*)—threefold; *trebl*e. L. *tripl*us. L. *tri*, three; *plus*, fold.

Trell (*treill*)—a latticed frame; *trell*is (lattice-work). F. *treill*e. L. *trichil*a, *tricl*a, an arbor.

Trem—tremble; *trem*ble, *trem*or, *trem*endous (causing to *tremble*), *trem*ulous. L. *trem*ere.

Trench—cut; *trench* (a ditch *cut* in the ground), *trench*ant (*cutting*), *trench*er (a wooden plate to *cut* or carve things on), re*trench* (*cut* down). F. *trench*er.

Trend—roll, turn round; *trend* (bend away, as if *turning round*). M.E. *trend*en.

Trepid—trembling, agitated; *trepid*ation, in*trepid*

(fearless, not *trembling*). L. *trepid*us. Low L. tre-
pere, to turn round.

Tri—three; *tri*ad (a union of *three*), *tri*angle, *tri*brach
(a poetic foot having *three short* syllables), *tri*dent (a
three-toothed spear), *tri*ennial (occurring once in
three years), *tri*foliate, *tri*glyph (the *three-grooved*
tablet in the Doric frieze), *tri*hedron, *tri*lateral, *tri*o,
*tri*ple, *tri*pod, *tri*sect, *tri*vial (the *three roads* to
knowledge: grammar, rhetoric and logic, satirized
as medieval thinking during Enlightenment). L. *tri*.

Tri—See *trit*; de*tri*ment.

Trib—race, family (like the three original families in
Rome); *trib*une (the chief of a *tribe*). L. *trib*us. L.
tres, *tri*, three.

Trib—rub, waste away; dia*tribe* (an abusive harangue,
a *wasting away* of time). G. *trib*ein.

Tribul—a threshing sledge with spikes; *tribul*ation
(affliction, as if under the *threshing sledge*[10]). L.
*tribul*um. L. *ter*ere, to rub.

Tribut—assign, allow, grant, pay; at*tribute* (*grant to*),
con*tribute* (*pay together*), dis*tribute* (*grant*, or
place, *apart*), re*tribut*ion (a *paying back*), *tribut*e
(a sum *paid*), *tribut*ary (*paying tribute* to). L.
*tribu*ere, *tribut*us. L. *trib*us, a tribe.[11]

Tric—hindrances, vexations, wiles, snares; in*tric*ate
(involved, as if by *hindrances*), ex*tric*ate (to disen-
tangle, as from *snares*), in*trig*ue (to plot, to *insnare*).
L. *tric*æ.

Triev—See *trov*.

Trigon—triangle; *trigon*ometry (the science that *measures triangles*). G. *trigon*on. G. *tri*, three; *gonia*,
angle.

Trin—by threes; *trin*ity. L. *trin*i. L. *tres*, *tri*a.

Trit—rub; at*trit*ion (*rubbing* against), de*trit*us (loose
matter *rubbed* down), detriment (a *rubbing* away),
*trit*urate (to grind, *rub*), *trit*e (worn out, *rubbed*

away), try (to test, as by *rubbing* the corn out of straw), tribulation (trial, as with a *flail*). L. *ter*ere, *trit*us.

Triumph—a public rejoicing over a victory. L. *triumph*us.

Triv—See *trov*.

Troch (*trech*)—run; *troch*ee (a *running* measure), *truck* (a wheel *runner*), *truck*le-bed (a bed running on *trucks*, or *wheels*). G. *trech*ein.

Trogl—hole, cave; *trogl*odyte (*cave*-dweller). G. *trogle*.

Tromb—trumpet; *tromb*one (the great *trumpet*). It. *tromb*a.

Trop—a turn; *trop*ic (the circle at which the sun *turns*), *trope* (a figure, or *turn*, of speech), *trop*hy (a monument of the rout of an enemy who *turn* to flight, a memento of victory[12]), helio*trope* (the flower that constantly *turns* to the *sun*). G. *trope*. G. *trep*ein, to turn.

Trov—find; *trov*er (an action arising out of the *finding* of goods), treasure-*trove* (treasure *found*), con*trive* (invent, *find* out), re*trieve* (recover, *find* again). O.F. *trov*er. O.F. *trove*.

Truc—fierce, wild, cruel; *truc*ulent. L. *trux*, *truc*is.

Trud; trus—thrust; de*trude* (*thrust down*), ex*trude* (*thrust out*), in*trude* (*thrust into*), ob*trude* (*thrust against*), pro*trude* (*thrust forth*), abs*truse* (difficult, *thrust away* from ready apprehension). L. *trud*ere, *trus*us.

Trunc—stump, staff; *trunc*ate (cut off, and make a *stump*), *trunk* (the stem, or *stump*, of a tree), *trun*cheon (a marshal's short *staff*), *trounce* (to beat with a *stick*). L. *trunc*us.

Tuber—a swelling; *tuber* (a rounded, *swelling* root), pro*tuber*ant (*swelling* forward). L. *tuber*.

Tuit—watch, protect, look; *tuit*ion (the sum paid for

the training, and therefore *watching* over, of a pupil), in*tuit*ion (an inward insight or instinct, a *looking upon*), *tut*elar (*protecting*), *tut*elage (*guardianship*), *tut*or (a *guardian*). L. *tu*eri, *tuit*us.

Tum—to swell, surge up; *tum*id (*swollen*), *tum*ulus (a mound, or *swell*, of earth), *tum*ult (a *surging up* of a crowd), *tum*efy (*cause* to *swell*), in*tum*escence (the act of *swelling*). L. *tum*ere.

Tunic—an under-garment. L. *tunic*a.

Turb—disturb, drive; *turb*id (*disturbed*), *turb*ulent (very *disturbing*), dis*turb* (*drive apart*), per*turb* (*disturb thoroughly*). L. *turb*are. L. *turb*a, a crowd (or confused mass).

Turbo—spindle, reel; *turb*ot (a fish having the rhomboidal form of a *reel*). L. *turbo*.

Turg—swell out; *turg*id (*swollen*). L. *turg*ere.

Turp—base, wicked; *turp*itude. L. *turp*is.

Turr—tower; *turr*et (a *little tower*), *tow*er. L. *turr*is.

Tus—strike; con*tus*ion (a severe bruising, a *striking together*). L. *tund*ere, *tus*us.

Tut—See *tuit*.

Twi—double; *twi*ce, *twi*bill, *twi*g (a shoot, causing its branch to *double*), *twi*light (the *double*, or doubtful, light[13]), *twi*n, *twi*ne, *twi*st. A.S. *twi*.

Tympan—drum; *tympan*um (the *drum* of the ear). L. *tympan*um. G. *tumpan*on. G. *tupt*ein, to strike.

Typ—a blow, impression, model; arche*typ*e (the original *model*), anti*typ*e (the copy formed *against* the *model*), *typ*e (a *model*). G. *tup*os. G. *tupt*ein, to strike.

Typh—smoke, mist, stupor; *typh*us (the *stupor* fever). G. *tuph*os. G. *tuph*ein, to smoke.

Tyrann—lord, master, sovereign; *tyran*t (a cruel *master* or *ruler*). G. *turann*os.

NOTES

[1] The famous Roman laws of the *Twelve Tables* were so called because they were inscribed on *tables* of brass for their preservation. These laws were framed by a body of men called *decemvirs* because of their number. The laws were taken mainly from the institutions of other nations, and were modified so as to meet the peculiar conditions at Rome. In this respect a wisdom was displayed that afterward was exemplified in the making of the Constitution of the United States. To retain what had been found good in the old and well tried, and to try only as few novelties and experiments as were absolutely unavoidable, was the principle upon which our great fundamental law was based. It is, therefore, an historical instrument, the development or outcome of the experience of all the ages in the work of government. This is why it stands the strain of use. Constitutions framed on abstract theories of social order have been snapped like frail threads when placed as restraining harness upon masses that were following out historical tendencies.

[2] The English law permits a testator to fix a line of descent for the real estate which he holds in *fee (absolutely)*. The great estates in England are all *entailed*, being only life interests to the holders. They are entailed in the line of the eldest son, according to the there prevailing law of *primogeniture*. A father can not dispose of his son's estate nor keep him out of his inheritance under the *entail*.

[3] This use of the word originated as a university pun.

[4] When Jeannie Deems went to London to plead with the Queen for the life of her sister, she besought the Duke of Hamilton to procure her an audience with the royal lady. Before entering the presence of the Duke, she arrayed herself in the national plaid, saying that "the heart of MacCallummore will be as cold as death can make it when it does not warm to the *tartan*."—"*Heart of Midlothian*," by Scott.

[5] In their career of conquest the Romans encountered all forms of heathenism, different countries having different divinities and different forms of worship. The Romans re-

spected all those religions, and even formally adopted the gods of the conquered countries. And they finally erected in the city a temple dedicated, not like the others, to individual gods, but to *all* the gods of the Roman Empire. This hospitality to their divinities and tolerance of their religion, together with other wise concessions, tended to reconcile the conquered races to the dominion of Rome and to consolidate the vast empire. When Christianity came preaching the one true God, and the worthlessness of *all* the *gods*, the Roman government assailed it with the most bitter persecution. For three hundred years the Christians were driven to caves in the earth, or torn by wild beasts to make a Roman holiday, until at last a Roman emperor, Constantine the Great, the founder of Constantinople, was converted. Christianity spread over the empire; the gods of the Pantheon were abolished, and the Pantheon itself became a Christian church.

[6] The tide is due to the attraction of the moon and, to some extent, to the attraction of the sun. The rising is called the *flood*, and the falling the *ebb* tide. When the sun and moon are in conjunction or opposition, we have our highest tide, called *spring tide*, as the result of their joint attraction. This occurs at new moon and full moon. When the moon is in the first or last quarter, the sun is then in a position to partly neutralize or overcome the moon's attraction. We then have the lowest tide, called *neap tide*. The tide rises simultaneously on opposite sides of the earth. This is due, in the first place, to the moon's attraction pulling the loose water up from the solid earth, and, in the second place, to its pulling the solid earth away from the loose water on the other side. A corresponding depression of the waters or low tide occurs on the sides of the earth that are at right angles to the direction of the moon's attraction.

The conformation of the land may cause an exceptionally high tide, as in the Bay of Fundy. Here the wide entrance receives a long section of the tidal wave, which, as it advances to the interior angle, is forced together and upward until it reaches the phenomenal height of sixty feet and upward.

Hence the language of the proverb, "Time and *tide* wait for no man."

[7] One of the recognized properties of matter is divisibility. The process of division may be carried beyond what the eye is

capable of seeing by making use of fine instruments and a powerful microscope. The particles obtained by the extreme limit of physical separation are susceptible of further division, and the mind can conceive of their being divided and subdivided. But it conceives an ultimate limit to this process of division, and the particles thus obtained are called *atoms* because they were thought *not* to be susceptible of further *division*. Ana*tomy*, Epi*tome*, Litho*tomy*, Phlebo*tomy*, *Tome*.

8 The trap rock is formed by passing upward in a molten condition through a fissure in the earth's crust and cooling so as to occupy the fissure. The compression in such a narrow space while cooling tends to give it the columnar structure. The trap-rock is very hard, and thus capable of resisting to a remarkable extent the action of the elements. When the adjacent crust is torn and worn away, the face of the trap formation with its apparently immortal columns towering in the air, presents to the eye a highly interesting, or even magnificent, spectacle. Among the famous examples of this formation are the Palisades of the Hudson River, the Giant's Causeway in Ireland, and Fingal's Cave on the Island of Staffa.

9 When Crœsus, the famous King of Lydia, was in possession of his great wealth and in the pride of his power and opulence, he was visited by Solon, the renowned legislator of Athens, and one of the Seven Wise Men of Greece. The monarch, desirous of making an impression upon his distinguished visitor, took the latter through his treasury, ablaze with wealth in every conceivable form. As the philosopher gave no sign, the king endeavored to penetrate his thoughts by asking him whom he considered the happiest person that he had yet encountered. After a period of reflection, greatly to the astonishment of the monarch, Solon mentioned some obscure individual in Athens. This poor man, he stated, had brought up a large family of boys and girls, but not one of whom had gone astray. After such a glorious achievement, he was further privileged, in his old age, to die in the front of battle fighting for his country. Greater cause of happiness to an individual had not come under his notice. Being questioned again to the same purport, he mentioned a certain poor widow of Sparta. On the approach of the Olympian games, her two sons, desirous of securing their mother a favorable seat, and failing to find their cattle in time, hitched themselves to her chariot and

dashed away to Olympia. This act of maternal piety produced such universal applause that the boys were permitted to lodge in the temple of Apollo. In the morning they were found dead, the god having adopted and taken them unto himself.

The mortified king, in his impatience, at last asked directly: 'How about me?" "Alas!" replied Solon, "no one can be pronounced happy till after his death, for he can not tell what reverses may be in store for him." The force of this remark came home to Crœsus afterward, when, despoiled of his kingdom and wealth by the conquering Cyrus, he was led forth a miserable captive to die on the funeral pyre. In the anguish of the moment he groaned aloud, "Oh! Solon! Solon!" Cyrus was curious to know why he called on Solon; and being told of the incident in the treasury, he was so moved that he decided to spare the life of his unhappy captive, and ever afterward he kept him near his person.

[10] Hence the phrase "under the *harrow* of *affliction*."

[11] Hence tribute meant literally the sum *paid* by a conquered *tribe*.

[12] The American Indian bears away the scalp-lock of his slain enemy, as a trophy of his prowess. The ancient warrior secured as his trophy the weapons and defensive armor of the foe who fell beneath his arm. The removal of these *spoils* left the body nearly or entirely naked. The spoils of a king, or commander-in-chief, were called at Rome the *spolia opima*, and were carefully preserved in the temples as trophies of the highest value. Pythagoras could visit a Greek temple eight hundred years after the siege of Troy and take down the arms of Euphorbus. (See *Metempsychosis*.)

[13] Twilight is due to the refraction of the sun's rays in passing through our atmosphere. As refraction is a bending of rays of light out of their original direction, there may be a partial illumination even from a luminary that has become entirely invisible, as may be seen in the ability to read in the shadow of a wall or other object obscuring the sun. Twilight prevails until the sun has descended thirteen degrees below the horizon. This limit is reached most rapidly at the equator and more slowly in

the higher latitudes, on account of the position of the plane of the horizon relative to the axis of rotation. The short day on an Arctic winter, therefore, has some compensation in the longer twilight; and the region of total obscurity in the north has the further aid of the *aurora borealis*.

U

Uber—be fruitful (or abundant, like *flowing milk*[1]); ex*uber*ant (abundant, extremely *fruitful*). L. *uber*-are. L. *uber*, an udder.

Ubiqu—everywhere; *ubiqu*ity (being present *everywhere*). L. *ubique*. L. *ubi*, where.

Ud—See *sud*.

Ulcer—sore; *ulcer* (a running *sore*). L. *ulcus, ulceris*.

Ulm—elm; *ulm*aceous. L. *ulmus*.

Ulter—beyond; *ulter*ior (further, more *beyond*). O.L. *ulter*.

Ultim—last; *ultim*ate (the *last*), *ultim*atum (the *last* proposition for settlement), *ultim*o (*last* month), pen*ult*(*im*) (*almost* the *last* syllable in a word, the *last* but one). L. *ultimus*.

Umbell—a parasol; *umbel* (a *parasol*-shaped inflorescence). L. *umbell*a. L. *umbr*a, a shade.

Umbr—shade; ad*umbr*ate (*shadow* forth), *umbr*ella (a *shade* from sun and storm), *umbr*age (offense, the *shadow* of suspicion), pen*umbr*a (*almost* a *shadow*). L. *umbr*a.

Un—one; *un*animous (of *one mind*), *un*icorn (the fabulous horse with *one* straight *horn* in the center of his forehead), *un*iform (alike, regular, of *one form*), *un*ion (a forming of *one*), *un*ique (exceptional, like only its *one* self), *un*it (a single *one*), *un*ite (to form into *one*), *un*ity (*oneness*), *un*iversal (general, *turned* into *one* whole), *un*iverse (the *universal*, or entire, creation), *un*iversity (a higher school, in which all, or *universal*, branches are taught), *on*ion (a plant whose several folds adhere in close *union*), tri*une* (consisting of *three* in *one*). L. *un*us.

Unct—See *ungu*.

Und—wave, flow; *und*ulate (to *wave*), ab*ound* (*overflow*), in*und*ate (*flow in* upon), red*ound* (*flow back*), red*und*ant (*overflowing, flowing back*). L. *und*a.

Ungu; unct—anoint; *ungu*ent (an *ointment*), *unct*ion (*anointing*). L. *ungu*ere, *unct*us.

Ur (*our*)—tail; cyno*sure* (an object attracting attention, like the north star in the end of the *dog tail* of the Little Bear), col*ure* (one of two circles passing through the solstitial or equinoxial points, and giving, where cut by the horizon, the appearance of the *docked tail* of a horse), squ*irre*l (ski*ure*l, the little animal whose bushy *tail* casts a *shadow*). G. *our*a, a tail; *col*os, docked; *ski*a, a shadow.

Urb—city; sub*urb* (near the *city*), *urb*ane (courteous, after the manner of *cities*). L. *urb*s.

Usur—use, interest; *usur*y (excessive *interest*). L. *usur*a. L. *uti, us*us, to use.

Usurp—employ, acquire, seize. L. *usurp*are.

Ut—use; *ut*ensil (an article of *use*), *ut*ilize (make *useful*), *ut*ility (*usefulness*). L. *ut*i.

Util—useful; *util*ity, *util*ize. L. *util*is. L. *ut*i, to use.

Uv—grape. L. *uv*a.

Uxor—wife; *uxor*ious (excessively fond of a *wife*), *uxor*icide (the killing of a *wife*). L. *uxor*.

NOTES

[1] A *fruitful* land *flows* with *milk* and honey.

V

Vac—be empty, at leisure; *vac*ation, e*vac*uate, *vac*uum.

Vacc—cow; *vacc*inate (to inoculate with virus taken from a *cow*). L. *vacc*a.

Vacill—reel; *vacill*ation (changing about, unsteady, as if *reeling* on the feet). L. *vacill*are.

Vacu—empty; *vacu*um, e*vacu*ate, *vacu*ous, *vacu*ity. L. *vacu*us. L. *vac*are, to be empty.

Vad; vas—go; e*vad*e (to shun, escape, *go* out), in*vad*e (*go* into), per*vad*e (*go* through). L. *vad*ere.

Vag—wander; *vag*abond, *vag*rant, *vag*ue, *vag*ary (a strange, or *wandering*, notion), extra*vag*ant (*wandering* beyond proper limits). L. *vag*ari.

Val—valley; *val*e, a*val*anch (a rush of loosened snow toward the *valley*). F. *val*. L. *val*lis.

Val—be strong, be worth, be of use; *val*id, *val*iant, *val*or, *val*ue, in*val*id, a*vail*, con*val*esce (grow *strong*, or well, again), counter*vail* (*be strong* against), pre*vail* (*be strong* over). L. *val*ere.

Val (*valr*)—the slain, slaughter; *val*halla (the *hall of the slain*, the paradise of the Northmen[1]). Icel. *valr*.

Vale—farewell; *vale*dictory (see *dict*). L. *vale*. L. *vale*re, to be strong.

Valetudin—health; *valetudin*ary (having poor *health*). L. *valetud*o, *valetudin*is. L. *val*ere, to be strong.

Vall—a rampart; circum*vall*ation (the placing of a *rempart around*), inter*val* (a space between, like the space *between* the *rampart* of a camp and the soldiers' tents[2]), *wall*. L. *vall*um. L. *vall*us, a stake, palisade.

Valv—leaf of a folding-door; *valv*e, bi*valv*e. L. *valv*a, *valv*æ.

Van—empty, vain; *vain* (*empty*, useless), *van*ity (*emptiness*), *van*ish (to disappear, and leave its place *empty*), e*van*escent (*vanishing* away), *vaunt* (to make *vain* or *empty* boasts). L. *van*us.

Vandal (*wandel*)—wander; *Vandal* (a barbarian, a member of one of the *wandering* tribes that overthrew the Roman Empire[3]). Ger. *wandel*n.

Vanqu (*vinc*)—conquer. L. *vinc*ere.

Vapid—stale. L. *vapid*us. L. *vapp*a, palled wine.

Vapor—vapor, breath; *vapor*, e*vapor*ate (pass off in *vapor*). L. *vapor*.

Vari—diverse, of many kinds; *vari*ous, *vary*, *vari*egate. L. *vari*us.

Varic—dilated vein; *varic*ose (permanently *dilated*). L. *varix*, *varic*is. L. *var*us, crooked.

Varic—straddling, diverging; pre*varic*ate (to be untruthful, to shift ground, or *straddle*), di*varic*ate (*diverging* apart). L. *varic*us. L. *var*us, crooked.

Variol—small-pox; *variol*oid (a *form* of *small-pox*). L. *variol*a. L. *vari*us, varied, spotted.

Vas—vessel; *vas*e, *vas*cular (having little *vessels*), extra*vas*ate (to draw *out* of the proper *vessels*), *ves*sel. L. *vas*.

Vast—great; *vast*. L. vastus.

Vast—lay waste; de*vast*ate. L. *vast*are. L. *vast*us, great.

Veer—See vir.

Veget—quicken, enliven; *veget*able (a plant fir or able to *live*). L. *veget*are. L. *veget*us, lively. L. *veg*ere, to quicken, arouse.

Veh—carry, bring; *veh*icle, vehement (impassioned, being *carried* out of one's mind), in*veigh* (*bring* against), *vein* (the vessel which *carries* the blood back to the heart[4]). L. *veh*ere.

Vel—veil; re*veal* (bring into view, put back the *veil*), *veil*. L. *velu*m, a ship's sail. L. *veh*ere, to carry, propel.

Veloc—swift; *veloc*ity, *veloc*ipede. L. *velox, veloc*is.

Velop—wrap, cover; en*velop* (*cover* in), de*velop* (*uncover*). O.F. en*volop*er

Ven—sale; *ven*al (corrupt, *selling* influence[5]). L. *ven*us, *ven*um.

Ven; vent—come; con*ven*e (*come* together), con*ven*ient (suitable, *coming* together), co*ven*ant (an agreement or *coming* together), inter*ven*e (*come* between), par*ven*u (a new arrival, just *come* through), re*ven*ue (*income, come* back), souv*en*ir (a remembrance, a *coming* into mind), super*ven*e (*come* upon, after), *ven*ue (the arrival or *coming* of a court), ad*vent* (*come* to), ad*vent*ure (a *ventur*y), con*vent* (an assembly, or *coming* together), con*vent*ion (a *coming* together), e*vent* (a result, *outcome*), in*vent* (find out, *come* upon), pre*vent* (anticipate, *come* before), *vent*ure (a *coming* upon). L. *ven*ire, *vent*us.

Ven—hunt; *ven*ison. L. *ven*ari.

Ven—vein; *ven*ous, *ven*esection. L. *ven*a.

Vend—sell; *vend*ible. L. *vend*ere.

Vener—reverence; *vener*able. L. *vener*ari. L. *venus, vener*is, love.

Veng—avenge; *veng*eance, a*veng*e, re*veng*e. F. *veng*er. L. *vindic*are, to lay claim to. L. *vindex, vindic*is, a claimant.

Veni—pardon; *veni*al (*pardonable*). L. *veni*a.

Vent—wind; *vent*ilate. L. *vent*us.

Vent—See *ven*.

Ventr—belly, stomach; *ventr*al, *ventr*icle, *ventr*iloquist. L. *venter, ventr*is.

Ver—spring; *ver*nal. L. *ver*.

Ver—true, truth; *ver*acious (*truthful*), *ver*ify (make out to be *true*), *ver*ity (a *truth*), *ver*dict (a *truthful* report), a*ver* (affirm to be *true*), *ver*y (in *truth*), *ver*isimilitude (an appearance of *truth*). L. *ver*us, true.

Verb—word; *verb*al (by *word* of mouth), *verb*atim (*word* for *word*), *verb*ose (*wordly*), *verb* (the asserting *word* of a sentence), pro*verb* (an old saying, a public *word*). L. *verb*um.

Verber—scourge, whip; re*verber*ate (to *whip* or beat back). L. *verber*.

Verd—flourish, be green; *verd*ant. F. *verd*ir. O.F. *verd*, green. L. *virid*is, green.

Verd—green; *verd*ant, *verd*igris (the *green* rust of bronze). O.F. *verd*. L. *virid*is.

Verg—tend, incline; con*verg*e, di*verg*e. L. *verg*ere.

Verg—wand, loop, ring, edge; *verg*er (the *rod-bearer*), *verg*e (the *edge* or *brink*). F. *verg*e. L. *virg*a.

Verm—worm; *verm*in, *verm*icelli, *verm*icular, *verm*ilion (of the color of the cochineal insect or *worm*). L. *verm*is.

Vern—home-born slave; *vern*acular (so thoroughly native to a country that it is possessed by the *home-born slaves*[6]). L. *vern*a.

Vers—dwell; con*vers*e (associate, *dwell with*). L. *vers*ari. L. *vert*ere, *vers*us, to turn.[7]

Vert; vers—turn; *vers*e (a line, or *turn*, of poetry), *vers*ion (a translation or *turning* into another language), *vert*ebra (a turning section of the spine), *vert*igo (giddiness, a *turning* round and round), *vert*ex (the highest point, like the zenith, the *turning* point of the stars), *vort*ex (a *whirlpool*), ad*vers*e (*turned toward* or against), ad*vert* (*turn to*), ad*vert*ise (inform, *turn to*), a*vert* (*turn aside*), anni*vers*ary (the *return* of the *year*), contro*vers*y (a quarrel or turning *against*), con*verse* (dwell, *turn* about, talk *with*), con*vert* (*turn completely*), di*vers* (*turned apart*), di*verse* (*turned apart*), di*vert* (*turn apart*), di*vorce* (a separation or *turning* apart), in*vert* (*turn over*), mal*versation* (*ill*-conduct or *turning* in office), ob*verse* (*turned toward*), per*vert* (ruin, *turn thoroughly*), pro(re*ver*)se (direct, or *turned forward*, discourse), re*verse* (*turned back*), re*vert* (*turn back*), sub*vert* (*turn under*), trans*verse* (*turned across*), tra*verse* (*turned across*), *vers* (a line or turn), *versed* (skilled, *turned*). L. *verte*re, *versus*.

Vesic—bladder; *vesicle*. L. *vesica*.

Vesper—the evening star; *vespers* (an *evening* service). L. *vesper*.

Vest—garment, clothing; *vest*, *vest*ment, *vest*ure, *vestry* (the wardrobe or place for *clothing*), di*vest* (strip off, *unclothe*), in*vest* (*clothe in*), tra*vesty* (a mockery like a disguise or change of *clothes*). L. *vestis*.

Vestibul—a fore-court; *vestibule* (an ante-chamber, or *fore-court*). L. *vestibulum*. L. *ve*, separate from; *stabulum*, an abode. L. *stare*, to stand.

Vestigi—foot-track; *vestige* (*track*, trace), in*vestig*ate (*track* out). L. *vestigium*.

Veter—old; *veteran*, in*veter*ate (lasting a *long time*). L. *vetus*, *veteris*.

Veterin—belonging to beasts of burden; *veterin*ary. L. *veterinus*.

Veto—I forbid. L. *veto*.

Vex—carried; con*vex* (*carried* together). L. *vehere*, *vexus*.

Vex—harass. L. *vexare*. L. *vehere*, *vexus*, to carry, convey.

Vi—way, road; *viaduct* (a *road* conducted over a stream or valley), de*viate* (go from the *way*), de*vious* (going out of the *way*), ob*viate* (prevent, come against in the *way*), ob*vious* (evident, lying in the *way* against), per*v*ious (allowing a passage or *way* through), pre*v*ious (on the *way* before), con*vey* (be with in the *way*), con*voy* (accompany, be with in the *way*), en*voy* (a messenger sent on his *way*), in*voi*ce (an account of goods sent on their *way*), *voy*age. L. *vi*a.

Viand—food; *viand*s. F. *viand*e. L. *vivenend*a. L. *viv*ere, to live.

Vibr—swing; *vibr*ate. L. *vibr*are.

Vic—a change, turn; *vic*issitude, *vic*ar (a deputy who takes his *turn* at the duties of the office). L. *vic*is.

Vicari—deputy; *vicari*ous (by *deputy*), *vicar* (a *deputy*). L. *vicari*us. L. *vic*is, turn, change, succession.

Vice—in the place of; *vice*gerent (ruling *in the place of*), *vice*roy (*in the place of* the king). L. *vice*.

Vicin—near; *vicin*ity. L. *vicin*us. L. *vic*us, village, street.[8]

Vict—live; *vict*uals (food by which we *live*). L. *viv*ere, *vict*us.

Vict—See *vinc*.

Victim—victim. L. *victim*a.

Vid; vis—see, appear; e*vid*ent (being *seen* clearly), pro*vid*e (*foresee*), *vis*ion, *vis*ible, *vis*it (go to *see*), *vis*or (the face, or *seeing* part, of a helmet), *vis*ta (a *view*), *vis*ual. L. *vid*ere, *vis*us.

Vigil—awake; *vigil*, *vigil*ant. L. *vigil*. L. *vig*ere, to be lively.

Vigor—vigor; in*vigor*ate. L. *vigor*. L. *vig*ere, to be lively.

Vil—base; *vil*e. L. *vil*is.

Vill—farm-house; *vill*a, *vill*age (a collection of *farm*-houses), *vill*ain (an abandoned wretch, like some of the early *farm*-slaves). L. *vill*a.

Vin—wine; *vin*e (the *wine* plant, the grape), *vin*tage, *vin*egar (the *eager*, or sharp, *wine*). L. *vin*um.

Vinc; vict—conquer; con*vinc*e (*conquer* with), e*vinc*e (thoroughly *conquer*), in*vinc*ible (*unconquerable*), *vanqu*ish, e*vict* (*conquer* out), *vict*or. L. *vinc*ere, *vict*us.

Vindic—lay claim to, avenge; *vindic*ate, *vindic*tive. L. *vindic*are.

Viol—treat with force; *viol*ate, *viol*ent. L. *viol*are.

Vir—man; *vir*ile (*manly*), *vir*ago (a scolding, *man-like* woman), *vir*tue (*manly* excellence), decem*vir* (one of the *ten men* who once ruled Rome), trium*vir* (one of the *three men* who once ruled Rome). L. *vir*.

Vir—poison; *vir*us, *vir*ulent. L. *vir*us.

Virgin—a maid. L. *virgo*, *virgin*is.

Virid—green; *virid*ity. L. *virid*is.

Vis—See *vid*.

Vit—life; *vit*al. L. *vit*a.

Viti—vice, fault; *viti*ate. L. *viti*um.

Vitr—glass; *vitr*eous, *vitr*ify, *vitr*iol (the *glassy* substance). L. *vitr*um.

Vitul—calf; *vitul*ine, *veal*, *vell*um (*calf's* skin), *viol* (an instrument first used at a festival at which a *calf* was sacrificed). L. *vitul*us.

Vituper—blame; *vituper*ate (to *blame* violently). L. *vituper*are. L. *viti*um, fault; *par*are, to prepare.

Viv—live; *viv*acity (*liveliness*), *viv*ify (to give *life* to), *viv*id (*lively*), *viv*iparous (producing *live* young), *viv*isection (cutting up *alive*), re*viv*e (*live* again), sur*viv*e (*outlive*). L. *viv*ere.

Voc—voice; *voc*al (belonging to the *voice*), *voc*iferate (shout aloud, lift up the *voice*), *viva voce* (with the living *voice*). L. *vox*, *voc*is.

Voc—call; *voc*ation (a *calling*), ad*voc*ate (plead, *call upon*), a*voc*ation (a diversion, a *calling away* of the attention), con*voc*e (*call together*), e*voc*e (*call out*), in*voc*e (*call upon*), pro*voc*e (*call forth*), re*voc*e (*call back*), *vouc*h (to warrant, *call* upon in support of). L. *voc*are. L. *vox*, *voc*is, the voice.

Vocabul—name, word; *vocabul*ary (a list of *words*), *vocable* (a *term* or *word*). L. *vocabul*um. L. *voc*are, to call. L. *vox*, *voc*is, the voice.

Vol—wish, will; *vol*ition. L. *vol*o, I wish.

Vol—fly; *vol*ley (a *flight* of shot), *vol*ant, *vol*atile (tending to disperse or *fly* away). L. *vol*are.

Volu—See *volv*.

Volunt—free-will; *volunt*ary (of one's own *free-will*). L. *volunt*as. L. *vol*o, I wish.

Volupt—pleasure; *volupt*uous (full of *pleasure*), *volupt*uary (one devoted to sensual *pleasures*). L. *volupt*as. L. *volup*, *volupe*, agreably. L. *vol*o, I wish.

Volv; volu; volut—roll; circum*volve* (*roll around*), con*volve* (*roll together*), de*volve* (roll down), e*volve* (*roll out, unroll*), in*volve* (*roll in*), re*volve* (*roll again*), *volu*me (a book, formerly a *roll* of papyrus or parchment), *volu*ble (fluent, having the words *rolling* out with ease), re*volu*tion (an overturning or *rolling* back[9]), re*volt* (an overthrow or *rolling* back of authority), *vault* (a chamber with a curved or *rolled* roof), *volut* (a spiral scroll, or *roll*, on a capital). L. *volv*ere, *volut*us.

Vom—vomit. L. *vom*ere.

Vor—devour; *vor*acious, de*vour*, herbi*vor*ous, carni*vor*ous, omni*vor*ous (*devouring* all things). L. *vor*are.

Vot—vow; *vot*ive (promised with a *vow*), *vot*ary (one paying religious *vows*), de*vote* (give up, *vow* away fully[10]), de*vout* (very *devoted*). L. *vov*ere, *vot*us.

Vot—a wish; *vote* (the expression of one's *wish* or will). L. *vot*um. L. *vov*ere, *vot*us, to vow.

Voy—See *vi*.

Vulg—the common people; *vulg*ar, di*vulg*e (publish abroad among the *people*). L. *vulg*us.

Vulner—a wound; *vulner*able,[11] in*vulner*able. L. *vuln*us, *vulner*is.

Vulp—fox; *vulp*ine (*fox*-like). L. *vulp*es.

Vuls; vult—pluck, tear; con*vuls*ion (a *plucking* to-gether), re*vuls*ion (a *plucking* back), *vult*ure (the beast that *tears* dead bodies). L. *vell*ere, *vuls*us.

NOTES

[1] Among the ancient Northmen it was regarded as a disgrace to die of disease or from the effects of old age. It was deemed a privilege and special honor to fall in the full vigor of manhood in the uproar of battle while spilling the blood of enemies. Such a death admitted the deceased to *Valhalla*, or the hall of slain heroes, there to pass an eternity of enjoyments, consisting mainly in drinking the blood of enemies from human skulls. Such a belief made the Northmen brave and cruel to the extreme. Their atrocities have filled many a page of history and legend. The Mohammedans were inspired to desperation in battle by a doctrine somewhat similar. They were taught to believe that the houris, a class of most beautiful females, were waiting in the paradise of the blest to receive at once the souls of those who fell in battle, and to minister to their pleasure thoughout all eternity.

[2] In marching forth to the conquest of the world, the Romans fortified every camp they occupied, if only for a single night, surrounding it with a *rampart* and a corresponding ditch or moat. In the case of a camp of any permanency, the rampart became something formidable. So great were those earth-works that many of them may be traced today, after the lapse of nearly two thousand years. The Romans forced their language everywhere in the west by bringing into the presence of the barbarians things which the latter had never used, and for which, conse-quently, they had no names. They were therefore compelled to use, or try to use, the Roman, or Latin, terms. The Roman legions were finally dispersed from Britain, but the great Roman works remained. In giving us the word *wall*, the conquering Anglo-Saxons were endeavoring to pronounce the Roman word *vall*um.

[3] The three tribes of barbarians that came at intervals to ravage the old and corrupt empire were the Goths, Vandals, and Huns. Of these, the Vandals exhibited the greatest ferocity and the spirit of mad destruction. They destroyed through mere wantonness whatever monuments or other works of art came within their power. Hence, a willful ruining of what is beautiful is called an act of *vandalism*. Most conquerors have evinced a disposition to remove works of art to their own capitals; but the Vandals acquired undying notoriety by their disposition to destroy.

[4] A *vein* is *that which carries*, or propels, the blood onward to the heart. The propelling power in the vein is principally the elastic quality of its tissue, which pressing upon the blood, forces it onward; though there is also an impetus received from the violent flow of arterial blood. Hence the vein is literally and in fact a *'propeller.''* The movement in the vein is sluggish so there is little danger from severing it and causing an external flow of venous blood.

[5] the term *mercenary* to sordid motives, or an unprincipled struggle after gain; the term *venal* is applied to the corrupt condition resulting from *mercenary* motives. Thus, a *mercenary* press *seeks* improper gains; a *venal* press has realized or is in the enjoyment of improper gains. Another distinction is that between *hire* and *sale*; the *mercenary* engages to perform specific services at a fixed rate; the *venal* person has transferred himself wholly to the *purchaser* of his service.

[6] In ancient times the slavery of the white race prevailed all over Europe. As the home-born slave was entirely uneducated, his speech and other traits were regarded as those peculiarly *native* to the soil. Education in ancient Rome caused the use of many Greek terms (as learning came from Greece), thereby disturbing the purity of Latin speech. Hence, in any country the *vernacular* speech is that used by the young and uneducated classes. The English *vernacular* is overwhelmingly Anglo-Saxon, though the English language is derived mainly from Latin and Greek sources; that is, the majority of English *words* are of Latin and Greek origin, while the English *vernacular* is almost exclusively Anglo-Saxon.

[7] The act of *dwelling* was compared to *turning* one's self about.

[8] Houses in the same *street* are in the same *vicinity*.

[9] The term *revolution*, however, is restricted to a revolt that is successful. Hence the American *revolt* become a *revolution*. In like manner the *revolt* in England against the kings of the Stuart dynasty became by its success a *revolution*. But it became a revolution in a double sense; for, whereas the monarchs claimed to rule by divine authority, the revolution settled the principle that they ruled by virtue of the choice of the people. Since the English Revolution, England has been virtually a republic, though retaining a hereditary executive with limited powers and restricted functions.

[10] The ancient Romans had a superstition that a general could *devote* his enemies to destruction by including himself in the vow. It was tried on two occasions by the Decil, father and son, each of whom rushed into the ranks of the enemy to save the Roman army as by a miracle. On both occasions the Romans were victorious. At a later time, Arnold Winkelried devoted himself for the Swiss, and enabled them to win a victory, though he did not expect a miraculous interposition.

[11] Thetis, the goddess mother of Achilles, dipped him when an infant into the river *Styx* in order to render him *invulnerable* to mortal weapons. She held him by the heel, thus keeping the water from that part, and, consequently, leaving it subject to mortal laws. When the arrow of Paris found entrance here, the hero yielded up his life in accordance with the dying prophecy of Hector:

> "Phœbus and Paris shall avenge my fate,
> And stretch thee here before the Scæan gate."
> —*Pope's Iliad.*

W

Wal (*wealh*)—foreign; *wal*nut (the *foreign* nut), *Wales*[1] (the *Foreign* Land). A.S. *wealh*.

NOTES

[1] The word *Wales* means the land of the *wealhs*, or foreigners. The Anglo-Saxon conquest of Britain continued through a period of two hundred years. It was finally limited by natural obstructions in the north and west. Behind the mountains in the one quarter and the morasses in the other, the severed remnants of the stubborn race that made such trouble for imperial Cæsar, seven hundred years earlier, still bade defiance to the invader. The brave western Celts became *foreigners* on the very soil which they had occupied for untold ages. The foiled conqueror flung an epithet over the region which his arms could not subdue. Like many another opprobrious epithet, it was finally adopted as a term of honor, and the name of the region will embody forever the chagrin and spite of an enemy from afar. Six hundred years after the failure of the Saxon conquest the Welsh submitted to be incorporated into the English nation. But they dictated conditions which forever saved their pride and required each English sovereign to style his eldest son and heir the *Prince of Wales*. So that instead of conquering the *foreign* region, Saxon and Norman England submitted to be ruled forever by a line of Welsh princes.

X

Xanth—yellow. G. *xanthos*.
Xiph—sword; *xiph*oid. G. *xiphos*.
Xyl—wood; *xyl*ography, *xyl*ophone. G. *xule*.

Z

Zo—animal; *zo*ology (the science of *animals*), *zo*-diac (a belt of the heavens containing twelve constellations, named almost entirely after *animals*), *zo*ophyte (an *animal plant*). G. *zo*on.

Zo—life; a*zo*ic (without *life*), a*zo*te (nitrogen, which destroys *life*). G. *zo*e.

Zon—belt, girdle; *zon*e. G. *zon*e.

Zyg—join; sy*zyg*y (*conjunction*). G. sy*zyg*os.

Zym—ferment; *zym*ology (the doctrine of *fermentation*), *zym*otic (relating to epidemic diseases, in which a poison works through the body like a *ferment*). G. *zym*oo.

PREFIXES

A—without, not. G. *a*. G. *an*. G. *ana*.
A—to, toward, into, at. F. *a*. L. *ad*.
A—from. L. *a*. L. *ab*.
A (for *ex*)—out; *a*mend. L. *ex*.
A—off; *a*down. A.S. *of*.
A—on; *a*foot, etc.
Ab—from, away. L. *ab*.
Abs—from, away. L. *abs*.
Ac (*ad*)—to, toward, unto, at. L. *ad*.
Ad—to, toward, unto, at. L. *ad*.
Af (*ad*)—to, toward, unto, at. L. *ad*.
Ag (*ad*)—to, toward, unto, at. L. *ad*.
Al—the. Ar. *al*.
Al (*ad*)—to, toward, unto, at. L. *ad*.
An—without, not. G. *an*. G. *ana*.
Ana—up, back, again. G. *ana*.
Ante—before. L. *ante*.
Anti—against. G. *anti*.
Ap (*ad*)—to, toward, unto, at. L. *ad*.
Apo—from, off. G. *apo*.
Ar (*ad*)—to, toward, unto, at. L. *ad*.
Arch—chief. G. *archi*.
Archi—chief. G. *archi*.
As (*ad*)—to, toward, unto, at. L. *ad*.
At (*ad*)—to, toward, unto, at. L. *ad*.

Be—to cause. A.S. *be*.
Bi—double. L. *bi*. L. *dui*, twice. L. *duo*, two.
Bis—twice. L. *bis*.

Cata—down, thoroughly. G. *cata*.
Co—together, with. L. *con*. L. *cum*.
Col (*con*)—together, with. L. *con*. L. *cum*.
Com (*con*)—together, with. L. *con*. L. *cum*.
Con—together, with. L. *con*. L. *cum*.
Contra—against, opposite. L. *contra*.
Cor (*con*)—together, with. L. *con*. L. *cum*.
Counter (*contra*)—against, opposite. L. *contra*.

De—down, from, away. L. *de*.
De—apart, away, un. F. *di*. O.F. *des*. L. *dis*.
Des—apart, away, un. F. *dis*. L. *dis*.
Di—double. G. *di*. G. *dis*.
Dia—through, between, across. G. *dia*.
Dis—apart, away, un. L. *dis*.

E—out. L. *e*. L. *ex*.
Ec—out. G. *ec*.
Ef (*ex*)—out. L. *ex*.
El (*en*)—in. G. *en*.
Em (*en*)—in. G. *en*.
En—in. G. *en*. F. *en*. L. *in*.
Epi—upon, to, besides. G. *epi*.
Eu—well. G. *eu*. G. *eus*, good.
Ex—out. L. *ex*. G. *ex*.

For—intensely, utterly; *for*bear, *for*bid, *for*fend, *for*get, *for*give, *for*go, *for*lorn, *for*sake, *for*swear. A.S. *for*.

Il (*in*)—in, into, on, upon. L. *in*.
Il (*in*)—not. L. *in*.
Im (*in*)—in, into, etc. L. *in*.
Im (*in*)—not. L. *in*.
In—in, into, etc. L. *in*.

In—not. L. *in*.
Inter—among, between. L. *inter*.
Ir (*in*)—in, into, etc. L. *in*.
Ir (*in*)—not. L. *in*.

Mal—bad. F. *mal*. L. *mal*us, bad.
Meta—among, with, after, over. G. *meta*.
Mis—ill, wrong. A.S. *mis*.
Mis (*mes*)—ill, bad; *mis*chief, *mis*creant, *mis*nomer, etc. O.F. *mes*. L. *min*us, less.
Mono—single, sole. G. *mono*. G. *monos*.

Non—not. L. *non*. L. *ne*, not; *un*us, one.

Ob—toward, against, at, before, upon, over, about, near. L. *ob*.
Oc (*ob*).
Of (*ob*).
Omni—all. L. *omni*. L. *omnis*, all.
Op (*ob*).

Pan—all. G. *pan*.
Par—through; *par*terre, *par*venue. F. *par*. L. *per*.
Para—beside. G. *para*.
Per—through. L. *per*.
Peri—around, about. G. *peri*.
Poly—many. L. *poly*. G. *polu*. G. *polus*, much
Port—toward; *port*end. O.S. *port*.
Post—after, behind. L. *post*.
Pre—before, beforehand. L. *pre*, *præ*. L. *præ*, before.
Preter—beyond. L. *preter*. L. *præter*, beyond. L. *præ*, before.
Pro—before, forward. L. *pro*.
Pros—toward. G. *pros*.

Proto—first. G. *protos.*
Pur—before, forward. O.F. *pur.* L. *pro.*

Re—again, back. L. *re.*
Red—again, back. L. *re.*

Se—away, apart, aside. L. *se.*
Sed—away, apart, aside. L. *se.*
Sub—under, after. L. *sub.*
Suc (*sub*).
Suf (*sub*).
Sum (*sub*).
Sup (*sub*).
Super—above, over. L. *super.*
Supra—above, beyond. L. *supra.* L. *superus.*
Sur (*sub*).
Sur—above, over. F. *sur.* L. *super.*
Sus (*sub*).
Syl (*syn*).
Sym (*syn*).
Syn—together. G. *sun.*

Tra (*trans*).
Trans—beyond, across, over. L. *trans.*

Un—not. A.S. *un.*
Un—reverse; *un*lock, etc.